THE BRITISH ATLANTIC EMPIRE
BEFORE THE AMERICAN REVOLUTION

The British Atlantic Empire before the American Revolution

Edited by

Peter Marshall

and

Glyn Williams

FRANK CASS

First published 1980 in Great Britain by
FRANK CASS AND COMPANY LIMITED
Gainsborough House, Gainsborough Road,
London, E11 1RS England

and in the United States of America by
FRANK CASS AND COMPANY LIMITED
c/o Biblio Distribution Centre
81 Adams Drive, P.O. Box 327, Totowa, N.J. 07511

British Library Cataloguing in Publication Data

The British Atlantic Empire before the American Revolution.
  1. North America—History—Colonial period, ca. 1600–
  1775
  2. Great Britain—Colonies—America
  I. Marshall, Peter, *b. 1926*
  II. Williams, Glyn
  III. 'Journal of Imperial and Commonwealth history'
  970.03   E45

ISBN 0–7146–3158–2

This group of studies first appeared in a Special Issue
on 'The British Atlantic Empire before the American
Revolution' of *Journal of Imperial and Commonwealth
History*, Vol. VIII, No. 2, published by Frank Cass
& Co. Ltd.

Printed in Great Britain by
The Bourne Press, Bournemouth

Contents

Notes on the Contributors   vii

Preface   1

The Empire and the Provincial Elites:
An Interpretation of some Recent Writings on the
English Atlantic, 1675–1740   **I. K. Steele**   2

The Board of Trade and London-American Interest Groups
in the Eighteenth Century   **Alison G. Olson** 33

Warfare and Political Change in
Mid-Eighteenth Century Massachusetts   **William Pencak**   51

British Government Spending and the
North American Colonies 1740–1775   **Julian Gwyn**   74

The Seven Years' War and the American Revolution:
the Causal Relationship Reconsidered   **Jack P. Greene**   85

Old Whigs, Old Tories and the American
Revolution   **Paul Langford**   106

Notes on the Contributors

I. K. Steele is Professor in the History Department of the University of Western Ontario. He is the author of *The Politics of Colonial Policy: The Board of Trade in Colonial Administration 1696–1720* (Oxford, 1968) and a number of articles.

Alison G. Olson is Professor in the History Department of the University of Maryland. She has written *The Radical Duke* (Oxford, 1961), *Anglo-American Politics 1660–1775* (Oxford, 1973) and many shorter studies.

William Pencak is Andrew Mellon Research Fellow at Duke University. He has published a number of articles on New England in the eighteenth century.

Julian Gwyn is Professor in the History Department of the University of Ottawa. He is the author of *The Enterprising Admiral: the Personal Fortune of Admiral Sir Peter Warren* (Montreal, 1974) and is the editor of *The Royal Navy and North America* (London, 1973).

Jack P. Greene is Andrew Mellon Professor in the Humanities at the Johns Hopkins University. He is the author of a number of books, has edited several selections of documents and has contributed to many collections of studies on Colonial America and the Revolution. Among his books are *The Quest for Power* (Chapel Hill, 1963) and *Landon Carter* (Charlottesville, 1967).

Paul Langford is Fellow and Senior Tutor of Lincoln College, Oxford. He has written *The First Rockingham Administration* (Oxford, 1973), *The Excise Crisis* (Oxford 1975) and *Modern British Foreign Policy: The Eighteenth Century* (London 1976) as well as many articles.

Preface

The dynamism within the American colonies in the fifty years or so before the outbreak of the crisis of the 1760s that was to lead to the Revolution has never been in doubt. Recent historical writing has amply demonstrated it. Population grew, new land was settled, economies expanded and diversified, social structures became more complex, colonial assemblies won more power and new political ideologies were formulated. By contrast, British imperial influence on the colonies has often been portrayed both as somewhat ineffectual in practice and as tradition-bound and unchanging in its aims, at least until the period of the Seven Years' War. This is the picture that emerges from the deservedly classic accounts of the imperial system written by Charles M. Andrews, George L. Beer and Lawrence Harper. They described how the institutions of trade regulation and constitutional supervision were devised in the later seventeenth century and pointed out the relative lack of institutional change before the 1750s. A number of recent scholars have, however, suggested that lack of institutional change does not necessarily mean that the imperial system was either static or ineffectual. It seemed to us that it would be valuable to devote an issue of this Journal to a reassessment of the imperial system before the revolution.

The articles written at our invitation suggest a number of ways in which the 'imperial factor' was of real importance in colonial life and show that there was dynamism on the British side as well as in the colonies. The links that bound mother country and colonies together were much more varied than the formal channels of authority set up in the previous century. For instance, both Professor Steele and Professor Olson show how London's spectacular growth enabled London-based interests, commercial, religious and ethnic, to exercise a powerful influence in the colonies. They stress that colonial elites were generally more inclined to cooperate with British interests than to oppose them. Three contributors concentrate on the important consequences for the colonies of the increasing scale of imperial warfare. Dr. Pencak and Professor Greene expose the political and social strains produced by war; Professor Gwyn emphasises economic opportunity. Finally, Dr. Langford shows that English Whig doctrine was not inert. Ideological change took place on both sides of the Altantic, as the Americans were to discover in the 1760s. Although none of these scholars would deny that important changes in British attitudes to the colonies took place in the Grenville era, they make it clear that Anglo-American relations developed on both sides of the Atlantic throughout the eighteenth century. Braudel's famous phrase applies to this as to an earlier period, 'L'Amerique ne commande pas seul'.

P.J.M.
G.W.

The Empire and Provincial Elites: An interpretation of some recent writings on the English Atlantic, 1675-1740

by

I. K. Steele

Amid a fiery blaze, visible sixty miles at sea, 'Some gentlemen took care to preserve Her Majesties Picture that was in the Town-House'.[1] It was a small gallantry, to be expected of men of their rank in the Queen's dominions, but not quite what we have come to expect in Boston, Massachusetts in 1711. These gentlemen, like those who passed a New Hampshire law requiring all members of their House of Assembly to wear swords,[2] were among those who were turning colonies into English Atlantic provinces. Yet their story belongs too easily and too exclusively to American colonial rather than British imperial history.

A whole certainly can be much less than its parts if the whole is the written history of the first British empire. Fifty years ago *The Cambridge History of the British Empire* was launched with a spacious and well-manned volume entitled *The Old Empire from the Beginnings to 1783*,[3] and the 'imperial school' of American colonial history was flourishing. Although two generations of scholars have revolutionised every aspect of this subject—including its boundaries—this has been accomplished with little deliberate interest in the history of the first British empire as a whole.[4] The habit of drawing Clio in national costume seems as ubiquitous as ever, and the empire is easily seen as an unusable past or a mild embarrassment to its successor states. The neglect of this subject owes even more to the fact that the new ways in history are specialised and comparative. Scholarly attention has been shifting from structures to functional units, from theory to practice, and from the general to the particular. These trends have meant that the first British empire has continued to attract less scholarly interest than have its successor states.

A review of some recent literature from the perspective of the English Atlantic empire draws attention to several themes, and concentration upon the lifetime 1675 to 1740 brings 'provincial' themes into sharpest focus. By 1675 the English Atlantic political economy was well beyond the pioneer dispersal stage, and patterns of much subsequent development were already present. This was the lifetime between the founding of the Lords of Trade and the Cartagena expedition. It was the long lifetime between the founding of the Royal African Company and the Stono rebellion, or between the founding of the Royal Observatory and Harrison's solution to the problem of longitude. This was also the span between Wycherly's *The Country Wife*

and Thomson's *Rule Britannia,* and between the Atlantic mission of George Fox and that of George Whitefield. Despite the well-known centrifugal tendencies that operated in this period, colonial fathers could die in 1740 without hearing a whisper of the coming of the American Revolution. In this provincial lifetime the integration, specialisation, and interdependence that grew in London's more immediate economic, social and political hinterlands[5] was carried to the Atlantic colonies with notable success.

Most Englishmen lived in London's provinces, whether in rural England, provincial towns, or transatlantic colonies. The county, town, or colony was the context within which most of life was lived;[6] with the 'English nation' as a general boundary between friends and enemies and a metaphor for the public good. Compared to the lifetime before 1675, migration within England, between England and the colonies, or even between colonies, was less endemic[7]—with the notable exceptions of the city of London, the colony of Pennsylvania, and the forced migration of Africans to the New World colonies. English population grew very little, grain prices were modest and quite stable, and no crises of subsistence occurred there or in the colonies.[8] In these respects, too, the comparisons with the previous lifetime are striking. The mortality crisis of the 1640s, the economic and political problems of the 1620s and 1640s, and what historians have called *The Crisis of the Aristocracy,* 'the storm over the gentry', or 'the general crisis of the seventeenth century',[9] all point to the tensions and disruptions that prompted internal migration, migration to continental Europe, and a major early Stuart migration to the new world. Studies of county life in this earlier lifetime have confirmed the general picture, but have also documented the strength of provincial life, and its power to resist centralisation by early Stuart or Cromwellian government.[10] Social history, especially local studies of villages, cities, and counties, have challenged the historical assumptions of a unified England with outlying colonies. London's provinces existed in some variety on both sides of the Atlantic, and the new world provinces were not automatically different for being united to the metropolis by water rather than by land.

Appreciation of the links between various aspects of life is one of the special challenges of historical study, and a tendency towards 'total history' has long been part of British imperial history.[11] Yet a scholar's assumptions, research subjects, methods, and preoccupations all tend to emphasise one aspect, be it economic, or social, or political, and to regard the other two as subsidiary subjects if not dependent variables. This exploration of the provincial life of the English Atlantic is organised to focus, in turn, upon each of these aspects.

The century after the restoration of Charles II has special attraction for economic historians concerned with the origins of industrial development and 'modernisation'. E. A. Wrigley's suggestive model, outlining the importance of London's growth in England's economic unification,[12] can usefully be extended to include the English Atlantic. If the agriculture, industry, and crafts of England were being transformed to respond to the phenomenal growth of the London market, the economic survival of the transatlantic provinces depended upon the development of marketable staples or related activities. London was the major source of credit, the major market, the logical entrepôt, though this natural preference had to be reinforced by war, by trade legislation, and by colonial administration. Economic specialisation in the colonies presumed maritime access to markets, and also presumed sea-borne sources of most needed goods. Thus interdependence grew with specialisation and economies of scale: plantations were among the prototypes of industrial production, profitable but vulnerable elements in the emerging English Atlantic economy.

Although the economic history of the English Atlantic has not been subjected to recent synthesis,[13] the field has been ably surveyed in the broader comparative studies by Ralph Davis and K. G. Davies.[14] The best short economic histories of pre-industrial England. including those by C. Wilson, L. A. Clarkson and D. C. Coleman,[15] are forced, by the recent riches of their field, to adopt a customs officer's perspective on the 'foreign plantations'. Studies of overseas trade and the shipping industry all assert the importance of the staple trades in the English re-export trade and in ship utilisation.[16] Yet the colonial staple trades are now likely to be seen primarily as sources of profit for London merchants and the English government, and are seldom credited with transforming England to anything like the degree claimed by some pamphleteers at the time and some historians since.[17]

By 1675 those who had migrated to escape the Old World were succeeded or outnumbered by those who intended to reap the harvest of the New World. Effort to improve upon a rude sufficiency drew colonists into the English Atlantic market economy.[18] The wilderness may well have been a subsequent source of colonial uniqueness, but it was at the edge of the real development of these provinces. Access to sea-borne commerce was more advantageous to colonists than to most other Englishmen.

Discovery and development of a marketable staple product was crucial to the shape of colonial societies, as H. A. Innis, M. H. Watkins, R. F. Neill, R. E. Baldwin, and D. C. North have emphasised.[19] Ironically, the first of the staples Innis studied, *The Cod Fisheries*,[20] could support contrasting economic and social structures in Newfoundland and New England. The English Newfoundland fishery remained West Country based into the eighteenth century, with international rivalry and fishing interests both helping to retard settlement on the island itself. C. Grant Head has emphasised the increased role of the 'wintering people' in the onshore fishery after the 1730s, and the shift of West Country fishermen from the onshore fishery to the formerly French-dominated Banks fishery proper.[21] In contrast, New England fisheries supported local village life from the beginning, but could reach out to Canso or Newfoundland with minimal local commitments. As the most perishable and difficult staple to regulate, fish was not susceptible to the entrepôt market structure of other colonial staples. However much it might be prized as a nursery of seamen and a source of foreign earnings, the fishery remained a staple of limited fiscal potential and administrative interest.[22]

Like the Newfoundland fishery, the English fur trade could operate as an English-based extraction trade or as a colonial traffic supporting a major colonial town like Albany. E. E. Rich's institutional study is the basis for the more recent work on the Hudson's Bay trade.[23] A. J. Ray and A. Rotstein have explored the price mechanisms and Indian perceptions of the trade,[24] and G. Williams has documented the continuing lure of the North-West Passage through the eighteenth century.[25] Although the northern English approach to the fur trade generated little local development beyond the Bay factories, the New York fur trade was funnelled through the substantial town of Albany in the new world, and was free of monopoly in its English markets even after fur was 'enumerated' in 1722. The economics of the Albany fur trade have received attention recently,[26] though less than have other features of the life of the Indians who traded at Albany.[27] The fur trade and the fish trade have been the basis for a staple theory of economic growth, yet the range of possible economic structures, the limited ancillary trades, and the comparatively small scale of both trades make them poor examples of the English Atlantic staples.

The sugar trade, that prize of English Atlantic commerce, has long been blessed with good economic historians. The foundation works of Richard Pares put him in a category by himself,[28] and the comprehensive volumes by Noel Deerr[29] have also survived as major reference works, as has Frank Wesley Pitman's strangely-titled *The Development of the British West Indies, 1700–1763*.[30] R. S. Dunn's scholarly and well written *Sugar and Slaves*[31] is a comprehensive study that includes a sound synthesis of the economic aspects of the rise of the planters in the later Stuart period. The economics of integration are more extensively traced in R. B. Sheridan's *Sugar and Slavery*. Sheridan divides West Indian economic historians into 'neo-Smithian' critics of the value of colonies and 'neo-Burkean' advocates of the conviction that empire paid.[32] However strange it might seem to apply a neo-Burkean lable to a Marxist argument that English industrialisation owed much to the profits of the sugar trade, this debate goes on, with Sheridan as a self-proclaimed 'neo-Burkean'.[33] But whatever the contentions on that issue, all are agreed that the sugar trade was the exemplar of imperial economic integration accomplished in the lifetime after the construction of the Navigation Acts and the agencies for their enforcement. The loss of the European re-export trade in sugar was a significant blow early in the eighteenth century, but the trade to England itself grew favourably. The sugar trade rested firmly on credit from the Royal African Company, London merchants, and affluent relatives.[34] Those colonists who could command the most metropolitan credit on the best terms (for land, slaves, and sugar equipment) won against their less cosmopolitan neighbours.[35] This capital and labour intensive trade was firmly bound to the metropolis.

The shuttle of the English sugar fleets to and from the English islands was neither the beginning nor the end of the sugar trade. The loggers, fishermen and seamen of New England; the farmers, millers and merchants of New York and Pennsylvania; these were all linked to the trade in much lighter bondage than that of the African slaves. Richard Pares and Byron Fairchild have sketched aspects of the lumber and provisions trade to the English sugar islands.[36] The slave trade has had considerable treatment;[37] the Irish provision trade to the islands,[38] the molasses trade, and the rum trade from the islands have also had their historians.[39] Studies of the development of merchant elites in Boston and Philadelphia[40] suggest the important place of the West Indies trade in the creation of these dynasties. J. F. Shepherd and G. M. Walton, as well as D. C. North and R. P. Thomas,[41] have found that shipping promoted New England capital accumulation, and the Massachusetts shipowners have been studied intensively.[42] For North American merchants, the sugar colonies were a major avenue of profit, especially prized for bills of exchange on London: New England trade directly to England was in furs, skins, train oil, masts and naval stores, but these returns did not cover the cost of English and European goods imported from the metropolis.[43]

Before 1740 the English colonies did not have extensive trade beyond the empire, though there were beginnings that deserve more study than they have received. The trade in fish to Mediterranean Europe was a direct trade that could be profitable but was subject to heavy competition. The trade to the foreign West Indies was more lucrative, especially to the French islands. By the 1730s two new trades from North America to southern Europe were growing in importance. These were the rice trade from South Carolina, which stayed with English carriers by prescription even though the trade was direct,[44] and the grain trade,[45] which was destined to become a more important source of profits for New York and Philadelphia merchants. Despite these initiatives, which can easily be exaggerated by hindsight, the English empire was, to a noticeable extent, bound together by the needs and opportunities of the sugar trade during the provincial lifetime discussed here.

Tobacco, the other great staple of the English Atlantic, generated less intercolonial trade than did sugar, but was responsible for more international traffic in Europe after re-export from Britain. J. M. Price has unravelled the complexities of the marketing of tobacco, initially in its connection with Russia, but most recently and masterfully in its links to the French tobacco monopoly.[46] The market crisis of the 1670s had accelerated the shift to slave labour and larger holdings, which in turn financed the rise of the gentlemen planters. As A. C. Land's research has suggested, the tobacco economy was financed on networks of local debt, much of it ultimately owed to English creditors.[47] By 1740 the shift to Glasgow as the main British entrepôt was a signal of changes in colonial tobacco marketing and credit arrangements. While the London-based agency system still prospered, this new element of consequence was changing the nature of the marketing of Chesapeake tobacco.[48]

The slaves, who grew much of the tobacco — and even more of the sugar and rice — have been the focus for much recent economic history of both slavery and the slave trade.[49] Eric Williams' ranging and provocative *Capitalism and Slavery*[50] is still a legitimate starting point for recent debates on the origins of racist attitudes,[51] the rate of return in the slave trade and slavery,[52] and the abolition movement.[53] *The Royal African Company,* by K. G. Davies, is a thorough study of the monopoly company that flourished and failed under the last Stuarts. The African involvement in the slave trade was a significant omission in the Williams thesis, and this aspect of the trade has been illuminated by the works of I. A. Akinjogbin, P. D. Curtin, K. Y. Daaku, D. Forde, A. J. H. Latham, R. Law, M. Priestley, W. Rodney, and

R. P. Thomas with R. N. Bean.[54] The scale of the forced migration of Africans to the new world has been carefully charted by Curtin[55] and this black maritime trade has been surveyed by D. P. Mannix, M. Craton, and Bean.[56] London's dominance in the slave trade, as in the tobacco trade, would lessen before the middle of the eighteenth century, but Liverpool and colonial slavers were of little consequence in the lifetime before 1740.[57] English dominance in the English Atlantic slave trade served to reinforce the economic powers that integrated the colonial staple trade into a unified and interdependent economic unit.

Whatever the motives of migrants, the initial economic development of colonies involved grafting these areas to existing economies by the production of marketable staples. It was natural that migrants turned to their own metropolis for needed goods and for the credit to acquire land, labour, and equipment to create returns which paid for imports. The trust that was necessary for business was easier to give to those who share the same family, the same religion, the same language and, when all else failed, the same laws.

Yet such natural inclination did not dominate all colonial Englishmen. Dutch initiative in English colonial sugar development was a clear and early indication that Dutch credit, shipping, and processing industries offered English planters better terms than their own country could. In the third quarter of the seventeenth century English governments consistently and decisively used laws, wars, and elaborate enforcement agencies to exclude the Dutch from what were certainly not to be 'foreign plantations'.

The rather futile debate over the primacy of merchant wealth or state power in the development of these economic policies has calmed.[58] C. D. Chandaman's *The English Public Revenues, 1660–1688*[59] documents the fiscal value of the customs revenues on tobacco and sugar, important income for Charles II and especially James II. Their drive for tighter control of the colonies can now be seen as efficient royal estate management. James II was the last king to control the customs revenues collected in England, revenues which financed expansion of his army. Pursuit of permanent colonial revenues was not so decisively checked after 1689, remaining an active political issue into the eighteenth century.

The burdens of the Navigation Acts upon colonial development has been an enduring topic of research. Although bedevilled by the unfathomable dimensions of smuggling and illegal trade,[60] the attempt to measure the price of empire goes on. Computer-assisted research has added new dimensions to this subject, yet the new methods have tended to confirm the classic assessments of L. A. Harper and O. M. Dickerson,[61] that the costs of empire for North American white colonists were modest.[62]

Economics of development is a current concern which has drawn additional attention to the economic history of England and her colonies in the pre-industrial period. Whether approached from the hypotheses of Watkins, W. W. Rostow, J. A. Ernst and M. Egnal, or North and Thomas,[63] the economic development of the English Atlantic in the period 1675 to 1740 did not seriously strain existing economic and political structures. The disruptions of war, the fiscal troubles of the 1730s, French colonial competition, and the problems revealed by the Molasses Act were all strains, but not evidence that the structures were themselves economically inadequate.

As relatively new economic ventures, the colonial trades were opportunities for practising new economic ideas. Commercial capitalism was less restrained by law and custom in these new areas,[64] and the social variety of the colonies adds to their interest for scholars studying cultural influences on economic activity. From an earlier academic concern with the connection between Protestantism and capitalism, recent attention has shifted to the secularising of economic virtue or revisions in the perceived relationship between the self and society. The general inquiries of S. Diamond and Richard D. Brown[65] pose questions that are receiving intriguing answers in the works of C. B. MacPherson, J. E. Crowley, J. G. A. Pocock, A. O. Hirschman and J. O. Appleby.[66]

Urban studies are one of the new preoccupations of historians that promise insights for the economic history of the English Atlantic. The frontier was an influence favouring colonial uniqueness, but the towns and cities of the English Atlantic shared many problems and perspectives. Carl Bridenbaugh's *Cities in the Wilderness*[67] was a herald for this new field. Despite the literature of the economic geographers, historians have seldom approached the analytical sophistication of J. M. Price's 'Economic Function and the Growth of American Port towns in the eighteenth century'.[68] The economic histories of important provincial ports in England set a high standard, illustrated by recent work on Bristol, Liverpool and particularly the studies of Exeter and Hull.[69] The leading towns of provincial America have also been studied, though economics is seldom the dominant theme. Studies of the economic development of the American seaboard town during rapid population growth (Philadelphia), slow growth (New York), and stagnation (Boston) would add to our understanding of development,[70] especially if English ports in similar circumstances were studied for comparison.

It was ships and shipping that laced together the ports of the English Atlantic. Studies of the shipbuilding and shipping industries have improved our descriptions of the merchant marine,[71] but much more can be done with surviving records. Although economic, political and social exchanges depended upon the communication facilities of the various trades, remarkably little has been done on the pace and pattern of the distribution of news in the English Atlantic.[72] Although Alan Pred[73] has demonstrated the importance of access to market news for the later growth of New York, nothing has been done to establish the routes of market news in the earlier period.

Economic attraction of colonial specialisation and interdependence lured men in England and the colonies to pursue the integration of the English Atlantic in the lifetime after 1675. There were some colonial statutes that gave advantages to their own merchants and shipowners, and there were objections to imperial legislation and its enforcement,[74] but the building of the English Atlantic economy was not seriously challenged from within. The empire was the context within which the emerging colonial elites found the resources for their own advancement.

Social history of the English Atlantic during these years has, for a variety of reasons, received comparatively little direct attention.[75] When the 'imperial school' of American colonial history prospered, social history was not fashionable, and the political economy of the English Atlantic empire easily became the whole of its history.[76] But a much more important reason why the empire is seen without social history is that much of the exciting social history of the last fifteen years has drawn attention to small communities. These 'community studies', built on parish records, local censuses, court records and town records, have tended to atomise and specify.[77] What Namier did for English political history, the new wave of local studies has done for social history. Expansive assertions about life in 'England' or ₄America' are retreating before measured studies of regional differences and their transplant and adaptation to the new world,[78] and before careful specific comparisons on a world-wide basis.[79] In time, new general patterns can be expected to emerge from this detailed work, allowing better social description of larger social groupings.

English population in the century after 1650 has been explored by scholars seeking the relationship between population growth and the onset of industrialisation. The years 1675–1730 are now seen as having very little population growth.[80] For the landed and monied elites, this demographic stability brought consolidation of estates, less political competition, a trade in the export of foodstuffs, and comparative social peace. Generally good harvests,[81] together with transportation improvements which minimised local shortages in an integrating English economy,[82] broke the traditional connection between poor harvests, increased death rates, and the redirection of capital resources into food and food production.[83] The onset of more rapid population increase in the 1730s marked the end of this hiatus, and there are some reasons for thinking that the changes in population were fairly independent of economic determinants, though bringing economic consequences.[84] Understandably, the period 1675–1730 did not see much English emigration to the colonies.

Colonial population growth patterns in the same period varied widely. In many colonies the recruiting of labour had been the main immediate concern in promoting migration. The result was a predominantly male population assembled in order to extract wealth, not to start a satellite community. The predominance of males among slaves, servants and masters limited the prospects of family formation and inhibited the emergence of genuine provincial, or creole, societies. The early Chesapeake colonies and the English West Indies were affected in this way,[85] though less so than were Newfoundland or Hudson Bay. If the sex ratios dictated that births and marriages would be fewer than deaths, the disease environment reinforced that tendency.[86] Most of the staple colonies were not demographically self-supporting in the seventeenth century, as the trade in slaves and servants illustrated, and the English Caribbean remained that way in the eighteenth century as well.[87]

The dramatic population growth rates usually attributed to colonial North America were neither universal nor immediate. Only those new colonies that attracted migrating families,[88] like the Puritan and Quaker settlements, would grow quickly from within rather than from immigration.[89] Founding families could accumulate and transmit property more effectively than most other frontiersmen, giving heirs additional opportunities. Quite naturally, economic stability and social stratification, or the foreclosing of opportunity, would come first to the demographically mature and economically limited New England colonies. The demography of the colonies varied greatly, particularly in the seventeenth century, and these differences had essential social and economic implications. Although the demography of the colonies differed from that of the communities from which the migrants came, the subsequent trends in colonial development, particularly in English North America, were towards sex ratios, age distributions, and marriage ages that were more like those in England than had been true at the founding of the colonies.[90]

Social mobility would appear to be one of the clearest contrasts between the older and newer sides of the English Atlantic. Alan Everitt and Lawrence Stone have explored aspects of elite recruitment in early modern England;[91] Stone's work indicates that there were four routes to rapid social advancement: marriage, the law, government office, and the colonies. The first three of these 'rapid' routes to the top of hierarchies presupposed the leisure and resources needed to gain considerable education, if only in manners. Were the Dick Whittingtons of 1675 to 1740 using the colonies as their route to social power in England?

Sugar was the only colonial staple that generated profits sweet enough to allow the most successful to flee the unhealthy colonies and relocate in gentlemanly comfort, if not opulence.[92] Physical survival in the islands was one prerequisite for success, but since poor whites outnumbered rich ones, survival was not enough. Sugar was expensive to produce: a planter needed capital and credit, both to start and to build a plantation fortune. English sources of credit would favour the well-to-do, or those judged most likely to honour debts, understand business, and answer letters. Sugar made fortunes, but seldom for those who went out as indentured servants. Men who were illiterate were as unlikely to find fortunes in the sugar trade as they were in the law, government office, or the genteel marriage market. It is likely that there was more opportunity for a woman servant to make her fortune in the seventeenth-century colonial marriage mart,[93] but this was a chance that became remote in most colonies as demography changed.

Other avenues of rapid social mobility in Restoration England could be pursued in the colonies as well, even if the colonies in themselves were a less than splendid social escalator. With the hard pioneering life over in most of the colonies, the religious leaders were increasingly joined by attorneys and doctors from England and Scotland who saw opportunities in migration.[94] Expansion of government offices could, as in Lord Berkeley's Virginia or Joseph Dudley's Massachusetts, afford access to land and local power.[95] What has been called *The Migratory Elite* of the second British Empire,[96] had its precursors in the first. The migration of merchants into Massachusetts after 1650 represents another aspect of this process.[97] New migrants with capital, credit, royal or proprietary favour found opportunities in the colonies. The development of the newer colonies of the Jerseys and Pennsylvania provided a wider spectrum of mobility, though the advantages of the migrant of the 'middling sort' were substantial. While political developments in the north gave opportunity to new men in the later Stuart period, social developments in the Chesapeake gradually strengthened the locally-born elite.[98] The Carolina frontier offered most of its new white inhabitants a rude sufficiency, with the economic and political prizes going to the experienced and well-to-do West Indian planters.[99] It would be surprising if those with the most advantages did not gain most from the development of new areas, new products, and new markets in the 'provincial lifetime'.

These same developments tended to limit the opportunities for indentured servants, who earlier could have hoped to become landowners and enjoy minor offices. The work of Russell Menard and Lorena Walsh on seventeenth-century Maryland[100] needs imitation wherever sources permit, but recent studies present a plausible picture of increasing stratification and lessening social mobility.[101] Again, as in other aspects of recent work in the area, colonial Englishmen's social existence is increasingly being seen as quite like life in the old world in many respects and colonial developments often served to lessen the differences as time went on.

In ways that are associated with the ideas of Harold Innis and Marshall McLuhan,[102] the English Atlantic was a paper empire. From laws and instructions to governors, sea captains, or agents, from letters and newspapers, or even from mundane bills of lading, it is evident that the English Atlantic was a society that rewarded literacy. This 'literal' culture developed patterns of thought, styles of argument, and views of life that were quite different from the oral traditions that had been inherited and which continued to condition the minds of the illiterate members of the same society.[103] For some, literacy was a badge of reformed Christian civilisation, but for others, literacy was a prerequisite for participation in the economic, social and political leadership of the English Atlantic. Illiteracy was linked to dependency, whether that of wife and children, or of the oral culture of Indians and African slaves. Anthropologist Robert Redfield has made a telling distinction between the 'Great Tradition' and the 'Little Tradition' as coexisting and competing perspectives within a society.[104] In the English Atlantic the Little Tradition was oral and local; the Great Tradition was literate and cosmopolitan. The successful provincial had some loyalty to each.

Literacy has become of increasing concern to scholars of early modern England and America. Although the sources are less than ideal, the findings tend once again to reduce the presumed contrasts between English and colonial residents. It is difficult to measure literacy from the signing or marking of wills, but such is the nature of the best evidence about colonial literacy. An adult male literacy rate of about 60 per cent, and female literacy at about 35 per cent, is indicated for heads of households in colonial North America in 1660. Although this rate would not change much in Virginia in the next century, K. A. Lockridge has found that male literacy in New England rose dramatically to 70 per cent by 1710 and to 85 per cent by 1760. The implications of this finding need further study, but suggest that the correlation between status and literacy was not maintained amid declining opportunity in eighteenth-century Massachusetts.[105] Fragmentary evidence on literacy elsewhere in English America suggests that white literacy rates were comparable to those of England, though slave illiteracy meant that the plantation colonies were notably less literate than England. It seems safe to assume that only a minority of the adults in England or America could read and write well enough to do so regularly. Whenever information was power, the written word was quicker, more accurate, more complete, exclusive, and it also allowed careful re-readings. In religion, in politics, in family life, and in business, the English Atlantic functioned primarly through, and for, the literate.

Education transmits and preserves more than it innovates, and recent work on American provincial education has re-emphasised the continuities between England and America.[106] New England's strenuous efforts to extend literacy and piety now seem less a special reaction to the fears of barbarism among their children in a frontier society[107] than a feature of Calvinist confidence in The Book. The public education laws of New England and of Scotland were established by visibly devout legislators, although the fruits of mass male literacy would come in less devout times. Education to preserve the faith, to preserve civility, and to transmit useful skills seems to have concerned colonials in varying degrees, in keeping with various traditions in Britain, but without any special fervour or neglect that was uniquely colonial.

Provincial newspapers first emerged in the 1690s, bringing local inter-pretations of events and cosmopolitan intrusions upon local life.[108] The *Worcester Postman* (1690) and the *Stamford Mercury* (1695) were the first two English provincial papers, but it is significant that the *Edinburgh Gazette* (1699) and the *Boston News-Letter* (1704) were next, preceding a flood of new English provincial papers during the next 15 years. The *Boston News-Letter* was so thoroughly committed to delivering court and English news that it has been ignored by historians seeking 'American' culture.[109] Whatever official censorship was applied to this first North American newspaper, its 300 subscribers[110] bought their weekly allotment of metropolitan news because they wanted it. Perhaps there was no apology for a newspaper that was overwhelmingly reprinted from English papers because no apology was necessary.[111]

Books and their ideas are recognised as an English Atlantic trade of consequence, but the general subject has not received nearly the attention recently lavished on the transit of political ideas,[112] or upon the colonial production of books.[113] Colonial contribution to the Royal Society may have been marked by provincial deference and search for recognition in the metropolis,[114] but N. Fiering has demonstrated how colonial men of letters could keep abreast of new ideas from Europe.[115] The Charlestown Library Society boasted of cultural provincialism in its simple Latin motto, 'Et Artes trans mare currunt'.[116]

Gentlemanly learning was firmly bound to 'home', but we cannot presume that the world of piety and practical knowledge was not also an English Atlantic one. Most visibly transatlantic, the Quaker community exchanged regular epistles and frequent visits of 'ministering Friends' who travelled to share and strengthen the faith.[117] Although New World Puritanism participated in the theological wars of England more fully in the mid-seventeenth century, religious links continued after the Restoration.[118] Anglicanism was the English empire's official faith, and its place in the colonies tended to grow with the age of the settlements, with the conscious sponsorship of the government, and with the efforts of the Society for the Propogation of the Gospel.[119] The surge of revivalism with which this period ended was itself a transatlantic phenomenon, for George Whitefield and John Wesley could speak to both English and colonial religious sensitivities.

London fashions were regarded with necessary ambivalence in all her provinces. Display of current fashions was a sign of London connections, perhaps advertising links with men of moment in the capital. The migrating elites updated colonial manners and fashions. This was not only true of royal or proprietary governors and their entourages: it was also true of what might be called the professions of pretence—the poorly regulated world of physicians, surgeons, advocates and attorneys. Fashion was a badge of gentility and civility that was worn in most inappropriate circumstances.[120] Denunciation of such foppery could also be imported in either secular or religious guise, but the provincial ridicule of pretence revealed a defence mechanism of those who felt culturally inferior.[121] Such inferiority could naturally lead provincial Englishmen on either side of the Atlantic to denounce London's sins while imitating them, and to exalt in the clean and wholesome moral climate of their own communities while importing the latest cultural whimsy from London. Nor should it be surprising if the provincial well-to-do did more of the imitating and the rest of colonial society did more of the denouncing.

Much of the recent social history of the period 1675–1740 has tended to qualify or contradict the easy assertions about how different the new world was from the old in fertility of its people, literacy, and even opportunity. This trend not only narrows the differences between colonial provinces and those on the home island, it suggests cultural continuity as a major value held by colonisers and their children. One of the general questions that emerges from such a sketch, and leads to a consideration of political culture, is 'How did the new elites elicit or impose social order in these relatively new communities?'

Imperial and colonial politics were vehicles for local social control, and ones which served an emerging elite by assisting, confirming and defending their new social position. English Atlantic politics have long fascinated historians, and the effort lavished on this field has been inspected frequently by a generation of reviewers.[122] The mesmerising power of the American Revolution, which fractured a polity regardless of whatever else it did or did not do, ensures continuing attention to political subjects. Unfortunately, this concern can also make colonial grandfathers into veterans of their grandsons' revolution. Provincial ambivalence was as evident in politics as in social life, for politics invited both the integration of the empire and the integration of the colony to resist that metropolitan initiative. The king's name was more than a distant benediction of would-be local grandees, for he sent demanding messages and messengers as well. In discussing the politics of integration, it is useful to notice some work concerning political institutions and ideas before considering the larger literature on political practice.

The history of English political institutions received much scholarly attention early in this century,[123] and recent studies of 'Anglo-American' politics have added comparatively little to that inheritance. The shift of attention has been a dramatic one. Institutional history that presumed more continuity than change was once written as a broad structural analysis of subjects such as royal governorships, the customs service, or the Board of Trade.[124] Recent studies tend to emphasise short term political changes as they affected institutions, resulting in more immediacy to particular historical situations and in more narrative structuring of monographs.[125] 'Whig history' has been so effectively ousted that processes like the 'origins of cabinet government' or 'the rise of the colonial assemblies' can be seen primarily as the accidental institutional consequences of politics.[126]

Local political institutions affected political integration decisively, and those of provincial England contrasted sharply with those of the colonies. County political life had its managers, its lord-lieutenants, county courts and locally-oriented J.P.s, but efforts to insulate the counties from central control were hampered by political institutions.[127] Parliament was the major political vehicle through which to resist royal or executive centralisation: yet Parliament was itself a centralising, homogenising force. Incorporated towns and cities were in a slightly stronger position, with some political institutions and needs that brought them closer to the transatlantic colonies. A chartered town had courts, an elite that was less hereditary than in the county, and might have a significant population of immigrants and limited social deference.

Charter and precedent were both usable in building the political institutions of the colonies into formal, and eventually formidable, protectors of local rights. Charters were not inviolate, but were rightly seen by royal servants as screening chartered and proprietary colonies from some of the centralising efforts of the royal administration.[128] Colonial assemblies, born under charter government but existing in all colonies by 1700, gradually became power centres which imitated the English House of Commons in resisting proprietors, governors, and eventually Parliament itself.[129] Strengthening of local assemblies was directed against executive power, but this process was also drawing power from the local level to the provincial, and can be seen as part of the consolidation of provincial elites.[130]

Colonial provinces may have had a usable institution for resisting royal initiative, but they also had a strong centralising office, that of governor. The monarch was not equal in all of his dominions. The colonial governor had a royal veto which lasted beyond 1707, when it was last used in England. The governor had the power to prorogue, recall, and dissolve colonial assemblies, a power which Parliament had weakened by 1690. In addition, the colonial governor had direct control over the judiciary in his colony.[131] English political institutions would undergo substantial changes in the lifetime after 1675, but the existence of colonial assemblies ensured that colonial efforts to emulate English Whiggery produced different results.

In theory, as well as practice, the defence of English provincial autonomy depended upon limiting the power of the king and his ministers, even though Lockean formulations of the rights of the subject could serve Whig ministries as well as their opponents in Parliament and in the counties.[132] Whig aristocrats and oligarchs believed their battle cries about liberty as they attacked placemen, standing armies, and life revenues for the king. In the corridors of Whitehall or Westminister, or in the somewhat different atmosphere of the colonial assemblies, gentlemen, merchants, and slaveholders found Whiggery, including that of the more radical *Eighteenth-Century Commonwealthman,*[133] entirely appropriate in the struggle for power against the king's representatives. The English Atlantic of the early eighteenth century shared the developing Whig political theory. It became more widespread in the colonies less because they were some inherently 'liberal fragment'[134] than because the emerging political community found this approach appealing and useful, particularly as it was shared by the dominant English political figures.

The practice of politics in the English Atlantic has received a great deal more attention in the last twenty years than has the theory. The atomisation of English politics owes much to the work of L. B. Namier, the first major piece of which appeared (like the first of the *Cambridge History of the British Empire*) fifty years ago.[135] Namier's major impact on scholarship came after the second World War, when his approach influenced scholars in English and then American colonial studies.[136] The approach, which perceives politics as the idea-free art of gathering power for patronage, has appealed both to those historians who are suspicious of ideology and to those whose ideas lead them to emphasise the economic interpretation of political behaviour. Namier's approach was also supportive of the strong biographical tradition in the writing of English political history, and gave added significance to local and county history as well. Namier's interpretation and method were developed to understand the generation after 1760, and it is the rather zealous application of this approach to Queen Anne's reign that has been very effectively challenged.[137]

Imperial politics of the English Atlantic between 1675 and 1740 exhibited phases, yet there were persisting forces of political integration throughout this period. The monarchy was a shared symbol of social and political order, lending its name to laws, charters and court proceedings. This symbolism had its uses in all the king's provinces, but was of particular concern in areas where social mobility was more common and deference was less so. The gentlemen merchants of incorporated towns like Hull or Leeds, for example, saw the charter and baronetcies as legitimising their social and political leadership in communities that included immigrants who had never touched their forelock to a merchant. The royal garrison at Hull might even supplement the night watch over property.[138] Local notables called courts into session in the king's name, but they rightly suspected the assizes[139] as centralising legal power as effectively as did appeals to higher courts and the lawmaking power of Westminster. The crown was a stabilising symbol, but much of politics was aimed at exploiting that symbol while eroding the crown's real power.

The crown was not only the formal font of order, it was also at least the formal source of the political patronage that supported many English aristocrats, and the pretensions of officeholders on both sides of the Atlantic. Sophisticated political use of the offices in the gift of the crown was justly feared as a power to overcome all legislative resistance.[140] Transatlantic provinces were particularly subject to the integrating power of royal patronage. A new royal governor could bring trouble for the calculations and pretensions of the colonial elite. His power over a few appointments was less important than his nominations for council seats, his control of the magistracy, and his influence over land grants. Governorships were brief and the lobbying of colonials and their agents to oust, obtain, or keep governors was itself a system that bound colonial leadership to English politics.[141]

Whatever the structural bias of imperial political institutions, they operated in the real and unpredictable world of all politics. The active monarchical drive for order and control that marked the period 1675 to 1688 was unique and formative. The crisis of 1688–9 was shared by the whole empire. The generation 1689–1714 saw several sharp shifts in political power. Then came the generation that achieved, and suffered, political stability. These phases are a simple framework within which some of the recent works of political historians can be viewed.

The English crown was an unusually active agent of political integration between 1675 and 1688. From the fiscal, diplomatic and political rubble of the last Dutch war, a sobered Charles II and his more sober and industrious younger brother, James, began rebuilding the monarchy's position. Opposition to royal resurgence crystallised into Whiggery, developed new weapons in electoral management, but lost the long and bitter fight to exclude James from the succession.[142] Customs revenues on imported colonial staples were a significant part of the royal revenues that were independent of Parliament. Bacon's Rebellion in Virginia hurt that revenue, and prompted closer political management of the colonies. From 1675 the new Lords of Trade and Plantatations began an administrative centralisation,[143] and launched the careers of William Blathwayt and Edward Randolph, names synonymous with this centralisation for the next generation.[144] In 1685 James gained the monarchy and the life revenues which, in the prosperity of his brief years, yielded enough to allow him more freedom from Parliament.[145]

The Glorious Revolution was an admission of failure: the king's political opponents had failed to stop him by constitutional means. The result was an acceptence of unconstitutional means, and significant adjustments to protect against recurrence, while insisting upon the preservative nature of the coup.[146] The colonial uprisings in the Dominion of New England and in Maryland have usually been seen as based upon local grievances, which seem sufficient causes.[147] What can easily be underestimated, as P. S. Haffenden indicates,[148] is that the Revolution was welcomed around the English Atlantic with few regrets and few Jacobites, indeed with something approaching unanimity. Apparently it mattered who was king of England: colonial revolutions occurred only where unofficial news of the royal changes arrived long before any official word reached the colonial executive.[149] In general, the revolution showed the political unity of the empire much more than it revealed its diversity.

War is an international test of the ability of a government to marshall resources. William brought a war against the powerful centralising French monarchy, and the war effort brought some of that state power which both the revolution and the war ostensibly opposed. Although there were political concessions to 'country' interests in the annual Parliaments, they were voting taxes for expanded government. The fiscal drain was from the North and West to the Southeast. from the landed to the manufacturing and service groups in the nation, and from the provinces to the metropolis.[150] For the colonies, the war and its successor would bring more military responsibilities than resources for the governors, but would increase the roles of the governor and the commander of the naval station ships. Assemblies bargained for privileges, paper money issues, or other concessions in return for supply, but an echo of the processes at work in England could be heard in the colonies when they were, rather intermittently, roused to war.[151] Colonials fought the French and did so as provincial Englishmen. As with the English governments of these war years, governors had varied success in harnessing factions for the war effort.[152] The assemblies would emerge stronger, and the governors weaker, as was true in England, but the wars made colonial dependency on metropolitan warmaking and peacemaking painfully obvious.[153]

Peace brought a respite from the government drive to assemble resources, eased the tax burden, and promised fewer initiatives at the expense of provincial life, or at least meant that local elites could manage these initiatives. The Whig political triumph was reinforced by helping the Tories commit political suicide, and by reducing the size of the electorate and the frequency of elections.[154] While radical Whigs pursued the wars of ideas, the managers of the government focused upon patronage as the purpose of power. Frank acceptence of the enjoyment of office brought consequences that are perhaps easiest seen in the well-documented colonial administrations. The quality of Newcastle's governors was uneven,[155] but that is less surprising or un-common than was the tendency for appointees to avoid initiatives that would be unpopular and to make compromises for personal peace or profit that permanently shrank the power of the governorship. Whatever power was not sacrificed that way was subject to more intense pressure from England. Patrons of the governor offered him candidates for those few offices that were still part of his direct patronage, offices he should have used to buy or keep political supporters from the local elite. The management of colonial politics had always reached to Whitehall: under Walpole and Newcastle the management of the House of Commons extended all the way to Jamaica and Virginia.[156]

Achieving 'political stability' in Walpole's England included what can still be called 'salutary neglect' of the colonies, if not political stability there as well.[157] 'Robinocracy' was factious Whiggery, tainted Whiggery, but still seen to be Whig by all but a few. Yet no colonial governor could be a Whig in office, though every one of them had to be a Whig to get that office. If the colonial executive threat to the liberties of the local elite had not been real, it would have been a most useful invention. The colonial assemblies were emulating the House of Commons of the recent past in defending 'country' values against the 'court'. This was not the road to independence, this was the political perspective of an emerging provincial elite anxious and able to consolidate their own power within the English Atlantic.[158] The triumph of the Whigs had been better institutionalised in the American and West Indian assemblies that it had been in England.

It was no coincidence that the 'English nation' mattered most to the people who mattered most. Those with economic, social, and political ties beyond the local level would include the nobility, the gentry, and the prominent merchants who were the leaders of county, town, or colony. These elites had a fascinating ambivalence towards the metropolis. On the one hand, they were the men of substance who could defend their localities from metropolitan interference; on the other hand, they could gain personal advantage in serving the court or the 'nation' as agents of centralisation.[159] They could resist royal or parliamentary initiatives with Whig thunder against tyranny, while exercising local political and legal power that was legitimised by the king's name. They could denounce the London stock-jobbers and goldsmiths while living on money borrowed in the metropolis for fashionable living, for land purchases, for industrial estate development, or even for lending to others in their locality. They could proclaim the moral superiority in the wholesome rural life while displaying their civility via the fashions of London. These paradoxical tensions, which were so cleverly exposed in later Stuart plays,[160] are enduring aspects of provincial life.

Recent scholarship suggests that when John Oldmixon claimed 'I have no notion of any more difference between Old-England and New than between Lincolnshire and Somerset'[161] he was stretching a truth less than was once thought. The emergence of English provincial history has destroyed the equation of London and England at the same time as American colonial studies have been challenging notions of a unique America, or what David Hall has called 'American exceptionalism'.[162] The links between what was happening in Stuart and Georgian England and the colonies were not a matter of parallels: the same processes of metropolitan integration were pulling at all London's provinces.

Of the major aspects of life, the economic attractions of specialisation, interdependence and integration recommended themselves to those provincials able to dominate the new staples of the colonies, or the older ones for the new English markets. The sea allowed colonial integration with little investment in roads or canals. At this provincial stage there was very little resistance, and obvious advantage to economic integration.

Although peopled by many from London's nearer provinces, the colonies began as social gatherings most unlike home. Demographic, economic, and political development all contributed to the emergence of new world provinces that were much more like the old than the founders would have imagined or intended. Gentility and civility served social purposes amongst provincial elites throughout the empire, mattering even more in London's more immediate hinterland, where political independence had been effectively lost. In colonial society, the elites could profitably accept English gentility as a social insulator which distinguished themselves from other colonists, Indians and slaves. The fall of the colonial governors was, and was intended to be, a constitutional replay of the fall of the Stuart monarchy. Colonial leaders maintained their local dominance through political institutions that served both to resist imperial initiatives and to integrate power within the colony itself. Success was not assured, and the generation of war after 1739 would upset the Whig empire in all of its parts, but colonial assemblies did represent a major source of power not available in the same way to English county and town elites. Colonial elites could serve themselves and call it serving the king or call it serving their electors. But they would have trouble claiming, as the slave or indentured servant might have done, (and as undergraduates continue to do), that 'The colonies exist for the benefit of the mother country'. Provincial elites were beneficiaries of empire. The ambiguity of being the vehicles of cosmopolitan influence and the defence against that influence did not produce great difficulties. The notion of 'stacking loyalties' has been used to good effect in other contexts,[163] but has been noticeably absent in explanations of provincials in the first empire. Virginians, like men of Devon, could hold their local loyalty firmly and yet fight as Englishmen. When loyalties clashed, the local one might triumph, but local elites drew power from the unity of the English Atlantic.

NOTES

1. *The Boston News-Letter,* no. 390, 8 Oct. 1711 and *The Diary of Samuel Sewall,* 3 vols. (Boston, 1878–1882), II, 323–4.
2. D. E. van Deventer, *The Emergence of Provincial New Hampshire, 1623–1741* (Baltimore, 1976), 218. An advertised horse race, with a 20 shilling entry fee and a £20 plate, hints at similar influences in Cambridge, Mass. by Sept. of 1715. *The Boston News-Letter,* nos. 594–6.
3. (Cambridge, 1929).
4. The imperial perspective is maintained by L. H. Gipson in *A Bibliographical Guide to the History of the British Empire, 1748–1776,* which is volume 14 of his *The British Empire before the American Revolution,* 15 vols. (Caldwell, Idaho & New York, 1936–70). Also see his 'The Imperial Approach to Early American History' in *The Reinterpretation of Early American History,* ed. R. A. Billington (San Marino, Cal., 1966), 185–99. Useful recent general bibliographies of American colonial history include: F. Freidel and R. K. Showman, *The Harvard Guide to American History,* 2nd ed., 2 vols. (Cambridge, Mass., 1974); A. T. Vaughan, *The American Colonies in the Seventeeth Century* (New York, 1971); J. P. Greene, *The American Colonies in the Eighteenth Century* (New York, 1969); Institute of Early American History and Culture, *Books about Early America* (Williamsburg, 1970) and its sequel *Books about Early America 1970–1975* (Williamsburg, 1976).
5. E. A. Wrigley, 'A Simple Model of London's Importance in Changing English Society and Economy, 1650–1750', *Past & Present,* no. 37 (July 1967), 44–70.
   The Scottish lowlands had an English provincial culture, but one with cultural, legal, political and economic aspects different from the English colonies. See: J. Clive and B. Bailyn, 'England's Cultural Provinces: Scotland and America', *The William and Mary Quarterly,* 3rd ser. (hereafter cited as *W&MQ),* xi (1954), 200–13; D. Daiches, *The Paradox of Scottish Culture: The Eighteenth Century Experience* (London, 1964); J. H. Burns, 'Scotland and England: Culture and Nationality 1500–1800', in J. S. Bromley and E. H. Kossman (eds.), *Britain and the Netherlands IV Metropolis, Dominion and Province* (The Hague, 1971), 17–41; and N. T. Phillipson,

'Culture and Society in the Eighteenth Century Province: The Case of Edinburgh and the Scottish Enlightenment', in L. Stone (ed.), *The University in Society* (Princeton, 1974), 407–48. The emergence of Scotland as a new exemplar for some American colonists in the generation after 1750 needs further study. See Andrew Hook, *Scotland and America 1750–1835* (Glasgow, 1975), chap. 2.

6. P. Laslett, *The World We have Lost* (London, 1965), chap. 3; W. G. Hoskins, *Provincial England* (London, 1963); A. M. Everitt, *The Community of Kent and the Great Rebellion, 1640–1660* (Leicester, 1966); and I. Roots, 'The Central Government and the Local Community', in E. W. Ives (ed.), *The English Revolution 1600–1660* (London, 1968), 34–47.

7. J. Cornwall, 'Evidence of Population Mobility in the Seventeenth Century', *Institute of Historical Research Bulletin*, xl (1967), 143–52; A. Everitt, 'Farm Labourers' in *The Agrarian History of England and Wales, IV: 1500–1640*, ed. J. Thirsk (Cambridge, 1967), 399–400; P. Clark, 'The Migrant in Kentish Towns, 1580–1640', in *Crisis and Order in English Towns 1500–1700*, eds. P. Clark and P. Slack (London, 1972), 117–163; P. Slack, 'Vagrants and Vagrancy in England 1598–1664', *Economic History Review*, 2nd ser. (hereafter cited as *EcHR*), xxvii (1974), 360–79.

8. E. L. Jones, 'Agriculture and Economic Growth in England, 1660–1750: Agricultural Change', *Journal of Economic History* (hereafter cited as *JEcH*), xxv (1965), 1–18; A. H. John, 'Agricultural Productivity and Economic Growth in England, 1700–1760', *ibid.*, 19–34; J. D. Chambers, *Population, Economy, and Society in Pre-Industrial England* (London, 1972). For the grain trade into Massachusetts see D. C. Klingaman, 'The Coastwise Trade of Colonial Massachusetts', *Essex Institute Historical Collections*, cviii (1972), 217–34.

9. L. Stone, *The Crisis of the Aristocracy, 1558–1641* (Oxford, 1965); J. H. Hexter, *Reappraisals in History* (London, 1961), 117–62; T. Aston, ed., *Crisis in Europe 1560–1660* (London, 1965).

10. A Everitt, *Change in the Provinces: the Seventeenth Century* (Leicester, 1969) is a suggestive general essay. Also see: Everitt, *Community of Kent;* J. S. Morrill, *Cheshire 1630–1660: County Government and Society during the English Revolution* (London, 1974); A. Fletcher, *A County Community in Peace and War: Sussex 1600–1660* (London, 1976); B. G. Blackwood, *The Lancashire Gentry and the Great Rebellion, 1640–1660* (Manchester, 1978).

11. W. F. Craven, 'Historical Study of the British Empire', *Journal of Modern History,* vi (1934), 40–1. This essay emphasises the first empire, and makes comparisons with later work possible.

12. Wrigley, *loc. cit.* On London investment in the provinces see J. D. Chambers, *The Vale of Trent, 1670–1800* (London, 1957) and compare J. R. Ward, *The Finance of Canal Building in Eighteenth Century England* (London, 1974); A. H. John, 'Aspects of English Economic Growth in the first half of the Eighteenth Century', *Economica*, xxviii (1961), 188. On the slow growth of 'country banks' in English provincial cities (cf. Edinburgh) see M. W. Flinn, *The Origins of the Industrial Revolution* (London, 1966), 52–4; D. C. Coleman, *The Economy of England 1450–1750* (Oxford, 1977), 147; and G. Jackson, *Hull in the Eighteenth Century: A Study in Economic and Social History* (London, 1972), chap. ix.

13. *Bibliography of British History: Stuart Period, 1603–1714,* 2nd ed., edited by G. Davies and M. F. Keeler (Oxford, 1970) remains the standard bibliography for the later Stuarts, and there are useful additions to be found in W. L. Sachse, *Restoration England, 1660–1689* (Cambridge, 1971) and in C. Wilson, *England's Apprenticeship, 1603–1763* (London, 1965). American colonial economic history was carefully reviewed by L. A. Harper, 'Recent Contributions to American Economic History: American History to 1789', *JEcH*, xix (1959), 1–24 and updated ten years later by G. R. Taylor's *American Economic History before 1860* (New York, 1969). Also see Freidel and Showman.

14. *The Rise of the Atlantic Economies* (London, 1973) and *The North Atlantic World in the Seventeenth Century* (London, 1974) respectively. There is also much that is suggestive in *The Cambridge Economic History of Europe:* vol. IV, *The Economy of Expanding Europe in the 16th and 17th Centuries*, E. E. Rich and C. Wilson (eds.), (Cambridge, 1967).

15. Wilson, *England's Apprenticeship;* L. A. Clarkson, *The Pre-Industrial Economy, 1500–1750* (London, 1971); and Coleman, *Economy of England.* Flinn, *Origins* emphasises the colonial markets in the period 1740–1760, see chap. iv.
16. See: E. B. Schumpeter, *English Overseas Trade Statistics, 1697–1808* (Oxford, 1960); P. Deane and W. A. Cole, *British Economic Growth, 1688–1959,* 2nd ed. (Cambridge, 1967) and N. F. R. Craft, 'English Economic Growth in the Eighteenth Century: A Re-Examination of Deane and Cole's Estimates', *EcHR,* xxix (1976), 226–35; R. Davis, *The Rise of the English Shipping Industry* (London, 1962) and his *English Overseas Trade 1500–1700* (London, 1963); and the studies gathered as *The Growth of English Overseas Trade in the 17th and 18th Centuries* (London, 1969) edited by W. E. Minchinton.
17. See Coleman, *Economy of England,* 196–201 for a cautious judgement. Davis, *Atlantic Economies* emphasises new world trade whereas Jones, *loc. cit.,* John, *loc. cit.,* and E. Kerridge, *The Agricultural Revolution* (London, 1967) present the case for agricultural growth, as does E. L. Jones, *Agriculture and the Industrial Revolution* (Oxford, 1975).
18. K. Lockridge, *A New England Town: The First Hundred Years* (New York, 1970); J. Demos, *A Little Commonwealth: Family Life in Plymouth Colony* (New York, 1970); and P. J. Greven Jr., *Four Generations: Population, Land, and Family in Colonial Andover, Massachusetts* (Ithaca, N.Y., 1970) are all valuable in appreciating the isolated community. J. T. Lemon, *The Best Poor Man's Country; A Geographical Study of Early Southeastern Pennsylvania* (Baltimore, 1972); R. L. Bushman, *From Puritan to Yankee: Character and the Social Order in Connecticut, 1690–1765* (Cambridge, Mass., 1967) and van Deventer, *Provincial New Hampshire* study somewhat larger subjects that demonstrate the impact of the market economy.
19. R. F. Neill, *A New Theory of Value: The Canadian Economics of H. A. Innis* (Toronto, 1972); M. H. Watkins, 'A Staple Theory of Economic Growth', *Canadian Journal of Economic and Political Science,* xxix (1963), 141–58; R. E. Baldwin, 'Patterns of Development in Newly Settled Regions', *Manchester School of Economic and Social Studies,* xxiv (1956), 161–79; D. C. North and R. P. Thomas, 'An Economic Theory of the Growth of the Western World', *EcHR,* xxiii (1970), 1–17.
20. (New Haven, 1940).
21. *Eighteenth Century Newfoundland* (Toronto, 1976).
22. The timber trade was another central feature of New England economics, best seen in the development of New Hampshire. See J. J. Malone, *Pine Trees and Politics: The Naval Stores and Forest Policy in Colonial New England 1691–1775* (Seattle, 1964) and van Deventer, *Provincial New Hampshire,* especially chap. v.
23. See his *The History of the Hudson's Bay Company, 1670–1870,* 2 vols. (London, 1958–9) and his more general *The Fur Trade and the Northwest to 1857* (Toronto, 1967).
24. A. J. Ray, *Indians in the Fur Trade: their role as trappers, hunters, and middlemen in the lands southwest of Hudson Bay, 1660–1870* (Toronto, 1974) and A. Rotstein, 'Fur Trade and Empire: An Institutional Analysis', Ph.D., thesis University of Toronto, 1967.
25. G. Williams, *The Search for the Northwest Passage in the Eighteenth Century* (London, 1962).
26. T. E. Norton, *The Fur Trade in Colonial New York, 1686–1776* (Madison, Wisc., 1974); D. A. Armour, 'The Merchants of Albany, New York 1686–1760', Ph.D. thesis, Northwestern University, 1965; S. E. Sale, 'Colonial Albany: Outpost of Empire', Ph.D. thesis, University of Southern California, 1973.
27. F. P. Prucha, *A Bibliographical Guide to the History of Indian-White Relations in the United States* (Chicago, 1977) is a full survey of recent work.
28. *War and Trade in the West Indies, 1739–1763* (Oxford, 1936); *A West India Fortune* (London, 1950); *Yankees and Creoles* (London, 1956); *Merchants and Planters* (New York, 1960).
29. N. Deerr, *History of Sugar,* 2 vols. (London, 1949).
30. (New Haven, 1917).
31. (Chapel Hill, 1972).
32. (Baltimore, 1973), 5–17.

33. The dabate can be followed in: R. B. Sheridan, 'The Wealth of Jamaica in the Eighteenth Century', *EcHR*, xviii (1965), 292–311; R. P. Thomas, 'The Sugar Colonies of the Old Empire: Profit or Loss for Great Britain', *ibid.*, xxi (1968), 30–45; R. B. Sheridan, 'The Wealth of Jamaica in the Eighteenth Century: a Rejoinder', *ibid.*, 46–61; R. K. Aufhauser, 'Profitability of Slavery in the British Caribbean', *Journal of Interdisciplinary History*, v (1974), 45–67; J. R. Ward, 'The Profitability of Sugar Planting in the British West Indies, 1650–1834', *EcHR*, xxxi (1978), 197–213.

34. See K. G. Davies, *The Royal African Company* (London, 1957), chaps. iv, vi; Sheridan, *Sugar and Slavery*, chaps. xii, xiii.

35. R. B. Sheridan, 'The Rise of a Colonial Gentry: A Case Study of Antigua, 1730–1758', *EcHR*, xiii (1961), 342–57; Dunn, *Sugar and Slaves*, especially chaps. ii, iv-vii.

36. Pares, *Yankees* and Fairchild, *Messrs. William Pepperrell, Merchants at Piscataqua* (Ithaca, N.Y., 1954).

37. See below, notes 51–7.

38. F. G. James, 'Irish Colonial Trade in the Eighteenth Century', *W&MQ*, xx (1963), 574–84, and his *Ireland in the Empire 1688–1770* (Cambridge, Mass., 1973).

39. G. M. Ostrander, 'The Colonial Molasses Trade', *Agricultural History*, xxx (1956), 77–84; W. D. Houlette, 'Rum Trading in the American Colonies before 1763', *The Journal of American History*, xxvii (1934), 129–52.

40. B. Bailyn, *The New England Merchants in the Seventeenth Century* (Cambridge, Mass., 1955) and F. B. Tolles, *Meeting House and Counting House* (Chapel Hill, N.C., 1948). W. I. Davisson and L. J. Bradley, 'New York Maritime Trade: Ship Voyage Patterns, 1715–1765', *New York Historical Society Quarterly*, lv (1971), 309–17 suggests the prominence of the island trade there as well.

41. *Shipping, Maritime Trade, and the Economic Development of Colonial North America* (Cambridge, 1972); North and Thomas, *loc. cit.* and D. C. North, 'Sources of Productivity Change in Ocean Shipping, 1600–1850', in R. W. Fogel and S. L. Engerman (eds.), *The Reinterpretation of American Economic History* (New York, 1971), 163–74.

42. B. and L. Bailyn, *Massachusetts Shipping, 1697–1714* (Cambridge, Mass., 1959).

43. This trade needs further study. Aspects of the naval stores trade are the focus of Malone, *Pine Trees*, and J. J. McCusker, *Money and Exchange in Europe and America, 1600–1775: A Handbook* (Chapel Hill, N.C., 1978) will ease the calculations here as elsewhere.

44. C. D. Clowse, *Economic Beginnings in Colonial South Carolina, 1670–1730* (Columbia, S.C., 1971); P. H. Wood, *Black Majority: Negroes in Colonial South Carolina from 1670 through the Stono Rebellion* (New York, 1974), chap. iv.

45. J. G. Lydon, 'Fish and Flour for Gold: Southern Europe and the Colonial American Balance of Payments', *Business History Review*, xxxix (1965), 171–83; D. Klingaman, 'The Significance of Grain in the Development of the Tobacco Colonies', *JEcH*, xxix (1969), 268–78; P. G. E. Clemens, 'From Tobacco to Grain: Economic Development on Maryland's Eastern Shore, 1660–1750', Ph.D. thesis, University of Wisconsin, 1974.

46. 'The Tobacco Adventure to Russia, 1676–1722', *Transactions of the American Philosophical Society*, new series, vol. li, pt. 1 (1961), 3–120; *France and the Chesapeake*, 2 vols. (Ann Arbor, Mich,. 1973).

47. 'Economic Base and Social Structure: The Northern Chesapeake in the Eighteenth Century', *JEcH*, xxv (1965), 639–59; and 'Economic Behavior in a Planting Society: The Eighteenth Century Chesapeake', *Journal of Southern History*, xxxiii (1967), 469–85.

48. J. M. Price, 'The Rise of Glasgow in the Chesapeake Tobacco Trade, 1707–1775', *W&MQ*, xi (1954), 179–200; T. M. Devine, *The Tobacco Lords* (Edinburgh, 1974); L. M. Cullen, 'Merchant Communities, The Navigation Acts and the Irish and Scottish Responses', and T. M. Devine, 'Colonial Commerce and the Scottish Economy, c. 1730–1815', both in *Comparative Aspects of Scottish and Irish Economic and Social History 1600–1900* (Edinburgh, 1977).

49. Bibliographies include: E. Miller, *The Negro in America: A Bibliography* (Cambridge, Mass., 1966); W. D. Jordan, *White over Black: American Attitudes Toward the*

Negro, 1550–1812 (Chapel Hill, N.C., 1968), pp. 586–614; J. M. McPherson, *Blacks in America: Bibliographical Essays* (New York, 1971); P. H. Wood, ' "I Did the Best I Could for My Day": The Study of Early Black History during the Second Reconstruction, 1960 to 1976', *W&MQ*, xxxv (1978), 185–225.
50. (London, 1944).
51. Williams' argument, that slavery led to discrimination, has been favoured by economic and by 'liberal' historians. O. and M. F. Handlin, 'Origins of the Southern Labour System', *W&MQ*, vii (1950), 199–222 and S. Elkins, *Slavery* (Chicago, 1959) are significant here. The primacy of prejudice as preceding and causing slavery has been argued by C. Degler, 'Slavery and the Genesis of American Race Prejudice', *Comparative Studies in Society and History*, ii (1959–60), 49–66 and by Jordan, *White over Black*. Jordan's 'Modern Tensions and the Origins of American Slavery,' *Journal of Southern History*, xxviii (1962), 18–33, exposed the false dichotomy of the debate and offered a sensible middle ground.
52. See above, note 33. Another centre of this debate concerns the period after 1760. Highlights include: R. W. Fogel and S. L. Engerman, *Time on the Cross*, 2 vols. (Boston, 1974); H. G. Guttman, *Slavery and the Numbers Game: A Critique of Time on the Cross* (Urbana, Ill., 1975). On the related question of the slavers' profits see R. P. Thomas and R. N. Bean, 'The Fishers of Men: The Profits of the Slave Trade', *JEcH*, xxxiv (1974), 885–914, and the following note.
53. R. Anstey, *The Atlantic Slave Trade and British Abolition, 1760–1810* (London, 1974); H. Temperley, 'Capitalism, Slavery and Ideology', *Past and Present*, no. 75 (May 1977), 94–118; S. Drescher, *Econocide: British Slavery in the Era of Abolition* (Pittsburgh, 1977).
54. I. A. Akinjogbin, *Dahomey and Its Neighbours, 1708–1818* (London, 1967); P. D. Curtin, *Economic Change in Precolonial Africa: Senegambia in the Era of the Slave Trade* (Madison, Wisc., 1975); K. Y. Daaku, *Trade and Politics on the Gold Coast 1600–1720* (Oxford, 1970); D. Forde, ed. *Efik Traders of Old Calabar* (London, 1956); A. J. H. Latham, *Old Calabar, 1600–1891* (London, 1973); R. Law, *The Oyo Empire c. 1600 – c. 1836* (Oxford, 1977); M. Priestley, *West African Trade and Coast Society, a family study* (London, 1969); W. Rodney, *A History of the Upper Guinea Coast, 1545–1800* (Oxford, 1970); Thomas and Bean, 'Fishers of Men'.
55. *The Atlantic Slave Trade: A Census* (Madison, Wisc., 1970).
56. D. P. Mannix and M. Crowley, *Black Cargoes* (New York, 1962); M. Craton, *Sinews of Empire: A Short History of British Slavery* (London, 1974); R. N. Bean, *The British Trans-Atlantic Slave Trade, 1650–1775* (New York, 1975).
57. G. Ostrander, 'The Making of the Triangular Trade Myth', *W&MQ*, xxx (1973), 635–44; H. S. Klein, 'Slaves and Shipping in Eighteenth-Century Virginia', *Journal of Interdisciplinary History*, v (1975), 383–412; P. G. E. Clemens, 'The Rise of Liverpool, 1665–1750', *EcHR*, xxix (1976), 211–25.
58. See D. C. Coleman, *Revisions in Mercantilism* (London, 1969).
59. (Oxford, 1975). Also see E. A. Reitan, 'From Revenue to Civil List 1689–1702', *Historical Journal*, xiii (1970), 571–88 and C. Roberts, 'The Constitutional Significance of the Financial Settlement of 1690', *ibid.*, xx (1977), 59–76.
60. T. C. Barker, 'Smuggling in the Eighteenth Century: The Evidence of the Scottish Tobacco Trade', *Virginia Magazine of History and Biography*, lxii (1954), 387–99; W. A. Cole, 'Trends in Eighteenth-Century Smuggling', *EcHR*, x (1958), 395–410; H. C. and L. H. Mui, ' "Trends in Eighteenth-Century Smuggling" Reconsidered', *ibid.*, xxviii (1975), 28–43, with Cole's rejoinder following, pp. 44–9.
61. O. M. Dickerson, *The Navigation Acts and the American Revolution* (Philadelphia, 1951). Slightly less optimistic estimates were offered by L. A. Harper, 'The Effects of the Navigation Acts on the Thirteen Colonies', in R. B. Morris (ed.), *The Era of the American Revolution* (New York, 1939), 3–39, and by C. P. Nettels, 'British Mercantilism and the Economic Development of the Thirteen Colonies', *JEcH*, xii (1952), 105–14.
62. R. P. Thomas, 'A Quantitative Approach to the Study of the Effects of British Imperial Policy upon Colonial Welfare: Some Preliminary Findings', *JEcH*, xxv (1964), 615–38 launched the new examinations. R. L. Ransom, 'British Policy and Colonial Growth: Some Implications of the Burden from the Navigation Acts'

JEcH, xxviii (1968), 427–35; P. McClelland, 'The Cost to America of British Imperial Policy', *American Economic Review*, lix (1969), 370–81; and G. M. Walton, 'The New Economic History and the Burdens of the Navigation Acts', *EcHR*, xxiv (1971), extended, challenged, and refined the Thomas argument. McClelland and Walton had another exchange in *ibid.*, xxvi (1973), 679–88.

63. Watkins, *loc. cit.*; W. W. Rostow, *The Process of Economic Growth* (Oxford, 1953) and *The World Economy* (London, 1978); J. A. Ernst and M. Egnal, 'An Economic Interpretation of the American Revolution', *W&MQ*, xxix (1972), 3–32 and M. Egnal, 'The Economic Development of the Thirteen Continental Colonies,1720– 1775', *ibid.*, xxxii (1975), 191–222; North and Thomas, *loc. cit.* and *The Rise of the Western World* (Cambridge, 1974).

64. J. O. Appleby, *Economic Thought and Ideology in Seventeenth-Century England* (Princeton, 1978), 53.

65. S. Diamond, 'Values as an Obstacle to Economic Growth: The American Colonies', *JEcH*, xxvii (1967), 561–75 and R. D. Brown, *Modernization: The Transformation of American Life 1600–1865* (New York, 1976).

66. C. B. MacPherson, *The Political Theory of Possessive Individualism: Hobbes to Locke* (Oxford, 1964); J. E. Crowley, *This Sheba, Self: The Conceptualization of Economic Life in Eighteenth-Century America* (Baltimore, 1974); J. G. A. Pocock, 'Virtue and Commerce in the Eighteenth Century', *Journal of Interdisciplinary History*, iii (1972–3), 119–34; A. O. Hirschman, *The Passions and the Interests: Political Arguments for Capitalism before its Triumph* (Princeton, 1977); Appleby, *op. cit.* Closely related are: J. M. Dunn, *The Political Thought of John Locke: An Historical Account of the Argument of the 'Two Treatises of Government'* (Cambridge, 1969) and J. A. W. Gunn, *Politics and the Public Interest in the Seventeenth Century* (London, 1969).

67. (New York, 1938).

68. *Perspectives in American History*, viii (1974), 123–86. See M. H. Ebner, *The New Urban History: Bibliography on Methodology and Historiography* (Monticello, Ill., 1973).

69. P. Corfield, 'Urban Development in England and Wales in the Sixteenth and Seventeenth Centuries', in D. C. Coleman and A. H. John (eds.), *Trade, Government and Economy in Pre-Industrial England: Essays presented to F. J. Fisher* (London, 1976), 214–47; Clark and Slack, *op. cit.*; P. McGrath (ed.), *Bristol in the Eighteenth Century* (Bristol, 1972); W. E. Minchinton, *The Trade of Bristol in the Eighteenth Century* (Bristol, 1957); Clemens, *loc. cit.*; W. B. Stephens, *Seventeenth-Century Exeter* (Exeter, 1958); W. G. Hoskins, *Industry, Trade and People in Exeter 1688– 1800*, 2nd ed. (Exeter, 1968); Jackson, *Hull*.

70. For Philadelphia, see: J. T. Lemon, 'Urbanization and the Development of Eighteenth-Century Southeastern Pennsylvania and Adjacent Delaware', *W&MQ*, xxiv (1967), 501–42; J. G. Lydon, 'Philadelphia's Commercial Expansion, 1720– 1739', *Pennsylvania Magazine of History and Biography*, xci (1967), 401–18; and J. K. Alexander, 'The Philadelphia Numbers Game: An analysis of Philadelphia's Eighteenth-Century Population', *ibid.*, xcviii (1974), 314–24. On New York, see: T. J. Archdeacon, *New York City, 1664–1710: Conquest and Change* (Ithaca, N.Y., 1976); B. M. Wilkenfeld, 'The Social and Economic Structure of the City of New York, 1695–1796', Ph.D. thesis, Columbia University, 1973. Provincial Boston has left few systematic sources, but see: J. A. Henretta, 'Economic Development and Social Structure in Colonial Boston', *W&MQ*, xxii (1965), 75–92; G. Warden, *Boston, 1689–1776* (Boston, 1970); and D. C. Klingaman, 'The Coastwise Trade of Colonial Massachusetts', *Essex Institute Historical Collection*, cviii (1972), 217–34,

71. Davis, *Shipping Industry;* Shepherd and Walton, *op. cit.*; Bailyn, *Massachusetts Shipping;* J. A. Goldenberg, *Shipbuilding in Colonial America* (Charlottesville, Va. 1976).

72. See: B. Bailyn, 'Communications and Trade: The Atlantic in the Seventeenth Century', *JEcH*, xiii (1953), 378–87; A. H. Cole, 'The Tempo of Mercantile Life in Colonial America', *Business History Review*, xxxiii (1959), 277–99; and the author's 'Time, Communication and Society: The English Atlantic, 1702', *Journal of American Studies*, viii (1974), 1–21 and 'Moat Theories and the English Atlantic,

1675 to 1740', Canadian Historical Association *Historical Papers 1978* (Ottawa, 1979), 18–33.

73. A. R. Pred, *Urban Growth and the Circulation of Informa tion* (Cambridge, Mass. 1973).

74. T. C. Barrow, *Trade and Empire: The British Customs Service in Colonial America, 1660–1775* (Cambridge, Mass., 1967) is particularly useful, though examples abound. L. V. Brock, *The Currency of the American Colonies, 1700–1764* (New York, 1975) documents another type of problem in this period. C. R. Haywood, 'The Influence of Mercantilism on Social Attitudes in the South, 1700–1763', *Journal of the History of Ideas*, xx (1959), 577–86, illustrate imitative aspects of the colonial situation.

75. Noteworthy examples of the genre include: M. Kraus, *The Atlantic Civilization— Eighteenth-Century Origins* (Ithaca, N.Y., 1949); F. B. Tolles, *Quakers and the Atlantic Culture* (New York, 1960); C. Bridenbaugh, *Mitre and Sceptre: Trans- atlantic Faiths, Ideas, Personalities, and Politics 1689–1775* (London, 1962); J. M, Price, 'One Family's Empire: The Russell-Lee-Clerk Connection in Maryland. Britain, and India, 1707–1857,' *Maryland Historical Magazine*, lxxii (1977), 165–225. Both English and American social history have expanded greatly. For bibliography see: Sachse, *Restoration England;* Freidel and Showman, *Harvard Guide;* G. N. Grob, *American Social History before 1860* (New York, 1970).

76. C. M. Andrews wrote *Colonial Folkways* (New Haven, 1919) and intended a volume of social history that remained unfinished at his death. See A. S. Eisenstadt, *Charles McLean Andrews* (New York, 1956), esp. 198–9.

77. New England has received more of this detailed social history than has the rest of the English Atlantic. Two stimulating essays that integrate elements of this new work are: R. S. Dunn, 'The Social History of Early New England', *American Quarterly*, xxiv (1972), 661–9 and J. M. Murrin', Review Essay', *History and Theory*, xi (1972), 226–75. Also see J. A. Henretta, *The Evolution of American Society, 1700– 1815: An Interdisciplinary Analysis* (Lexington, Mass., 1973).

78. S. C. Powell, *Puritan Village: The Formation of a New England Town* (Middletown, Conn., 1963); J. J. Waters, 'Hingham, Massachusetts, 1631–1661: An East Anglian Oligarchy in the New World', *Journal of Social History*, i (1968), 351–70; D. G. Allen, 'In English Ways: The Movement of Societies and the Transfer of English Local Law and Custom to Massachusetts Bay, 1600–1690', Ph.D. thesis, University of Wisconsin, 1974; T. H. Breen, 'Persistent Localism: English Social Change and the Shaping of New England Institutions', *W&MQ*, xxxii (1975), 3–38 and 'Transfer of Culture: Chance and Design in Shaping Massachusetts Bay, 1630–1660', *New England Historical and Geneological Register*, cxxxii (1978), 3–17.

79. L. de Mause (ed.), *The History of Childhood* (London, 1976) and P. Laslett (ed.), *Household and Family in Past Time* (Cambridge, 1972) are illustrations that include papers on the English Atlantic communities. The second of these has a substantial bibliography.

80. See E. A. Wrigley, *Population and History* (New York, 1969); M. W. Flinn, *British Population Growth 1700–1850* (London, 1970); and Chambers, *Population, Economy, and Society*. The substantial landowners also did no better than maintain their numbers, as T. H. Hollingsworth has shown in *The Demography of the British Peerage* (London, 1965). Some direct social consequences are studied in L. Stone 'Social Mobility in England, 1500–1700', *Past and Present*, no. 33 (April, 1966) esp. 47–8 and in C. Clay, 'Marriage, Inheritance, and the Rise of Large Estates in England, 1660–1815', *EcHR*, xxi (1968), 503–18.

81. Deane and Cole, 91 and note 17 above.

82. W. Albert, *The Turnpike System in England* (London, 1972) and G. L. Turnbull, 'Provincial Road Carrying in England in the Eighteenth Century', *Journal of Trans- port History*, new series, iv (1977), 17–39. Coastal shipping is thoroughly explored by T. S. Willan in *The English Coasting Trade* (Manchester, 1938) and *River Naviga- tion in England* (London, 1964). See P. Deane, *The First Industrial Revolution* (Cambridge, 1965), chap. v for implications.

83. Wrigley, 64–8.

84. See Flinn, *British Population* and Chambers, *Population, Economy, and Society*. The argument of T. McKeown and R. G. Brown, 'Medical Evidence related to

English Population Changes in the Eighteenth Century', *Population Studies,* ix (1955), 119–41 has been challenged by P. Razzell, 'Population change in eighteenth-century England. A Reinterpretation', *EcHR,* xviii (1965), 312–32.

85. See Dunn, *Sugar and Slaves,* chaps. viii–ix and E. S. Morgan, *American Slavery, American Freedom* (New York, 1975), chap. viii for general subject. For a specific study for Maryland, see R. R. Menard, 'Immigrants and their Increase: The Process of Population Growth in Early Colonial Maryland', and L. G. Carr, 'The Development of the Maryland Orphans' Court, 1654–1715' in A. C. Land *et al.* (eds.), *Law, Society and Politics in Early Maryland* (Baltimore, 1977), 88–110 and 41–62 respectively.

86. P. Curtin, 'Epidemiology and the Slave Trade', *Political Science Quarterly,* lxxxiii (1968), 190–216; R. R. Menard and L. S. Walsh, 'Death in the Chesapeake: Two Life Tables for Men in Early Colonial Maryland', *Maryland Historical Magazine,* lxix (1974), 211–27; D. B. and A. H. Rutman', Of Agues and Fevers: Malaria in the Early Chesapeake', *W&MQ,* xxxiii (1976), 31–60.

87. R. V. Wells, *The Population of the British Colonies in America before 1776; A Survey of Census Data* (Princeton, N.J., 1976) is an ambitious synthesis, but see D. B. Rutman, 'History Counts, or Numbers have more than Face Value', *Reviews in American History,* iv (1976), 372–8. J. Potter, in 'The Growth of Population in America 1700–1860', in D. V. Glass and D. E. C. Eversley (eds.), *Population in History* (Chicago, 1965), 631–88, lamented the lack of reliable work on immigration while suspecting its continuing importance into the eighteenth century. For the West Indies, see: Dunn, *Sugar and Slaves* and his 'The Barbados Census of 1680: Profile of the Richest Colony in English America', *W&MQ,* xxvi (1969), 3–30; and P. A. Molen, 'Population and Social Patterns in Barbados in the Early Eighteenth Century', *ibid.,* xxviii (1971), 287–300.

88. The history of the family has attracted considerable recent attention, with particular focus on old and New England. See: Laslett (ed.), pp. 125–203, 545–69; L. Stone, *The Family, Sex and Marriage in England 1500–1800* (London, 1977). For the American colonies, study might begin with: Demos, *op. cit.;* Greven, *op. cit;* K. A. Lockridge, 'The Population of Dedham, Massachusetts, 1636–1736', *EcHR,* xix (1966), 318–44; D. S. Scott, 'The Demographic History of Colonial New England', *JEcH,* xxxii (1972), 165–83; R. V. Wells, 'Quaker Marriage Patterns in a Colonial Perspective', *W&MQ,* xxix (1972), 415–42 and his *Population of the British Colonies;* R. W. Beales, Jr, 'In Search of the Historical Child: Miniature Adulthood and Youth in Colonial New England', *American Quarterly,* xxvii (1975), 379–98.

89. T. H. Breen and S. Foster, 'Moving to the New World: the Character of Early Massachusetts Immigration', *W&MQ,* xxx (1973), 189–222 prompts this obvious distinction. See R. P. Thomas and T. L. Anderson', White Population, Labour Force and Extensive Growth of the New England Economy in the Seventeenth Century', *JEcH,* xxiii (1973), 634–67. For the contrast to the south see: Menard, 'Immigrants and their Increase'; Dunn *Sugar and Slaves,* Tables 27, 30, 31; Morgan, *American Slavery,* 407–10.

90. See sources cited in note 88; K. A. Lockridge, 'Land, Population and the Evolution of New England Society, 1630–1790; and an Afterthought', in S. Katz (ed.), *Colonial America: Essays in Politics and Social Development* (Boston, 1971), 466–91; and see below, notes 93, 100, 101.

91. See *Past and Present,* no. 33 (April 1966) for Everitt's 'Social Mobility in Early Modern England' and Stone's 'Social Mobility in England, 1500–1700', 1–15 and 16–55 respectively.

92. Dunn, *Sugar and Slaves,* 200–1 argues that this course was seldom very profitable.

93. L. G. Carr and L. S. Walsh, 'The Planter's Wife: The Experience of White Women in Seventeenth-Century Maryland', *W&MQ,* xxxiv (1977), 542–71 is suggestive.

94. See, for instances, W. J. Bell, Jr., 'Medical Practice in Colonial America', *Bulletin of the History of Medicine,* xxxi (1957), 442–53; A. M. Smith, 'Virginia Lawyers, 1680–1776: The Birth of an American Profession'. Ph.D. thesis, Johns Hopkins University, 1967, 175–80, 301–18. Also see J. W. Schmotter, 'Ministerial Careers in Eighteenth-Century New England: The Social Context, 1700–1760', *Journal of*

Social History, ix (1975–6), 249–67 and J. M. Murrin, 'The Legal Transformation: The Bench and Bar of Eighteenth-Century Massachusetts', in Katz (ed.), 415–449.

95. B. Bailyn, 'Politics and Social Structure in Virginia', in J. M. Smith (ed.), *Seventeenth-Century America: Essays in Colonial History* (Chapel Hill, N.C., 1959), 90–115: Barrow, chap. iv; M. G. Hall, *Edward Randolph and the American Colonies* (Chapel Hill, N.C., 1960).

96. By F. Musgrove (London, 1963).

97. Bailyn, *The New England Merchants*, 110 ff.

98. D. W. Jordan, 'Maryland's Privy Council, 1637–1715', in Land *et al.* (eds.), 65–87; Jordan's 'Political Stability and the Emergence of a Native Elite in Maryland, 1660–1715', together with C. Shammas, 'English Born and Creole Elites in Turn of the Century Virginia', are to appear in the forthcoming *The Chesapeake in the Seventeenth Century: Essays on Anglo-American Society*, eds. T. W. Tate and D. Ammerman (Chapel Hill, N.C.).

99. R. Waterhouse, 'England, the Caribbean and the Settlement of South Carolina', *Journal of American Studies*, ix (1975), 259–81 compares migrants from England and from the West Indies. R. S. Dunn, 'The English Sugar Islands and the Founding of South Carolina', *South Carolina Historical Magazine*, lxxii (1971), 81–93.

100. R. R. Menard, 'From Servant to Freeholder: Status Mobility and Property Accumulation in Seventeenth-Century Maryland', *W&MQ*, xxx (1970), 37–64; L. S. Walsh, 'Servitude and Opportunity in Charles County, Maryland, 1658–1705', in Land *et al.* (ed.), 111–33.

101. Work not previously cited that bears on this theme for the period to 1740 includes: B. C. Daniels, 'Long Range Trends of Wealth Distribution in Eighteenth-Century New England', *Explorations in Economic History*, xi (1973–4), 123–35; S. B. Kim, *Landlord and Tenant in Colonial New York: Manorial Society, 1664–1775* (Chapel Hill, N.C., 1978); J. T. Lemon and G. B. Nash, 'The Distribution of Wealth in Eighteenth-Century America: A Century of Changes in Chester County, Pennsylvania, 1693–1802', *Journal of Social History*, ii (1968), 1–24; G. B. Nash, 'Urban Wealth and Poverty in Pre-Revolutionary America', *Journal of Interdisciplinary History*, vi (1976), 545–84; R. R. Menard, P. M. G. Harris and L. G. Carr, 'Opportunity and Inequality: The Distribution of Wealth on the Lower Western Shore of Maryland, 1638–1705', *Maryland Historical Magazine*, lxix (1974), 169–84; C. Shammas, 'The Determinants of Personal Wealth in Seventeenth-Century England and America', *JEcH*, xxxvii (1977), 675–89; R. Berthoff and J. M. Murrin, 'Feudalism, Communalism, and the Yeoman Freeholder: The American Revolution Considered as a Social Accident', in S. G. Kurtz and J. H. Hutson (eds.), *Essays on the American Revolution* (Chapel Hill, N.C., 1973), 256–88.

102. H. A. Innis, *Empire and Communications* (Oxford, 1950); M. McLuhan, *The Gutenberg Galaxy* (Toronto, 1962) and his introduction to Innis's other book on the subject, *The Bias of Communication* (Toronto, 1964).

103. W. J. Ong, *The Presence of the Word: Some Prolegomena for Cultural and Religious History* (New Haven, 1967) is seminal. R. Isaac shows the value of this approach in 'Dramatizing the Ideology of Revolution: Popular Mobilization in Virginia, 1774 to 1776', *W&MQ*, xxxiii (1976), 357–85 and 'Preachers and Patriots: Popular Culture and the Revolution in Virginia', in A. F. Young (ed.) *The American Revolution: Explorations in the History of American Radicalism* (DeKalb, Ill., 1976), 127–56.

104. R. Redfield, *The Primitive World and Its Transformation* (Ithaca, N.Y., 1953).

105. K. Lockridge, *Literacy in Colonial New England* (New York, 1974), 87–97. Lawrence Stone's 'Literacy and Education in England, 1640–1900', *Past and Present*, no. 42 (Feb., 1969), 68–139 was the starting point for much subsequent discussion. See R. T. Vann, 'Literacy in Seventeenth-Century England: Some Hearth Tax Evidence', *Journal of Interdisciplinary History*, v (1974–5), 287–93; R. S. Schofield, 'Illiteracy in pre-industrial England: the work of the Cambridge Group', *Educational Reports Umea*, ii (1973), 1–21; D. Cressy, 'Levels of Illiteracy in England, 1530–1730', *Historical Journal*, xx (1977), 1–23.

106. B. Bailyn, *Education in the Forming of American Society* (Chapel Hill, N.C., 1960) drew professional historians to this subject, as did E. S. Morgan, *The Puritan Family*, 2nd ed. (New York, 1966). L. A. Cremin, *American Education: The Colonial Exper-*

ience 1607–1783 (New York, 1970) is a major new synthesis, which includes an extensive bibliographical essay. J. Axtell, *The School Upon a Hill: Education and Society in Colonial New England* (New Haven, 1974) broadens perceptions of the subject.

107. J. Axtell's, 'The White Indians of Colonial America', in *W&MQ*, xxxii (1975), 55–88 documents this tension, which suggests the social utility of popular accounts of captivity and escape from Indian life.
108. R. M. Wiles, *Serial Publication in England Before 1750* (Cambridge, 1957) and his *Freshest Advice: Earliest Provincial Newspapers in England* (Columbus, Ohio, 1965).
109. R. L. Merritt, *Symbols of American Community, 1735–1775* (New Haven, 1966) was an innovative, though unconvincing, analysis of American colonial perceptions of themselves in newspapers.
110. See issue no. 799, 10 Aug. 1719.
111. Early colonial newspapers have not been subject to much recent analysis aside from Merritt. See: S. Kobre, *The Development of the Colonial Newspaper* (Gloucester, Mass., 1960); E. C. Lathem, *Chronological Tables of American Newspapers, 1690– 1820* (Barre, Mass., 1972); and F. L. Mott, *American Journalism: A History, 1690– 1960*, 3rd ed. (New York, 1962).
112. See notes 132–3 below.
113. Reprinting of the massive *The American Bibliography of Charles Evans*, 14 vols. (Worcester, Mass., 1956) and the extremely useful microfische edition of most of its contents *Early American Imprints, first series, 1639–1800*, ed. C. K. Shipton (Worcester, Mass., 1956–　) isolate colonially-produced work. Recent work includes C. W. Miller, *Benjamin Franklin's Philadelphia Printing, 1728–1766: A Descriptive Catalogue* (Philadelphia, 1974) and J. G. Riewald, *Reynier Jansen of Philadelphia, Early American Printer: A Chapter in Seventeenth-Century Nonconformity* (Groningen, 1970). For additional sources before 1970 see: Vaughan, *Seventeenth Century*, 108–9; Greene, *Eighteenth Century*, 86–7; and B. Hindle, *Technology in Early America: Needs and Opportunities for Study* (Chapel Hill, N.C., 1966), 75–6.
114. See R. P. Stearns, *Science in the British Colonies of America* (Urbana, Ill., 1970) and A. Oleson and S. C. Brown (eds.), *The Pursuit of Knowledge in the Early American Republic* (Baltimore, 1976).
115. 'The Transatlantic Republic of Letters: A Note on the Circulation of Learned Periodicals to Early Eighteenth-Century America', *W&MQ*, xxxiii (1976), 642–60. E. Wolf II has detailed the avid book collecting of James Logan in *The Library of James Logan of Philadelphia, 1674–1751* (Philadelphia, 1974). For references to Wolf's other articles on private libraries, and earlier work on the subject, see Greene, *Eighteenth Century*, 85–6.
116. F. P. Bowes, *The Culture of Early Charleston* (Chapel Hill, N.C., 1942), 61.
117. See especially F. B. Tolles, *Quakers and the Atlantic Culture* (New York, 1960).
118. The Congregational clergy have received considerable attention in recent years. See: D. D. Hall, *The Faithful Shepherd: A History of the New England Ministry in the Seventeenth Century* (Chapel Hill, N.C., 1972); J. W. T. Youngs Jr. *et al., God's Messengers: Religious Leadership in Colonial New England, 1700–1750* (Baltimore, 1976); J. Ellis, *The New England Mind in Transition: Samuel Johnson of Connecticut* (New Haven, 1973); E. Elliott, *Power and the Pulpit in Puritan New England* (Princeton, N.J., 1975). Among more recent general treatments see: F. J. Bremer, *The Puritan Experiment* (New York, 1976); J. W. Jones, *The Shattered Synthesis: New England Puritanism before the Great Awakening* (New Haven, 1974); and L. Ziff, *Puritanism in America: New Culture in a New World* (New York, 1973). A. G. Roeber, ' "Her Merchandise . . . Shall be Holiness to the Lord": The Progress and Decline of Puritan Gentility at the Brattle Street Church, Boston, 1715–1745', *New England Historical and Geneological Register*, cxxxi (1977), 175–94 is particularly useful here.
119. C. Bridenbaugh, *Mitre and Sceptre: Transatlantic Faiths, Ideas, Personalities, and Politics 1689–1775* (New York, 1962); J. Calam, *Parsons and Pedagogues: The S.P.G. Adventure in American Education* (New York, 1971).
120. See: R. S. Dunn, *Puritans and Yankees: The Winthrop Dynasty of New England 1630–1717* (Princeton, N.J., 1962), chap. ix; Dunn, *Sugar and Slaves*, chap. viii;

L. B. Wright, *The First Gentlemen of Virginia: Intellectual Qualities of the Early Colonial Ruling Class* (San Marino, Cal., 1940), chap. iii.

121. Caroline Robbins touches on this theme in 'What Makes a Revolutionary?' in *The American Revolution: A Heritage of Change*, J. Parker and C. Urness (eds.), (Minneapolis, 1975), 14–15. Also see J. P. Greene, 'Search for Identity: An Interpretation of the Meaning of Selected Patterns of Social Response in Eighteenth-Century America', *Journal of Social History*, iii (1970), 189–220.

122. J. P. Greene has made a special study of this subject, including his 'The Flight from Determinism: A Review of Recent Literature on the Coming of the American Revolution', *South Atlantic Quarterly*, lxi (1962), 235–59; 'The Plunge of the Lemmings: A Consideration of Recent Writings on British Politics and the American Revolution', *ibid.*, lxvii (1968), 141–75; 'Changing Interpretations of Early American Politics', in R. A. Billington, *The Reinterpretation of Early American History* (San Marino, Cal., 1966), 151–84; and *The Reinterpretation of the American Revolution, 1763–1789* (New York, 1968). See also: J. E. Illick, 'Recent Scholarship Concerning Anglo-American Relations, 1675–1775', in A. G. Olson and R. M. Brown, eds., *Anglo-American Political Relations 1675–1775* (New Brunswick, N.J., 1970), 189–212. R. Walcott's 'The Later Stuarts (1660–1714): Significant Work of the Last Twenty Years (1939–1959)', *American Historical Review*, lxvii (1961–2), 352–70 has been succeeded by R. R. Johnson's, 'Politics Redefined: An Assessment of Recent Writings on the Late Stuart Period of English History, 1660 to 1714', *W&MQ*, xxxv (1978), 691–732. For the subsequent period see W. A. Bultmann, 'Early Hanoverian England (1714–1760): Some Recent Writings', *Journal of Modern History*, xxxv (1963), 46–61.

123. F. W. Maitland, *The Constitutional History of England*, ed. H. A. L. Fisher (Cambridge, 1908) remains useful, as is D. L. Keir, *The Constitutional History of Modern Britain since 1485*, 8th ed. (London, 1966), and M. A. Thomson, *A Constitutional History of England, 1642 to 1801* (London, 1938). The constitution of the empire attracted attention from C. H. McIlwain in *The American Revolution: A Constitutional Interpretation* (New York, 1923) which was challenged by R. L. Schuyler, *Parliament and the British Empire* (New York, 1929). A. B. Keith, *Constitutional History of the First British Empire* (Oxford, 1930) is still useful. See H. Wheeler 'Calvin's Case (1608) and the McIlwain-Schuyler Debate' *American Historical Review*, lxi (1956), 587–97 and B. A. Black, 'The Constitution of Empire: The Case for the Colonists', *University of Pennsylvania Law Review*, cxxiv (1975–6), 1157–1211,

124. L. W. Labaree, *Royal Government in America* (New Haven, 1930); E. E. Hoon, *The Organization of the English Customs System, 1696–1786* (New York, 1938); and O. M. Dickerson, *American Colonial Government 1696–1765* (Cleveland, 1912) are durable examples of this approach.

125. T. C. Barrow's *Trade and Empire* (Cambridge, Mass., 1967) and the author's *Politics of Colonial Policy* (Oxford, 1968) illustrate this approach with reference to the customs and the Board of Trade respectively.

126. See J. H. Plumb, 'The Organization of the Cabinet in the Reign of Queen Anne', *Transactions of the Royal Historical Society*, 5th ser., vii (1957), 137–57 and J. P. Greene, *The Quest for Power* (Chapel Hill, 1963), the latter of which is an institutional history which does emphasize continuities.

127. See above note 10 and J. S. Cockburn, *The English Assizes, 1558–1714* (Cambridge, 1972). Christopher Hill's 'Puritans and "the Dark Corners of the Land",' in his *Change and Continuity in Seventeenth-Century England* (London, 1974) 3–47 explores related themes for an earlier period.

128. See P. S. Haffenden, 'The Crown and the Colonial Charters, 1675–1688', *W&MQ*, xv (1958), 297–311, 452–66; R. S. Dunn, 'The Downfall of the Bermuda Company: A Restoration Farce', *ibid.*, xx (1963), 478–512; the author's 'The Board of Trade, The Quakers, and Resumption of Colonial Charters, 1699–1702', *ibid.*, xxiii (1966), 596–619; D. S. Lovejoy, 'Virginia's Charter and Bacon's Rebellion, 1675–1676', in Olson and Brown, *Anglo-American Political Relations*, 31–51.

129. See Greene, *The Quest for Power* and his 'Political Mimesis: A Consideration of the Historical and Cultural Roots of Legislative Behaviour in the British Colonies

in the Eighteenth Century', *American Historical Review*, lxxv (1969–70), 337–60; F. G. Spurdle, *Early West Indian Government* (Palmerston North, N.Z., n.d.).

130. Van Deventer's *Provincial New Hampshire* develops this theme, especially pp. 181, 186. The same is apparent from E. M. Cook Jr., *The Fathers of the Towns* (Baltimore, 1976), chap vi and A. Tully, *William Penn's Legacy* (Baltimore, 1977). M. Zuckerman's controversial *Peaceable Kingdoms* (New York, 1970) argues for local power in the case of Massachusetts towns. See D. G. Allen, 'The Zuckerman Thesis and the Process of Legal Rationalization in Provincial Massachusetts', *W&MQ*, xxix (1972), 443–60 and Zuckerman's rebuttal, 461–8; L. K. Wroth, 'Possible Kingdoms: The New England Town from the Perspective of Legal History', *American Journal of Legal History*, xv (1971), 320–21. For Maryland comparisions see C. A. Ellefson, *The County Courts and the Provincial Court in Maryland, 1733–1763'*. Ph.D. thesis, University of Maryland, 1963.

131. B. Bailyn, *The Origins of American Politics* (New York, 1968).

132. I. Kramnick, *Bolingbroke and his Circle* (Cambridge, Mass., 1968); J. G. A. Pocock, 'Machiavelli, Harrington, and English Political Ideologies in the Eighteenth Century', *W&MQ*, xxii (1965), 547–83. See note 66 above.

133. C. Robbins, *The Eighteenth-Century Commonwealthman* (Cambridge, Mass., 1959) and J. G. A. Pocock, *The Machiavellian Moment: Florentine Political Thought and the Atlantic Republican Tradition* (Princeton, N.J., 1975). J. P. Greene and B. Bailyn have debated the relative importance of Roundhead and Whig contributions to American colonial political ideas in *American Historical Review*, lxxv (1969–70), 337–67. J. G. A. Pocock, *The Ancient Constitution and the Feudal Law* (Cambridge, 1957) and H. T. Colbourn, *The Lamp of Experience* (Chapel Hill, N.C., 1965) explore related themes in perceptions of history.

134. L. B. Hartz, *The Liberal Tradition in America* (New York, 1955) and his *The Founding of New Societies* (New York, 1964).

135. *The Structure of Politics at the Accession of George III*, 2 vols. (London, 1929). A revised, one-volume second edition appeared in 1957.

136. The impact can be seen most readily from the bibliographical essays: Walcott, 'The Later Stuarts'; Bultmann, 'Early Hanoverian England'; and Greene, 'The Plunge of the Lemmings'.

137. R. W. Walcott, *English Politics in the Early Eighteenth Century* (Oxford, 1956). E. L. Ellis, 'The Whig Junto in Relation to the Development of Party Politics and Party Organisation from its Inception to 1714'. D. Phil. thesis, Oxford University, 1961 was one of the first signs of the corrective trend. J. H. Plumb, *The Growth of Political Stability in England 1675–1725* (London, 1967) and G. Holmes, *British Politics in the Age of Anne* (London, 1967) re-established political parties in historical discussion of the period. See Johnson, 'Politics Redefined', 702–6.

138. Yet the local constables might also arrest press gangs. See the excellent case studies by Gordon Jackson, *Hull in the Eighteenth Century* (London, 1972) and by R. G. Wilson, *Gentlemen Merchants: The Merchant Community in Leeds 1700–1830* (Manchester, 1971). S. S. Webb, 'Army and Empire: English Garrison Government in Britain and America, 1569–1763', *W&MQ*, xxxiv (1977), 1–31 is a very useful guide to the extent of the garrisons, emphasising their service to centralisation rather than local social control and economic advantage.

139. Cockburn, *English Assizes*, *passim*.

140. See note 133 above.

141. S. N. Katz, *Newcastle's New York* (Cambridge, Mass., 1968) is an excellent case study of the processes involved.

142. See especially: J. R. Jones, *The First Whigs* (London, 1961); J. P. Kenyon, *Robert Spencer, Earl of Sunderland, 1641–1702* (London, 1958); K. H. D. Haley, *The First Earl of Shaftesbury* (Oxford, 1968); J. H. Plumb, 'The Growth of the Electorate in England from 1660–1715', *Past & Present*, no. 45 (Nov. 1969), 90–116; J. R. Western, *Monarchy and Revolution: The English State in the 1680s* (London, 1972); and J. Miller, *Popery and Politics in England 1660–1688* (Cambridge, 1973).

143. Haffenden, *loc. cit.*; R. S. Dunn, 'Imperial Pressures on Massachusetts and Jamaica, 1675–1700', in Olson and Brown, *Anglo-American Political Relations*, 52–75; A. G. Olson, *Anglo-American Politics 1660–1775: The Relationship Between Parties in*

England and Colonial America (Oxford, 1973), chap. ii. See also S. S. Webb, ' "Brave Men and Servants to His Royal Highness": The Household of James Stuart in the Evolution of English Imperialism', *Perspectives in American History,* viii (1974), 55–80 and compare J. C. Rainboldt, 'A New Look at Stuart "Tyranny": The Crown's Attack on the Virginia Assembly', *Virginia Magazine of History and Biography,* lxxv (1967), 387–407.

144. G. A. Jacobsen's *William Blathwayt, a Late Seventeenth Century English Administrator* (New Haven, 1932) has served admirably, but a needed reassessment has begun with S. S. Webb, 'William Blathwayt, Imperial Fixer: From Popish Plot to Glorious Revolution', *W&MQ,* xxv (1968), 3–21, and the sequel, *ibid.,* 373–415. Hall, *Randolph, passim.*

145. Chandaman, *English Public Revenues,* and C. Roberts, 'The Constitutional Significance of the Financial Settlement of 1690', *Historical Journal,* xx (1977), 59–76.

146. M. P. Thompson, 'The Idea of Conquest in Controversies ver the 1688 Revolution', *Journal of the History of Ideas,* xxxviii (1977), 33–46. See also: J. Carswell, *The Descent on England* (London, 1969); J. R. Jones, *The Revolution of 1688 in England* (New York, 1972) and D. H. Hosford, *Nottingham, Nobles, and the North: Aspects of the Revolution of 1688* (Hamden, Conn., 1976).

147. See L. G. Carr and D. W. Jordan, *Maryland's Revolution of Government, 1689–1692* (Ithaca, N.Y., 1974); D. S. Lovejoy, *The Glorious Revolution in America* (New York, 1972); and Archdeacon, *New York* for well-substantiated arguments from this perspective.

148. P. S. Haffenden, *New England in the English Nation, 1689–1713* (Oxford, 1974), chap.i.

149. The author's 'Time, Communications and Community', explores this problem in the less explosive context of Anne's accession in 1702.

150. On the fiscal problems, see Dickson, *op. cit.,* 1–77 and D. W. Jones, 'London Merchants and the Crisis of the 1690s', in Clark and Slack, *Crisis and Order,* 311–55. H. Horwitz, *Parliament, Policy and Politics in the Reign of William III* (Manchester, 1977) is excellent on the war's political impact. See also A. H. John, 'War and the English Economy, 1700–1763', *EcHR,* vii (1955), 329–44.

151. See Greene, *Eighteenth Century,* 18–21, for some recent work on the military aspects of the subject. Further study of the impact of war on the English Atlantic between 1689 and 1714 is needed. See Olson, *Anglo-American Politics,* chap. iii; G. B. Nash, *Quakers and Politics: Pennsylvania 1681–1726* (Princeton, N.J., 1968), chaps. iv-vi; Steele, *Politics of Colonial Policy,* chap. v.

152. For illustrations see J. D. Runcie, 'The Problem of Anglo-American Politics in Bellomont's New York', *W&MQ,* xxvi (1969), 191–217; S. S. Webb, 'The Strange Career of Francis Nicholson', *ibid.,* xxiii (1966), 513–48: and D. A. Williams, 'Anglo-Virginia Politics, 1690–1735', in Olson and Brown, *Anglo-American Political Relations,* 76–91.

153. G. S. Graham, *Empire of the North Atlantic,* 2nd ed. (London, 1958) and his *The Walker Expedition to Quebec* (London, 1953); G. M. Waller, *Samuel Vetch, Colonial Enterpriser* (Chapel Hill, N.C., 1960); and also see D. E. Leach, *Arms for Empire: A Military History of the British Colonies in North America, 1607–1763* (New York, 1973).

154. P. S. Fritz, *The English Ministers and Jacobitism between the Rebellion of 1715 and 1745* (Toronto, 1975); Plumb, 'The Electorate'.

155. P. Haffenden, 'Colonial Appointments and Patronage under the Duke of Newcastle, 1724–1739', *English Historical Review,* lxxviii (1963), 417–35 and Katz, *Newcastle's New York,* chap. ii.

156. J. A. Henretta, *'Salutary Neglect': Colonial Administration under the Duke of Newcastle* (Princeton, N.J., 1972); M. Kammen, *Empire and Interest: The American Colonies and the Politics of Mercantilism* (Boston, 1970), chap. iii; Olson, *Anglo-American Politics,* chap. iv; G. Metcalf, *Royal Government and Political Conflict in Jamaica 1729–1783* (London, 1965), chaps. i and ii.

157. J. P. Greene, 'The Growth of Political Stability: An interpretation of Political Development in the Anglo-American Colonies, 1660–1760', in J. Parker and C. Urness (eds.) *The American Revolution: A Heritage of Change* (Minneapolis, Minn.,

1975), 26–52. See also: T. E. Morgan, 'Turmoil in an Orderly Society: Colonial Virginia, 1607–1754; A History and Analysis'. Ph.D. thesis, William and Mary, 1976 and A. R. Ekirch, ' "Poor Carolina": Society and Politics in North Carolina, 1729–1771'. Ph.D. thesis, Johns Hopkins University, 1979.

158. Olson indicated the need for more intense work on the 1730s and 1740s in Olson and Brown, *Anglo-American Political Relations,* 12, and J. P. Greene more recently has drawn attention to the late 1740s in 'A Posture of Hostility: A Reconsideration of Some Aspects of the Origin of the American Revolution', American Antiquarian Society *Proceedings,* lxxxvii (1977), pt. 1, 27–68.

159. R. Syme, *Colonial Elites: Rome, Spain and the Americas* (London, 1958) is a suggestive general essay on the integration of colonial elites into empires.

160. See R. D. Hume, *The Development of English Drama in the Late Seventeenth Century* (Oxford, 1976), 122–7 and A. J. Weitzman, 'Eighteenth-Century London: Urban Paradise or Fallen City'? *Journal of the History of Ideas,* xxxvi (1975), 469–80.

161. *British Empire in America,* 2 vols. (London, 1708), I, 96.

162. D. D. Hall, 'Education and the Social Order in Colonial America', *Reviews in American History,* iii (1975), 181.

163. D. M. Potter, 'The Historian's Use of Nationalism and Vice Versa', *American Historical Review,* lxvii (1961–2), 924–50. Carl Berger, *The Sense of Power: Studies in the Ideas of Canadian Imperialism 1867–1914* (Toronto, 1970) explores related themes very effectively.

The Board of Trade and London-American Interest Groups in the Eighteenth Century

by

Alison G. Olson

The history of the eighteenth-century English Board of Trade has hardly been regarded as a success story by the historians who have written it. Created in 1696 to make recommendations on questions of imperial administration, nominate colonial officials to carry out their recommendations, and back up the provincial officials in office, the Board is commonly agreed to have failed at all its jobs. Either (by one set of accounts) power-hungry ministers did it in by overriding or ignoring its recommendations, stripping it of its important nominations, and appointing second-raters to the Board itself or (by another set of accounts) the Board's heavy-handed mercantile approach and indolence in backing up the officials charged with implementing it brought on it the hostility of colonists and royal officials alike. In either case the question seems not to have been whether the Board failed, but why.[1]

Recent studies of administration in developing countries (as Great Britain certainly was in the eighteenth century) suggest that it might be time for at least a partial rehabilitation of the Board's reputation. They suggest, by comparison, that the Board was performing a function that has hitherto been little emphasized, namely the accommodation of various pre-modern and modern interest groups that were emerging in eighteenth-century England.

The Board's establishment coincided in time with a period of rapid proliferation of London interest groups with American connections. There were three main types of these London—American groups, mercantile, ethnic, and ecclesiastic, each with its own political leverage, and since the Board was to specialize in mercantile and imperial problems the work of accommodating these London-American groups fell heavily upon it. In handling its work the Board sought their advice, often acceded to their demands, and built up a comfortable working relationship with each of them.

One of the most serious problems of emerging nations is the handling of competing interests; domestic political stability depends upon their doing so effectively.[2] By the standards of developing nations Britain was remarkably successful in accommodating interest groups in the early eighteenth century, and the Board of Trade appears to have contributed substantially to its success. The years of greatest British success, 1700 to 1760, coincided with the period of the Board's greatest activity. In the later eighteenth century after 1760, British success was considerably more limited and interest groups became increasingly dissatisfied with the status quo. This period, in turn, was coincident with a period of declining activity and influence for the Board of Trade.

Such an interpretation must begin with a definition of 'interest group'. Eighteenth-century writers like Edmund Burke identified increasingly differentiated interests within the governing community—a landed interest, a mercantile interest, a professional interest, and so on. But such broad, 'fixed' categories bore little relation either to the way men acted or to the kinds of groups that lobbied at various levels of government. Recent writers have laid more stress on interest groups functioning outside the centres of political power but have not developed a commonly accepted definition. Recognising, therefore, that any definition will be arbitrary, we may suggest 'a group that accepts the political system and attempts through bargaining with political authorities to improve its own position in it, operating from the borders of power, influencing but not directly making political decisions.' By this definition there were few transatlantic interests in existence before the Board's establishment in 1696: towns, guilds and chartered commercial companies had all functioned as interests in England but none (including the Hudson's Bay Company and the Royal African Company, surprisingly) was to develop American associations.[3] Among the groups that did come to be 'Anglo-American' as opposed to 'Anglo', a few dated back to the 1670s but in that early decade they lacked either American connections or an efficient lobbying organisation, or both. The Quaker Yearly Meeting, established in 1675, had by 1678 appointed a clerk to take down the heads of bills which might affect Quakers. Evidently the custom soon fell into abeyance, though after the settlement of Pennsylvania the meeting began regular correspondence with the Philadelphia Yearly Meeting on political as well as theological questions.[4] The Bishop of London had been given the administration of the Anglican church in the colonies in 1675, and began taking a fuller interest in them after 1689 when James Blair went to Virginia as the Bishop's first commissary, authorised to convene the local clergy and send back reports of their local grievances to the Bishop.[5] But by the early 1690s Virginia represented the only colony to have such relations with the Anglican church in England. General Baptists began meeting regularly after 1686 but by the early 1690s had not yet concerned themselves with American issues.[6] In the thirty-six years between the restoration of Charles II in 1660 and the Board's establishment in 1696, the Privy Council had received petitions from three interest groups; between 1686 and 1696 the old Lords of Trade, predecessors of the Board of Trade, had received four petitions from what might be called English interest groups, but two were from the would-be organisers of companies that never formed and one was from the proprietors of New Jersey.[7] Indeed, by the time the Board was created only two groups, the French Committee of London, set up to aid Huguenot refugees (and on occasion to help them get to America), and the London merchants trading to Virginia, could truly be said to constitute organised Anglo-American interests.[8]

Within a few years of the Board's establishment, however, this was no longer true. By 1701 the Quakers had established a committee to lobby members of Parliament, and by 1704 the London Meeting for Sufferings had begun corresponding regularly with yearly meetings in New England and the southern colonies as well as Philadelphia.[9] After 1701 the Anglican church began sending commissaries to every colony; and it also established the Society for the Propagation of the Gospel to work with Anglican communities overseas, mainly in the northern mainland colonies.[10] The same year the Society for Promoting Christian Knowledge was established, developing continental connections which led them to focus their attention on helping non-English communities in America.[11] In 1702, also, after a false start ten years earlier, ministers of the Three Denominations in London (Baptist, Presbyterian, Congregational) began meeting; in their first few years they did little but present formal addresses to the king but by 1715 they were intermittently becoming more active.[12] In 1706 American Presbyterians established a Presbytery in Pennsylvania and began corresponding with English Presbyterians as well as the General Assembly of Scotland.[13] Again in 1702, the Sephardic Jewish congregation at Bevis Marks established a Committee of Deputies to 'attend to the business of the nation which is before Parliament'.[14] The Huguenot Society, with connections in the Threadneedle Street Church, initiated its correspondence with American churches between 1699 and 1702;[15] the Lutherans were slow to organise as an interest but the first Lutheran chaplain was appointed to the royal chapel early in Queen Anne's reign, establishing political influence for the Lutheran communities at court.[16] Finally, our first record of three mercantile coffee houses, the Pennsylvania, New England, and Carolina coffee houses, dates from 1702, and the New York Coffee House was probably established shortly before this.[17] By 1706 English coffee house leaders were in informal correspondence with merchant groups in Charleston, Philadelphia, New York City, and Boston. The cumulative growth of Anglo-American interests is suggested by the fact that the Board received fifty-one petitions from such groups before 1709.

Though the actual circumstances surrounding the development of different groups varied, there were at least two general explanations for the development of Anglo-American interests. One was the rapid growth of London towards the end of the seventeenth century.[18] Interest groups, before 1760, at least, represented local interests, not national ones. But Londoners soon demonstrated a remarkable (by eighteenth-century standards) ability to speak for men of similar interests in provinces of England and the empire. The London Meeting for Sufferings, the Dissenting Deputies in and about London, the organisation of French churches in London, the Bevis Marks Committee, the network of Lutheran chaplains around the court and the SPCK, were composed of Londoners, but their role as spokesmen for the interests of all their co-religionists was rarely challenged by local associations. Similarly the London merchants, though at times competitors with the outport merchants, were with few exceptions their spokesmen in national politics, at least on American issues. It is significant here that London merchants could speak for Charleston merchants in much the same way that they spoke for merchants in Bristol and Norwich; London church lobbyists could speak for New York or Philadelphia church groups in the same way they spoke for church groups in the English provinces. The absence of national interests and the predominance of London over provincial interests in England and America allowed the Americans to fit easily into the pattern of English lobbying.[19]

Part of the importance of London lay simply in its proximity to the machinery of government. Londoners could respond more quickly than provincials to legislative or administrative threats, and they could be called upon more quickly for consultation. Part lay in the fact that Londoners developed a genuine acceptance of a pluralistic society long before the more homogeneous 'island communities' of the provinces were able to do so.[20] But the largest part came from sheer numbers: interest groups in London were more likely than those in the provinces to have the numbers and wealth sufficient to produce surplus resources which could be used to help colleagues elsewhere. Rapid growth was not always an asset: the influx of thousands of French refugees into London after the revocation of the Edict of Nantes in 1685 (eighteen French churches were established in the 1690s alone) greatly complicated the work of the Huguenot committee,[21] and the influx of hundreds of Axkenzim Jews into an area of a few blocks in London in the same decade presented an enormous challenge to the leadership of the existing Sephardic community.[22] But at the worst, a rapid growth in numbers could force a community to tighten its organisation to distribute evenly the available resources, and at best, when newcomers were assimilated and employed, large communities could tap resources beyond the immediate needs of their members. London's congregations and non-English communities supplied their provincial colleagues with bibles, books, even ministers; London's ethnic, ecclesiastical, and mercantile groups could use their surplus towards lobbying, supporting political agents, entertainment for politicians, legal fees, carriage fare, and the like.

A more general reason for the emergence of interests was the establishment of the eighteenth-century 'political nation' if, again being arbitrary, we define 'political nation' as the elite who governed England in the aftermath of the Glorious Revolution. For an interest group to operate from the 'borders of power' those borders must be defined, and it was in the reigns of William III and Anne that such a definition became possible (for England, though not for America). By Anne's death, or at least shortly afterwards, is arguable, some people were clearly 'in' the political nation, others were quite clearly out, and others—members of political interest groups—were in a stable position on the borders. Dissenters were left on the borders of the political nation by the combination of the failure of ecclesiastical comprehension and the passage of the Toleration Act in 1689, a pair of events which defined dissenters out of the established church, and hence largely out of the political nation, but established their right to existence on the fringes of that nation.[23] Immigrants were left on the borders by a combination of a parliamentary act of 1712, which repealed a general Naturalization Act passed three years before, and the fact that they could obtain denisation from the King or Parliament, which allowed them to own land but not to participate actively in politics.[24] Lesser merchants were left out of the financial nation by a combination of two things, the establishment of the national debt in 1696 (they could not subscribe) and the creation of London's financial directorate (the Bank, the Royal Assurance Company, the East India Company, and a number of other large mercantile companies either were created or consolidated their power in William's reign, and the lesser merchants were excluded from the directorships). They too, were on the fringes of power.[25]

The defining of the English political borders meant that interests no longer had hopes (as they had had from time to time in the Restoration) of being at the centre of power, but they also had no fears of being driven underground. No longer need they alternate, as the few existing Restoration interests had done, between wooing highly placed individuals in government and defensively protecting their people from these individuals by creating a state within a state. With a clearly defined position the London interests could devote themselves to systematic lobbying, helping colonial interests whose positions in the provinces were less well defined.[26]

In the same period interest groups were developing in the American colonies. The growth of colonial stability in contrast with the violent challenges to colonial leadership in the 1670s and 1680s created an environment in which interest groups could also develop, though their position was often far less clear than the position of their English counterparts. Immigration from England and the continent and the commercial growth of the colonies produced concentrations of colonists with similar interests though except for the merchant communities these were as likely to be island communities outside the provincial capital as neighbourhoods within it, since the capitals were too small to develop the concentrations found in London.

American interests were more vulnerable to local pressures and less capable of developing surplus resources than the interest groups in the imperial capital. They were also, in the last decade of the seventeenth century, far more directly affected by decisions made in London than they had been at any time earlier. After the Glorious Revolution five colonies came newly under temporary or permanent royal control which meant among other things that their governors were royal appointees guided by instructions prepared in London. Moreover, between 1685 and 1696 all the mainland colonies that had not previously done so were henceforth required to send their laws to England for review.[27] Aware for the first time of the uses of London politics, American interest groups turned to London interests to assist them in local politics. Religious groups sought the disallowance of provincial laws discriminating against them and the appointment of sympathetic colonial officials. Ethnic groups were more interested in getting good community land, exemption from provincial taxes, and easy naturalization. Individually colonial planters and merchants sought the London merchants' help in obtaining patronage and the approval of private provincial acts; as groups they were interested in getting British support for things like building lighthouses or opening up continental trade, favourable British review of some paper money issues, and the disallowance of provincial tax laws that discriminated against their mercantile or agricultural interests.[28]

The Americans solicited English help rather hesitantly at first, uncertain whether British interests would take colonial problems up as their own, uncertain also whether the cost—both in terms of money and in terms of the local stigma attached to appealing over the head of the provincial majority to an external authority—was worth it. They worked also by trial and error, on occasion sending laws too late for review, on other occasions sending laws that had expired or writing of rumoured laws that were never on the books.[29] Nevertheless, after a shaky start the London-American connections developed rapidly in the two decades after the Glorious Revolution: London mercantile leaders sought political favours for their leading American correspondents to keep them happy, London church groups spread the faith by helping co-religionists in America, and non-English communities in London became convinced that the best way to prevent the periodic overtaxing of their resources by inundations of unassimilated poor was to help fellow refugees settle directly in America. At least fourteen American interests, including Quakers in three colonies, Anglicans in two others, ethnic minorities in four provinces and merchant groups in three cities, sought help from their English counterparts in bringing matters before the British government in this period. Thus the Board was established in the very period that saw the rapid development of London-American interest cooperation.

The Board's duties were loosely defined—'to inspect and examine into the general Trade of our said Kingdom and the several parts thereof', 'to consider of some proper methods for setting on worke and employing the Poore of our said Kingdome', and 'to inform yourselves of the present condition of the respective plantations'.[30] With these functions, especially the last, the Board might have come to work with interests on any number of issues. But it came in practice to have four particular functions which were useful to the North American lobbies.

One such function was arranging the resettlement of non-English groups moving, sometimes via London, to America: the Board's negotiations with ship captains for reasonable transportation across the Atlantic and with governors and assemblies for assistance to refugees once they arrived were of vital concern to non-English communities in London. Another function was the nomination of members of the colonial councils, a subject of particular interest to members of the London mercantile communities who sought nominations as favours to colonial correspondents as a way of establishing the trust on which their pre-modern mercantile relationship depended.

Far more important to most trans-Atlantic groups were two other functions. One was the drafting of instructions for colonial governors. Occasionally the great officers of state would interpose and alter gubernatorial instructions in response to English pressure. After a request from Benjamin Avery, head of the Protestant Dissenting Deputies, the Duke of Newcastle looked into the 'instructions sent to Governor Shirley [of Massachusetts] and the difficulties which it is apprehended, they will occasion both to his Excellency and the province'.[31] But most of the instructions were drawn up by the Board of Trade, and these occasionally included specific instructions for the enactment of provincial laws.

As the second of its more important functions, the Board was empowered 'to examine into and weigh such Acts of the Assemblies of the Plantations respectively as shall from time to time be sent or transmitted hither for our approbation' and 'to set down and represent as aforesaid the usefulness or mischief thereof to our Crown, and to our said Kingdom of England or to the Plantations themselves in case the same should be established for Lawes there'. (Officially the Board's function was only advisory, but the Privy Council normally followed its recommendation.) One of the principles behind the examination of provincial legislation was that, as stipulated in the various provincial charters, colonial laws could not be repugnant to the laws of England. This examination thus became in effect an antecedent of the modern judicial review, and the fact that it was handled in its early stages by the Board gave English interests a chance to work there to obtain the allowance or disallowance of laws affecting their American associates.

The Board's main functions, then, were those of particular concern to the Anglo-American interests, and in handling the issues the Board was particularly responsive to their pressure. Since they often had a near monopoly of first-hand information on particular conditions in the colonies the Board sought them out when preparing its reports. When the Board wanted information about French Protestants who had landed at Jersey on their way to America, it consulted French ministers in London;[32] when it wanted information about the working of South Carolina's township law over the 1730s it consulted merchants trading to the colony;[33] when it wanted to know to know how Connecticut's ecclesiastical establishment was treating Quakers in 1705 it consulted two delegates from the London Meeting for Sufferings.[34]

The Board sought more than information from the various interests; it sought the opinions of rank and file members on various questions. At times it sent someone out to poll them: leading merchants, colonial agents, or agents hired by the merchants themselves were asked to solicit the opinions of merchants as a group on questions like the placing of lighthouses or the timing of convoys.[35] Twice a week its meetings were opened to the public and agents were sent to provide the interest groups in advance with notices of hearings the rank and file might usefully attend.[36] Just how many people could squeeze in at any one meeting is not clear but in 1711 the active members of the Virginia 'Trade' decided to attend en masse, and though there were up to 175 of them, they anticipated no trouble getting in.[37]

There is also evidence that individual members of the Board consulted privately with interests on particular affairs: it would be surprising, in fact, if they had not. Members of the Board tended to be country gentlemen with little personal identification with any Anglo-American interest except the Anglican church.[38] (The Bishop of London was an ex-officio member of the Board but he attended only six meetings in the eighteenth century, and while leaders of various interests, like the merchant William Baker[39] were occasionally considered for seats at the Board, the appointments never materialised.) Nevertheless, particular members did develop connections with particular interest groups—Martin Bladen with the Chesapeake merchants in the 1740s, for example.[40] James Oswald with Glasgow tobacco merchants the following decade,[41] Viscount Dupplin with the Dissenters in the same period[42]—and these men served as informal channels between the interests and the Board.

The Board thus made a point of consulting with interest groups; it also tended to follow their recommendations. In handling non-English migration to the colonies it followed closely the advice of non-English communities in London, working with them to arrange the departure of emigres from Europe, to regulate the living conditions aboard the ships on which they sailed, to instruct the governors to provide them tax free land for a decade after their arrival in the colonies, and to oversee their supplies for some times after they settled. On the nomination to colonial councillorships it is difficult to be sure how influential the merchants were, since merchants passed their nominations on through individual members of the Board (i.e. 'Buchanan pr. Col Bladen')[43] and the names of the merchants are not usually mentioned directly in the surviving lists of councillors and the men who nominated them. Probably merchant nominations accounted indirectly for 10–20 per cent of colonial councillorships (the Bishop of London accounted for another 5 per cent). This did not seem a small percentage to contemporaries: governors, who thought such nominations essential to the power of the governorship, were outraged by it.

It was in handling its two most important functions, however, the preparation of gubernatorial instructions and the review of provincial legislation, that the Board was most responsive to pressures from interest groups. Gubernatorial instructions were on occasion prepared explicitly to benefit particular interests. The Bishop of London helped to draft a Maryland act of 1700 establishing the Anglican church in that colony. The act was drawn up in London and transmitted to Maryland through the Governor's instructions.[44] Quaker pressure was responsible for Governor Hunter's instruction in 1709: 'You take care than an Act be passt in the General Assembly of your said Province to the like effect as that past here in the 7th and 8th years of his late Majesties reign Entituled an act that the Solemn affirmation and declaration of the People called Quakers shall be accepted instead of an Oath in the usual form'.[45] A 1734 instruction to Governor Gooch of Virginia directed him to get a law passed to exempt German settlers from payment of parish taxes for a longer time than stipulated by previous law; the source of pressure for this instruction is clear enough.[46] An instruction to South Carolina's Governor regarding the setting aside money to create townships was in response to a representation from 'planters and merchants trading to South Carolina'.[47] It is difficult, in fact, to find examples of instructions requested by ethnic and religious groups being turned down, and there were only a few such cases regarding the merchants.

The function on which the Board was most responsive to interest group pressure was the review of colonial legislation, partly because interest groups often had first-hand information about a particular law's 'usefulness or mischief' to a province, partly because most English laws were unclear when applied to a colonial situation. The Board could develop few principles and was forced instead to make a series of ad hoc decisions, for each of which it relied on information from English interests about the way in which their American correspondents would be affected. The English Toleration Act, for example, was one of those acts to which colonial acts were supposed to conform: it exempted Dissenters from the legal penalties which the Test and Corporation Acts imposed upon them. But how did the law apply when a Dissenting church was actually the established church in a province? In colonies where the Church of England was 'tolerated' but not established, did toleration extend to Bishops? Faced with these and innumerable other questions about the Toleration Act, the Board interpreted the act differently from colony to colony, on various occasions consulting the Bishop of London and representatives of Dissenting interests. Similarly, colonial laws were to conform to the Navigation Acts and were not to prejudice the trade of the mother country. But what taxes could colonial assemblies levy without in some way prejudicing the trade of the mother country? Governor Hunter of New York complained that 'by clamours of merchants or those self-interested, every sort of duty many be construed to affect the trade of Great Britain.'[48] Faced again with difficult interpretations, the Board turned to London merchants and agents of the colonial assemblies for advice.

Thus the Board became extremely responsive to interests in the matter of legislative review. The Board's records mention specifically only two cases where non-English representatives were consulted on particular provincial legislation,[49] but it is difficult to find any provincial acts reviewed otherwise than non-English groups would have wanted. Governor Spotswood referred to the Board's deference to merchants in 1718 when he complained that the London merchants trading to Virginia might as well draw up their own version of a tobacco inspection act to be passed in the colony, 'otherwise there is no pleasing them'.[50] The governor's complaint was fair enough: the only occasions on which the merchants' views were disregarded were rare ones on which they were clearly ill informed or those that concerned local affairs on which the Board thought it was not proper to interfere.[51] Most striking of all was the churches' role in legislative review. In the first twenty years of the century five of the colonies passed laws severely limiting the rights of religious minorities, and all five saw them disallowed by the Board. Over the rest of the century five more discriminatory acts were passed and in each case the Board decided in favour of the minority.

Not only was the Board responsive to interest group pressures; it was relatively more responsive to them than were other parts of the government —notably the ministers and parliament. Unlike the Board, ministers as a rule dealt only with the leaders of the interest groups and dealt with them only in person (one ill and elderly dissenter even felt obliged to apologise to the Duke of Newcastle for sending the Duke a letter he had dictated to his son rather than writing personally).[52] The net effect was probably to cream off the top of the interest groups from the rest of the membership. This was certainly true of Sampson Gideon, the highly placed London Jewish financier who left his Bevis Marks congregation; it was probably somewhat true of the Lutheran and Huguenot court chaplains, though they did make a point of preaching to London congregations on a regular basis. It is hard to say how much men like Samuel and Joseph Stennett maintained their closeness to their Baptist congregations after they became confidants of the Duke of Newcastle. Certainly they continued to earn the devotion and respect of fellow ministers. At the same time they seem to have been out of touch with the radical elements in their congregations from the mid-century on. One could go on to suggest doubts about Benjamin Avery, leader of the Dissenting Deputies, or even Micajah Perry, the Virginia tycoon of the 1720s who seems to have drifted away from his mercantile community in the next two decades. Somewhere between a boss, a tribal leader, and simply the wealthy member of the group, many of the eighteenth-century group leaders were partially detachable from the rank and file for whom they spoke.

Another problem the interests found in dealing with the great officers of state was that the kinds of demands which it was appropriate to make of ministers were less well defined than those that could be made of the Board of Trade. In working with ministers interest groups were likely to make some costly demands, demands that the ministers could not grant without antagonising substantial sections of the electorate. Dissenters demanded repeal of the Test and Corporation acts, foreigners demanded blanket naturalization laws, merchants sought to influence foreign policy or customs laws to their own advantage but to the considerable disadvantage of influential competitors. Restrained by political expediency from granting the interests' domestic demands, ministers were eager enough to encourage the Board of Trade to grant them 'cheaper' favours in America which were unlikely to arouse the ire of Englishmen: Englishmen were not reluctant to tolerate and encourage American interests, even if those interests were associated with their English rivals. Rarely was it necessary anyway to disoblige one English group in order to satisfy another on American questions because English lobbyists generally worked for removal of restrictions on their own associates but not for the imposition of restrictions on others.

Thus ministers often denied the highest aspirations of English interests while relying on the Board of Trade to 'neutralise' the groups as best they could. They denied the Dissenting Deputies' demand for repeal of the Test and Corporation Acts while assuring them that they would not appoint an American bishop.[53] They may well have felt able to oppose the Virginia merchants in the tobacco excise crisis because they had shortly before sponsored a law making it easier for the merchants to collect their debts in Virginia and had followed their wishes in reviewing a Virginia law for amending the staple of tobacco.[54] (Indeed, the lesser merchants who supposedly formed the backbone of London radicalism came hat-in-hand to the Board of Trade when American favours were at stake.) Similarly, while denying the non-English communities a general naturalization in England because there was too much local opposition, ministers did later pass such an act with the Board's support for non-English in the American colonies.

If English interests found the Board more accessible than the officers of state, they also found it easier to work with than Parliament, for appealing to Parliament could require organisation on a scale which many interests were too small or too immature to equal. At the very least the difficulties in approaching ministers repeated themselves since parliamentary success on any issue required the support of the ministers or at least the assurance that they were not hostile. Dissenters discovered this in 1716, for example, when they attempted unsuccessfully to force the ministers to repeal the occasional Conformity and Schism Acts. They re-learned the lesson in 1736 when they pressed Walpole for repeal of the Test and Corporation Acts and had to give up when he opposed them.[55] When Henry Pelham showed no enthusiasm for the establishment of an American bishopric in 1749 the Bishop of London had to back down on his campaign to get one.[56] When the London merchants responded to American complaints about their supposed inaction against the Townshend Acts by saying they could do nothing without the support of the ministry they passed on a well learned lesson.[57]

Even if ministers did not oppose them, interest groups found that it took far more resources and organisation to lobby Parliament than to lobby the Board. It was one thing to lobby Board members whose very appointment committed them to some interest in American affairs, but quite another thing to lobby several hundred members of Parliament who were largely indifferent to American affairs. It was necessary to establish committees to go over the voting records of M.P.s and call on those who might be sympathetic.[58] Merchants could call on M.P.s from London and the outports; dissenters could remind particular M.P.s of dissenting votes among their constituents.[59] When possible the committee had to publish pamphlets or broadsides and distribute them at M.P.s' homes or at the door of the House. Occasionally they resorted to log rolling (though this was not common until the middle of the century): the West India planter-merchant interest and the Irish linen interest once exchanged support on issues involving molasses and linen. Tobacco and wine merchants combined to seek the opening of French trade during Queen Anne's War.[60] But even the most considerable efforts might come to nothing and interests were driven back to seek pared down demands from the Board of Trade.

The amount of interest group activity before the Board in any one period between 1700 and 1760 was determined by a number of things. The size of the interest groups was one (other merchant groups were slower to develop numbers than the Virginians, while the Virginia group fell off in absolute numbers after the 1720s);[61] the relationship of leaders to the rank and file was another (the Virginia group, again, was hurt in the 1740s by the financial crash of some of its leaders and by the preference of other potential leaders to work on their own rather than with the community). Another determinant, and a more important one, was the presence or absence of clusters of issues which required sustained group activity, issues centred around the printing of paper money, for example, or the provincial interpretation of the Toleration Act. Still another was the relationship of the provincial governors with local interests and the governors' vulnerability to attack in England.

Particular groups waxed and waned over the decades: the Virginia merchants were quite active down to 1715, declined after that and were virtually dormant from the early 1730s to the mid-1750s; the New York merchants were particularly active from 1710 to the early 1730s and then declined, while South Carolina and Massachusetts merchants 'peaked' somewhat later. Ecclesiastical lobbies were particularly active in influencing judicial review down to the mid-1720s, then switched their emphasis to influencing the appointment and supervision of colonial governors. Non-English groups became active in the 1730s and 1740s. Whatever the group, the Board seems to have developed a comfortable working relationship with it at some occasion during the years before 1760.

In the years after the accession of George III, however, several related developments began to alter the Board's working arrangements with the Anglo-American interests. After 1764 the Board considered no petitions from Anglo-American lobbies, heard little testimony, and indeed sought none, from traditional Anglo-American interests. Its reports rarely mentioned the opinions of such interests; it appears to have ignored them in its recommendations. In its reviews of colonial legislation the Board referred only to the opinions of the legal advisor as to the compatibility of the laws with relevant British legislation, never mentioning the views of affected interests as to their workability in America. Hitherto the Board and their legal advisors had made ad hoc decisions about the relevance of English statutes to colonial legislation, bowing on occasion to the wishes of interests involved; now the Earl of Shelburne, briefly president of the Board in 1763, prepared a formal 'Table of Such English and British Statutes as are expressly or virtually extended to His Majestys Colonies in America'.[62] In such circumstances it is difficult to imagine that the Board could have been accommodating interest groups as it had done earlier in the century.

Basically, the Board's function of balancing off interest groups seems to have been a victim of the ministerial instability of the 1760s in a number of related ways. As a result of the ministerial upheavals, the Board suffered rapid turnovers in its own leadrship, a lack of clarity in its relation with the Secretary of State, and ultimately a reduction in its powers, all of which were bound to affect its relationship with interest groups. Between 1730 and 1760 the Board had had only three presidents, each one in office long enough to build up many connections with interests. Between 1761 and 1766 the Board had six, each in office for too short a time to build up such associations. After 1766 the Board was first dominated, then headed by Secretaries of State, and existed only as an office staff to them. Moreover the Board lost many of its powers over the decade, including the right to investigate colonial problems on its own initiative, and the right to receive memorials and petitions directly.[63]

One can make too much of these changes at the Board, however. The Presidents of the Board were replaced rapidly, but the rank and file membership changed much more slowly, giving some possible continuity in interest group connections. Even as a unit of the staff of the Secretary of State there was nothing to prevent their considering American problems; even after 1766 they continued to review colonial legislation, and there was nothing to prevent their consulting interest groups on this as they had before or receiving petitions from interest groups through the Secretary of State.

More important than changes in the powers of the Board were changes in the attitudes of the ministers which ultimately undercut the Board's relations with interest groups. In the early 1760s the core of Old Whigs who had dominated English politics since George I was dismissed from office by

George III. Their successors were men who represented not only a new generation of English politicians but also a new attitude to interest group politics. Many of the younger generation of politicians brought a new legalism to their politics, an interest in the consistent enforcement of law as an end in itself. A spin-off from the ideas of English legal reformers of the mid-eighteenth century, the new legalism vastly restricted the discretion given the Board in its interpretation of the application of British and colonial laws. No longer could the interpretation of British statutes as a standard of colonial legislation be left flexible; no longer could colonial officials who winked at the laws but got along well with Anglo-American interests be encouraged in office.[64]

Moreover the retirement of the Old Whigs brought uncertainty on the part of their successors about whether the interests were more loyal to the government or to the Old Whigs themselves. With the exception of the Marquis of Rockingham's ministry, 1765-6, ministers who succeeded the Old Whigs in office did not share their concern to placate English interests; indeed it is doubtful that they understood the reasons for the Old Whigs' assumption that political stability depended in part on the successful accommodation of interest groups.[65] When Bute was Prime Minister, all the Baptist ministers responsible for distributing the Baptists' bounty were dismissed and no new ones hired because, as the Baptist leader Samuel Stennett wrote Newcastle, 'the Dissenters in general apprehend, they were honnored with your Grace's favor'.[66] George Grenville referred to Rockingham's administration as run by a club of merchants; Lord North advised the London merchants trading to America to return to their counting houses and leave matters to him.[67] Merchants did meet with members of Pitt's cabinet on the Paper Currency Act but little came of their efforts. Only the Rockingham administration worked regularly with the merchants, even offering a cabinet position to Sir William Baker, prominent New York merchant, utilising merchant support in the repeal of the Stamp Act, and drafting trade regulations with their cooperation.[68]

The interest groups for their part reacted with confusion to the separation of their traditional allies from the government. Hesitant to support a government that was indifferent to them, they were even more hesitant to go into opposition with the Old Whigs who could offer them no rewards and who were, moreover, less in need than the government of the interests' strongest weapon, information. Their dilemma was further complicated by the rise of 'agitational' interests around Wilkes at the end of the decade of the 1760s. Most members of the Anglo-American interests wanted nothing to do with Wilkes, despite his attraction for Americans. Only one-tenth of all the identifiable, politically minded American merchants, for example, signed a Wilkite petition late in 1775. But only one per cent signed the anti-Wilkite petition of 1769, suggesting that most of the American merchants wanted nothing to do with the Wilkite question on either side.[69] They 'did not meddle with politics'[70]—i.e. political agitation, as one Virginia merchant told his American correspondents. Baptist and Dissenting Deputies seem to have supported the Old Whigs through the election of 1768; in 1773, unsupported by the ministry they mounted their first public drive, verging on the agitational, for the abolition of compulsory subscription to the Articles of Religion.

Thus the decline of the Board's capacity to placate English interest groups by American favours can be seen as part of a decline in the concern of successive ministries to use them for this purpose. Like the bounty for the Baptists, the Board was cut off because two decades of ministries were not aware of the need to appease Anglo-American interests. This was a part, and not such a small one, of the cause of the unrest in England and America after 1775.

In its decline the Board was no longer able to serve the transatlantic interests as it had done before 1760, but in its heyday it had served them well. Retrospectively it emerges as an early example, if not indeed the earliest, of an institution sorely needed in any developing nation, namely, a clearing house for vital interest group demands. To the extent that it was, the Board made a useful—and hitherto unrecognised—contribution to the stability of eighteenth-century England and America.[71]

NOTES

1. For representative interpretations of the Board as a victim of ministerial ambitions see Oliver M. Dickerson, *American Colonial Government, 1696–1765* (New York, 1962 reprint of 1912 edn.), 67; Arthur Herbert Basye, *The Lords Commissioners of Trade and Plantations, Commonly known as the Board of Trade, 1748–1782* New Haven, 1925), 5, 25, 27, 30–1, and the most sophisticated recent treatment by I. K. Steele, *The Politics of Colonial Policy; The Board of Trade in Colonial Administration, 1696–1720* (Oxford, 1968), 170–2. For the other approach see Charles McLean Andrews, *The Colonial Period of American History: England's Commercial and Colonial Policy,* IV (New Haven, 1938).

2. On this see Gabriel Almond and G. Bingham Powell, *Comparative Politics, a Developmental Approach* (Boston, 1966), 35, 75–86; Gabriel Almond and James S. Coleman, *The Politics of the Developing Areas* (Princeton, 1960), 33–5; Myron Weiner, 'Political Participation: Crisis of the Political Process', in Leonard Binder *et. al., Crisis and Sequences in Political Development* (Princeton, 1971), 167–73; Samuel Huntington, *Political Order in Changing Societies* (New Haven, 1968), 36, 47, 79. On Britain see Graham Wootton, *Pressure Groups in Britain 1720–1970* (London, 1975), 1–47; Allen M. Potter, *Organised Groups in British National Politics* (London, 1961), 29; Samuel H. Beer, 'The Representation of Interests in British Government: Historical Background', *American Political Science Review,* LI (1957), 613–50 and Michael Kammen, *Empire and Interest* (New York, 1970), *passim.*

3. Leslie A. Clarkson, *The Pre-Industrial Economy in England, 1500–1750* (New York, 1972), 198; Charles Wilson, 'Government Policy and Private Interest in Modern English History', in *Economic History and the Historian, Collected Essays* (London, 1969), Ch. 9.

4. Douglas R. Lacey, *Dissent and Parliamentary Politics in England, 1661–1689* (New Brunswick, New Jersey, 1969), 106–7.

5. Alison G. Olson, 'The Commissiares of the Bishop of London in Colonial Politics' in Alison G. Olson and Richard Maxwell Brown, eds., *Anglo-American Political Relations, 1675–1775* (New Brunswick, N.J., 1970), 109–124.

6. Charles Edwin Whiting, *Studies in English Puritanism from the Restoration to the Revolution, 1660–1689* (London, 1968), 130.

7. J. W. Fortescue, ed., *Calendar of State Papers Colonial, America and the West Indies,* XIII (London, 1900) nos. 763, 2, 352, 396, 2466, 646; *Ibid.,* XIV (London, 1901) nos. 919, 949, XII (London, 1898) no. 1690.

8. There appears to have been a group of New England merchants that lobbied the earlier Lords of Trade in 1675/6 for stricter enforcement of the Navigation Acts, but the group did not reappear for a quarter century after that (MS. 'Journal of ye Lords of the Privy Council Committee for Trade and Plantations', I, 70, 109, 111, Pennsylvania Historical Society). One might also count the New England Company as a lobby, but its combination of Dissenters and Anglicans in a non-denominational missionary endeavour meant that it did not fit the pattern of other ecclesiastical lobbies. (See William Kellaway, *The New England Company, 1649–1776* (New York, 1962), 1–172, *passim*. For evidence of the Virginia lobby see *C.S.P. Col., A. and W.I.* XI (London, 1898), nos. 277, 1271, *Ibid.* XIV, no. 900; Leo Francis Stock, *Proceedings and Debates of British Parliaments about North America*, 5 vols. (Washington, D.C., 1924), I, 273–4, II, 5, 160; Great Britain, Public Record Office, Colonial Office 5/305, ff. 105–6, 143, 367. For evidence of Huguenot influence see *C.S.P. Col., A. and W.I.* XII, nos. 1354, 1741. One might consider the Quakers as a third lobby, but as late as the 1690s they still relied almost exclusively on the influence of individuals like Penn rather than on organised efforts of the meeting.

9. A. T. Gary, 'The Political and Economic Relations of English and American Quakers, 1750–1785', (Oxford, D. Phil, thesis, 1935), 32–3.

10. Olson, 'Commissaries of the Bishop of London', in *Anglo-American Political Relations*, 109–24.

11. W. K. Lowther Clarke, *The History of the S.P.C.K.* (London, 1959), Ch. 1.

12. Carl Bridenbaugh, *Mitre and Sceptre* (New York, 1962), 35–9; Address to New England ministers, Feb. or Mar., 1714–15, Cotton Mather to Dr. Daniel Williams *et. al.* (1715), Thomas Reynolds to Cotton Mather, 9 June 1715, 'Diary of Cotton Mather 1709–1724', *Massachusetts Historical Society Collections*, 7th Ser, VIII (Boston, 1912), 300–3, 317–19.

13. Leonard Trinterud, *Presbyterianism, the Forming of an American Tradition* (Philadelphia, 1949), 27–33; *Records of the Presbyterian Church in the United States of America, 1706–1788*, (New York, 1949), 52, 63, 224–5, 245, 351, 386; unknown to John Matthews, 1719, 'NYC Churches 30, II', New York Historical Society; 'Memorial and Petition of the Presbyterian Church in the city of New York to the Reverend and Honorable the Moderator and Members of the Venerable Assembly the Church of Scotland, Mar. 18, 1766' (reciting help the Assembly has given them over the century) Dartmouth MS D (W) 1778 /II/ 182, Staffordshire County Record Office.

14. *Bevis Marks Records: being contributions to the History of the Spanish and Portuguese Congregation of London Pt. I, The Early History of the Congregation from the Beginning until 1800* (Oxford, 1940), 35.

15. 'Threadneedle Street Letterbook, to and from', Huguenot Society Library, London. Letter of 27 Aug., 1699, 25 Aug., 1700, 19 May, 1700.

16. Garold N. Davis, *German Thought and Culture in England, 1700–1770* (Chapel Hill, 1969), 45.

17. Bryant Lillywhite, *London Coffee Houses* (London, 1963), 387, 408, 447–8.

18. E. A. Wrigley, 'A Simple Model of London's Importance in Changing English Society and Economy, 1650–1750', *Past and Present*, XXXVII (1967), 44–70.

19. For the concentration of non-conformists in London see Harry Grant Plum, *Restoration Puritanism, A Study of the Growth of English Liberty* (Chapel Hill, N.C., 1943), 71. For London's help to the provinces see Duncan Coomer, *English Dissent under the Early Hanoverians* (London, 1946), 56, and Bridenbaugh, *Mitre and Sceptre*, 36.

20. See Frank Tomkins Melton, 'London and Parliament, an Analysis of a Constituency, 1661–1702' (University of Wisconsin Ph.D. thesis, 1969) esp. 15, 164–6, 231.

21. Malcolm R. Thorpe, 'The English Government and Huguenot Settlement, 1680–1702' University of Wisconsin Ph.D. thesis, 1972) 71; 'The Archives of the French Protestant Church of London, A Handlist', comp. Raymond Smith *Huguenot Society Publications* L (London, 1972), 89–92.

22. Albert M. Hyamson, *A History of the Jews in England* (London, 1928), 188.

23. Raymond Clarke Mensing, Jr., 'Attitudes on Religious Toleration as expressed in English Parliamentary Debates, 1660–1919' (Emory University Ph.D. thesis, 1970) 153–4.

24. P. M. G. Dickson, *The Financial Revolution in England* (New York, 1967), 249–303.

25. See A. H. Carpenter, 'Naturalization in England and the American Colonies'. *American Historical Review*, IX (1903–4), 292–3; Caroline Robbins, 'A Note on General Naturalization under the Later Stuarts and a Speech in the House of Commons on the Subject in 1664', *Journal of Modern History*, XXXIV (1962), 168–177.

26. For representative examples of the behaviour of interest groups in the Restoration see Margaret Priestly, 'London Merchants and Opposition Politics in Chalres II's Reign', *Bulletin of the Institute of Historical Research*, XXIX (1956), 205–19; Gerald R. Cragg, *Puritanism in the Period of the Great Persecution, 1660–1688* (Cambridge, 1957); Whiting, *Studies in English Puritanism*, 20, 32, 63, 82, 95–6; J. R. Maybee 'Anglicans and Non Conformists, 1679–1704, A study of the Background in Swift's, A Tale of Tub' (Princeton University Ph.D. thesis, 1942) 14–189.

27. Elmer B. Russell, 'The Review of American Colonial Legislation by the King in Council', *Columbia University Studies in History, Economics, and Public Law*, LXIV (New York, 1915), 19–37.

28. This is not to suggest that the Americans had no way of forwarding their demands to London before the end of the century. Earlier, however, Americans had used highly placed individuals, friends or relatives, to put their case at court. See for example, Robert C. Black, Jr., *The Younger John Winthrop* (New York, 1966), Chs. 16 and 17; *William Fitzhugh and his Chesapeake World, 1676–1701*, ed. Richard Beale Davis (Chapel Hill, N.C., 1963), 351, n6; Richard S. Dunn, 'John Winthrop Jr. and the Narragansett Country', *William and Mary Quarterly*, 3d Ser. XIII (1956) 68–86; Bernard Bailyn, *The New England Merchants in the Seventeenth Century* (Cambridge, Mass., 1955), 174–7; Gary, 'The Political and Economic Relations of English and American Quakers, 1750–1785', Ch. 1.

29. New England Quakers did this, for example, in 1692, 1693, and 1695, when they asked English Quakers for help in obtaining the disallowance of laws that had already been approved (Arthur John Worrall, 'New England Quakerism, 1656–1830', Indiana University Ph.D. thesis, 1969, 86).

30. The Board's Commission is published in *Documents relative to the Colonial History of the State of New York*, ed. E. B. O'Callaghan, IV (Albany, 1854), 145–148.

31. Avery to Newcastle, 16 Feb., 1741, Add. Ms. 32, 699, f. 62. Avery was also concerned that Newcastle might suggest to the Massachusetts assembly the name of a particular person to be chosen as the colony's agent in London. He opposed this, partly because the legislature had already nominated Jasper Mauduit, well liked on the Exchange, and partly because the nomination was a local issue on which 'it is hoped, that his Majesties' servants here will hardly think fit to interpose' (Avery to Newcastle, 15 Dec. 1758, Add. Ms. 32, 886, f. 334).

32. 23 Mar. 1749/50, *Journals of the Board of Trade, 1749–53* (London, 1932), 46.

33. 3 July, 1735, *J.B.T. 1734–41* (London, 1930), 35.

34. 17 April, 1 June, 2 Oct., 1705, *J.B.T. 1704–9* (London, 1920), 127, 141, 165.

35. For example, in 1758 the Board asked the agent of Virginia and Maryland 'to take the opinion of the merchants and Traders to Virginia and Maryland upon the utility of a lighthouse so proposed . . .' James Abercromby to Gov. Fauquier, 28 Dec. 1758, Abercromby Letter Book, Virginia Historical Society. On 25 Feb. 1705/6 Mr. Blakeston was sent to poll the London merchants about the timing of convoys to Virginia. *J.B.T. 1704–9*, 226–7.

36. The Board's weekly schedule was arranged and ordered to be posted 'for the benefit of people who have business' on 20 Nov. 1717. *J.B.T. 1714/15–1718* (London, 1924), 296.

37. Micajah Perry to William Popple, 11 Oct. 1711, C.O. 5/1363, f. 333. In 1742 twenty Quakers attended the Board in a hearing on charges against the Pennsylvania assembly. (John Kinsey to Israel Pemberton, 4 mo 28, 1742, Pemberton Papers, Pa. Hist. Soc.) In 1734 'A large number of Friends' attended on the Pennsylvania Maryland boundary dispute. (London Meeting for Sufferings to Quarterly Meeting of Friends in Chester, Newcaslte, Kent, and Sussex counties, 12 mo 28, 1734, London Meeting for Sufferings, Epistles Sent, II, 495–6).

38. Some of the English merchants who had originally pressed for the creation of the Board in the 1690s had hoped that merchants might be represented on the Board, and some proposals went so far as to suggest an elected council of merchants (R. M.

Lees, 'Parliament and the Proposal for a Council of Trade, 1695–6', *English Historical Review*, LIV (1939), 46–7). But had some groups been represented and others not, the Board would have been regarded as partial; had all the important interests been represented, politicians might have distrusted the Board as a rival to Parliament.

39. On this see L. S. Sutherland, 'Edmund Burke and the First Rockingham Ministry', *E.H.R.* XLVII (1932), 46–72.

40. This is suggested by Bladen's passing on their nominations for councillorships (Recommendations for colonial councillors: Virginia. C. O. 324/48).

41. Oswald's connections are suggested in *Memorials of the Public Life and Character of the Right Honorable James Oswald of Dunniker* (Edinburgh, 1825), *passim*.

42. 6 Feb. 1753, *The Reverend Samuel Davies Abroad, The Diary of a Journey to England and Scotland*, ed. George William Pitcher, (Urbana, Ill., 1967), 69–70.

43. Recommendations for colonial councillors: Virginia, C. O. 324/48. All estimates of nominations are based on this volume.

44. 13 Feb. 1701, *Acts of the Privy Council, America and the West Indies* II (London, 1910), no. 814.

45. C. O. 5/995, f. 72, Instruction no. 60.

46. 14 Mar. 1734, *J.B.T. 1734–41* (London, 1930), 10.

47. Representation to the King, 10 June, 1730, C. O. 5/400, f. 286.

48. Hunter to William Popple, 1 Oct. 1718, C. O. 5/1124. ff. 52–4.

49. On 13 June, 1735 Purry's petition on behalf of a South Carolina appropriation act was considered favourably (*J.B.T. 1734–41*, 25). On 15 May, 1745 the Board consulted Moravian leaders about a New York act discriminating against them (*J.B.T. 1741–9*, London, 1931, 164–5). On 18 Nov. 1745, they read a letter from the Moravian agent in favour of a Pennsylvania naturalization act (*Ibid.*, 213–14).

50. Spotswood to Board, 27 Sept. 1718. C. O. 5/1365, ff. 1767.

51. Merchants trading to Jamaica were scolded in 1736: 'The Board then informed them that they are surprised the merchants should lay memorials before H. M. without proof'. 15 April, 1736, *J.B.T., 1734–41*, 102. On another occasion the legal adviser to the Board advised 'I am of opinion that the Merchants of London Trading to New York, are not proper to object to what debts ought to be allowed or disallowed, this being a thing which is absolutely in the power of The General Assembly'. West to Board, 22 April, 1719. C. O. 5/1124, ff. 64–71.

52. 'I am ashamed to think that I shou'd address such a Personage by an Amanuensis, but necessity has oblig'd me under much pain and weakness to dictate to my son these lines at my bedside'. Jos. Stennet to Newcastle 7 Nov. 1757, Add. Ms. 32, 867, f. 455.

53. For example, see Bridenbaugh, *Mitre and Sceptre*, 44–5; Maurice Armstrong, 'The Dissenting Deputies and the American Colonies', *Church History*, XXIX (1960), 302; Susan Martha Reed, *Church and State in Massachusetts* (Urbana, Ill., 1914), 141; Minutes of the Dissenting Deputies, 5 May, 1749 (Guildhall MS 3083/1 p. 315).

54. Board of Trade to King, 29 May, 1731, C. O. 5/1366, ff. 61–71.

55. Richard Burgess Barlow *Citizenship and Conscience, a Study in the Theory and Practice of Religious Toleration in England during the Eighteenth Century* (Philadelphia, 1862), 68–9, 82.

56. Arthur Lyon Cross, *The Anglican Episcopate and the American Colonies* (Cambridge, Mass., 1924), 122–5.

57. William Nelson to John Norton, 19 July, 1770, William and Thomas Nelson Letterbook, 1766–75; Jack M. Sosin, *Agents and Merchants* (Lincoln, Nebraska, 1965), 124; Michael Kammen, *A Rope of Sand* (Ithaca, New York, 1968), 199.

58. For an example of the Quakers' efforts to do this, see I. K. Steele, 'The Board of Trade, the Quakers, and Resumption of Colonial Charters, 1699–1702'. *W.M.Q.*, 3 Ser. XXIII (1966), 596–619. For a similar example, the efforts of the London merchants trading to Virginia, see Jacob Price, *France and the Chesapeake* (Ann Arbor, 1973), 512–29.

59. 'I take the liberty to acquaint your Grace, that agreeably to your Grace's request, our friends have wrote to a great number of Ministers and Gentlemen that have influence in the County of Essex, warmly recommending Mr. Luther to their favor. This, we have done not doubting upon your Grace's recommendation that he is a

steady friend to the present family and to our liberties civil and religious'. Samuel Stennet to Newcastle, 6 July, 1763, Add. Ms. 32, 949, f. 277. Dissenters threatened to withdraw their support from the ministry in 1716 'for without their support they cannot be chosen' (Barlow, *Citizenship and Conscience*, 69, citing William Matthews, ed., *The Diary of Dudly Ryder*, London, 1939, 361); Bridenbaugh, *Mitre and Sceptre*, 42.

60. Price, *France and the Chesapeake*, 578.
61. Jacob Price, 'The Economic Growth of the Chesapeake and the European Market, 1697–1775'. *Journal of Economic History*, XXIV (Dec., 1964), 510.
62. Shelburne Papers, V. 85 p. 250, William L. Clements Library, Michigan.
63. Administrative changes affecting the Board are summarised in Arthur Herbert Basye, *The Lords Commissioners of Trade and Plantations* (New Haven, 1925), Chs. III and IV.
64. On this, see Alison G. Olson, 'Parliament, Empire, and Parliamentary Law' in *Three British Revolutions*, ed. J. G. A. Pocock (Princeton, forthcoming).
65. The 'Old Whig' association with interest groups was most pronounced in the period of Henry Pelham and the Duke of Newcastle but it dated back to the beginning of the century. See Geoffrey Holmes, *British Politics in the Age of Anne* (New York, 1967), 105. For a good example of Newcastle's awareness of the importance of interest groups see the discussion of proposals to appoint an Anglican Bishop for the colonies, in Cross, *The Anglican Episcopate*, 114–25, App. A, 324–30.
66. This is calculated by comparing the number of American merchants listed in 'The Pro-American Petitioners of 11 October 1775', App. A of John A. Sainsbury, 'The Pro-American Movement in London, 1769–1782: Extra Parliamentary Opposition to the Government's American Policy', (McGill University Ph.D. thesis, 1975) with my own card list of merchants who signed any petition or testified before Parliament on the Board of Trade between 1763 and 1775.
67. Sosin, *Agents and Merchants*, 175–6.
68. Sutherland, 'Edmund Burke and the First Rockingham Ministry', *E.H.R.*, XLVII (1932), 46–72.
69. George Rude, 'The Anti-Wilkeite Merchants of 1769', *Guildhall Miscellany*, II (1965), 283–304.
70. Thomas Nelson to Samuel Athawes, 7 Aug. 1774, William and Thomas Nelson Letter Book 1766–1775, Va. Hist. Soc.
71. The author would like to thank Professor Donald Gordon and Professor I. K. Steele for their criticisms of the article and Professor Jon Butler for the use of his notes on the Huguenot correspondence. She also wishes to thank the General Research Board of the University of Maryland for financial assistance in preparing the article.

Warfare and Political Change in Mid-Eighteenth-Century Massachusetts

by

William Pencak[1]

'Join or Die.' So Benjamin Franklin warned his fellow American colonists shortly after the French and Indian War began in 1754. Beneath a diagram of a snake severed in thirteen pieces depicting the fragmented provinces of British North America, he lamented 'the extreme difficulty of bringing so many different governments and assemblies to agree in any speedy and effectual measures for our common defense and security, while our enemies have the very great advantage of being under one direction, with one council and one purse'.[2] Franklin's argument applied not only to the need for combination at this juncture among the mainland provinces. It articulated the particular case of a general truth: states hampered by internal bickering fail to mobilise their military resources effectively and rapidly find their domestic weaknesses compounded by impotence in foreign affairs.

Franklin need only have turned to eighteenth-century Europe for proof of his statement. Successful states developed efficient means of collecting taxes, conscripting soldiers, and neutralising resistance to political centralisation. Only such techniques could forge the principal tool of national survival—a competitive military establishment. The sorry decline of Poland, Sweden, and the Ottoman Empire from their seventeenth-century glory can be attributed to the monarch's inability to check the autonomy of the nobility. On the other hand, Prussia and England overcame the handicap of relatively small populations by developing brutal but effective means of recruiting respectively the most powerful army and navy in Europe, and succeeded in integrating the landowning class into civil and military administration. France, Austria, and Russia represented the intermediate case of large nations which eliminated local privileges and opposition intermittently and imperfectly, but maintained major power status through sheer size and periodically strong rulers. Nations able to neutralise the institution eighteenth-century Americans associated with liberty—the legislative assembly—survived and increased in strength; states too tender of the corporate privileges of their subjects deteriorated or expired.[3]

Yet the American colonies neither joined nor died during the great mid-century wars which finally eliminated the French menace. True, every mainland province furnished troops and supplies for the common cause, However. this voluntary cooperation proved so ineffectual that in addition to provincial levies, Britain had to furnish regular regiments greater in number than the French-Canadian forces in order to bring the war to an end. Even after Wolfe defeated Montcalm on the Plains of Abraham, British troops had to be summoned to deal with pockets of Indian resistance in Pennsylvania and South Carolina. Throughout the French and Indian War, British officers and administrators complained of soldiers who deserted or refused to fight outside their home colonies, merchants who traded with the enemy, and assemblies which incomprehensibly did not vote adequate supplies and quarters for the very troops which guaranteed their existence. Such resistance to a more centralised administration, understandable in terms of the eighteenth-century Whig ideology by which the colonists measured their freedom, appeared suicidal in the context of modern world history which has required nations to stand united or fall divided. Only the knowledge that eighty thousand French Canadians could never destroy them, coupled with the fact of assistance from the mother country, permitted the Americans the luxury of adhering to liberties rendered obsolete by the realities of European international politics.[4]

However, even if the North American colonies were united only minimally among themselves, it can be demonstrated convincingly that at least one province underwent, with respect to its *internal* government and administration, a transformation remarkably similar to the state-building process of the great European powers. Between the outbreak of King George's War in 1740 and the signing of the Peace of Paris in 1763, the Massachusetts General Court roused itself from a quarter-century of lethargy and achieved feats of taxation and mobilisation which Frederick the Great might have envied. Under the tutelage of William Shirley, governor from 1741 to 1756, the Bay Colony changed from one of the most truculent provinces in the empire to the most cooperative. However, the province's mobilisation contained the seeds of its organisers' destruction: the suffering engendered convinced the people that both imperial and local leaders posed serious threats to their liberties and well-being.

To effect this about-face, the very nature of Massachusetts' political system had to change. A legislature primarily concerned with obstructing Britain's plans to strengthen royal authority and with resolving disputes presented by towns and individuals became an active body which designed and implemented vast military campaigns. A potent faction devoted to the royal prerogative developed virtually *ex nihilo* supplanting the influence of the previously dominant country faction which had convinced the assembly that any increase in the governor's power destroyed popular liberty. New systems of finance and public administration, and a new sense of mission emerged. For a quarter century, Massachusetts waged total war.

Massachusetts' pre-eminence among the American colonies in fighting King George's (1740–1748) and the French and Indian (1754–63) wars is indisputable. In the latter conflict, the Bay Colony outspent Virginia, the second most zealous province, £818,000 sterling to £385,000 collectively, or £20 to £14 per adult male. Annual levies from 1755 to 1759 numbered approximately 7000 soldiers; 5000 men were mustered in 1760 and 3000 per year until 1763. Such an army for a province with approximately 50,000 adult males meant that war was being waged on a scale comparable to the great wars of modern times.[5] And in King George's War, Massachusetts had the field almost to itself. Aside from grudging and minimal support from New York, the other New England colonies, and even Britain, the expedition which conquered Louisbourg in 1745 and the abortive Canada and Crown Point campaign of the following year were projected, manned, and supplied almost entirely by the Bay Colony.[6]

During King William's and Queen Anne's Wars, in 1690, 1706, 1709, and 1711, Massachusetts had prepared massive but unsuccessful expeditions to eliminate French power in Canada. Following the Peace of Utrecht in 1713, however, Massachusetts' government lost much of its energy. The province devoted itself to settling the recently won frontier, trying to solve the perplexing problem of a rapidly depreciating currency, and foiling the efforts of royal governors to increase their power at the expense of the lower house. Localism, ideological wrangling, stalemate, and stagnation best describe the politics of the interwar period. At this time 'the legislative agenda,' as Michael Zuckerman has noted, 'was substantially set by petitions from the towns and their inhabitants'.[7] The General Court functioned, as its name implies, primarily as a court, settling disputes that became too hot to handle on the town level, determining the ownership of frontier lands, granting licenses to sell liquor, and voting an annual budget of approximately £10,000 sterling. Most of the money went to pay the salaries of the legislators, judges, and the handful of soldiers who garrisoned Boston's Castle William and a few outposts in Maine. During the legislative session of 1743–1744, for instance, the last year before the Louisbourg campaign, 307 resolves passed. General provincial business accounted for only 98, and most of these consisted of routine matters such as voting salaries for all provincial officials from the governor to the door-keeper, approving the accounts of the county treasurers, and passing on bills to entertain various dignitaries. Over two-thirds of the business consisted of ajudicating items of interest to particular towns and individuals.[8]

In addition to settling local problems, the three branches of the Court devoted much of their energy to defining the limits of their respective powers. Beginning in 1720, Governor Samuel Shute (1716–1723) insisted that he had a right to veto the assembly's choice of its speaker, especially when it selected the obnoxious Elisha Cooke, who had repeatedly referred to Shute as a 'great blockhead' and once accosted him, while intoxicated and semi-dressed, late at night on a Boston street. The matter was only resolved in 1726 when the Privy Council forced the deputies to accept an Explanatory Charter which decided the case in Shute's favour.[9]

A similar dispute occurred when the home government saddled Shute's successor, Lieutenant-Governor William Dummer (1723–1728), with an instruction requiring the annual redemption of Massachusetts' paper currency—which derived its value by being redeemable for taxes in specified years—to forestall the inflation which had begun to affect British creditors. The house responded by refusing to vote any appropriations at all in 1727 until Dummer caved in and violated his orders. Massachusetts managed to circumvent instructions reducing its money supply until 1741, when parliamentary intransigence led to the abortive Land and Silver Bank schemes which nearly tore the province apart.[10]

The remaining two governors during the interwar years fared no better.

William Burnet (1728-1729) spent his entire year and three months in Massachusetts insisting that the assembly should permanently guarantee the executive a salary of at least £1000 sterling per year. Such an act would prevent the governor from pleasing his constituents at the expense of his superiors. This controversy dragged on until 1735. Burnet's successor Jonathan Belcher (1730-1741) finally worked out a compromise whereby the governor obtained an annually voted grant, but the house in turn promised that it would equal £1000 sterling and be voted at the beginning of each year's session, instead of at the end after the governor had approved all of the assembly's votes.[11] The last of these jurisdictional disputes occurred when Belcher had to persuade the house that all money appropriated for the treasury by the deputies be spent merely with the approval of the governor and council for each specific disbursement. The lower house refused to yield this right from 1730 to 1733, and responded to Belcher's demands by voting no money at all for nearly two years. As in the case of the Explanatory Charter, a sharp warning from the crown changed the deputies' minds.[12]

The nature of political conflict in peacetime Massachusetts must be defined if the changes produced by war are to be fully appreciated. As noted, the principal controversy centred on the division of powers within the General Court. When not handling local business, the assembly spent its time arguing with the governor and council. *House Journals* for the 1720s and 30s contain hundreds of pages of messages in which both sides based their arguments primarily on the province charter and English precedents, with the assembly claiming the powers of the House of Commons, derived from the charter clause guaranteeing all the rights of Englishmen. The 'Old Whig' appeal to the natural rights of man and the 'New Whig' attack on executive corruption were conspicuous by their absence. Ideological debate, while intense, utilised a common language and did not delve deeply into the relationship of society and government. Both sides confined themselves largely to technical points of law.

The composition of factions between Queen Anne's and King George's wars also contrasted markedly with future patterns. No effective prerogative party existed in the legislature, since on every disputed point the interests of Massachusetts and Britain clashed rather than coincided. For example, many of the house's denials of the governor's power over the speaker passed unanimously. The most favourable vote Burnet ever obtained on the permanent salary was a 54 to 18 rejection. Even this vote occurred on a watered-down proposition which guaranteed payment only for one particular executive's administration, and angered Burnet as much as the deputies.[13] In 1732, the assembly refused by 56 to 1 to supply the treasury unless it could control specific appropriations. True, the house reversed itself on this issue by 55-25 in 1733 under threat of the king's displeasure, just as it 'submitted to' (rather than 'accepted of') the Explanatory Charter by 48-32.[14] But such compliance clearly occurred under duress. Only Governor Belcher began to form a party loyal to himself and thereby successfully stifled the opposition from 1735 to 1739.[15] This faction can hardly be considered a court party, however, since Belcher spent much of his energy persuading Britain not to insist on the question of the permanent salary and to postpone redemption of the paper money supply. The governor had rather assumed leadership of the country faction.

The popular faction's one-sided dominance during the interwar period is explained by the fact that leadership in the assembly was concentrated in a few powerful hands. If service on fifteen committees—which examination of the *House Journals* suggests is a plausible dividing line between political leaders and the rank-and-file—be taken to indicate prominence, only 27 of 104 towns represented supplied any leader at all. If a deputy is counted once for every year he attained this position, seven towns provided 61 per cent of this select group. Boston headed the list with 32 per cent; with rare exceptions, all four of the capital's assemblymen appeared as leaders. Only Charlestown, Braintree, Ipswich, Salem, Northampton, and Roxbury supplied more than four per cent. Certain individuals (such as Speakers Edmund Quincy of Braintree and William Dudley of Roxbury) who served repeatedly account for the importance of these towns.[16]

Most of the leading political figures between 1713 and 1740 belonged to an extended kinship network, centred on Boston, which embraced the first families of Massachusetts. Even the few men who adhered to the unpopular governors' standards were related to their opponents. The famous Elisha Cooke, who founded the Boston Caucus in 1719 and led the popular party until his death in 1737, counted three of his brothers-in-law, Oliver Noyes, John Clarke, and William Paine, among his principal supporters in the house. But Clarke was also the brother-in-law of Cotton Mather, who consistently favoured the royal governor. Elizabeth Clarke, John's sister, was married to Elisha Hutchinson, that family's patriarch in the early eighteenth century. All the Hutchinsons except William, a Caucus supporter, favoured the prerogative. One of Cooke's uncles was Nathaniel Byfield, a brother-in-law of Governor Joseph Dudley (1702–1715) who turned against his kinsman's administration during its final years. If we go one step further, two of Dudley's three daughters had married sons of councillors Samuel Sewall and Wait Winthrop while their fathers were feuding violently with the governor.[17] However violent the rhetoric of peacetime political conflict, it was tempered by the fact that all the participants belonged to an elite which both the populace and representatives entrusted with the government.

Peacetime politics thus were plagued with superficial contention, but the system was essentially stable because administration was not expensive, government was stabilised through elite family participation and did not impinge on the lives of people except through request or mild taxation, and political issues rarely went beyond discussion of legislative prerogatives. But around 1740, two events shattered this political framework almost simultaneously: the currency crisis and the Great Awakening. Compelled by Britain to withdraw all except £30,000 of its £390,000 in circulation by 1741, two groups in Massachusetts tried to sidestep the order by creating private currencies—a Land Bank with province-wide support and a Silver Bank, favoured primarily by wealthy Boston merchants. The province overwhelmingly supported the Land Bank. Only 11 of the 43 deputies who opposed the measure in 1740 were re-elected in 1741, whereas 33 of the 63 who supported it retained their seats. Opposed by Governor Belcher and both

British and Massachusetts merchants, the Bank was ultimately declared illegal by Parliament, which provoked its supporters to threaten violent revolution. The situation was defused because Belcher was removed at the height of the crisis (ironically enough, because the ministry had been misinformed by his political opponents that he actually favoured the Land Bank) and was replaced by Advocate General William Shirley, who managed to liquidate the Bank to the satisfaction of most parties.[18]

The Awakening revived popular interest in religion at the same time that the Bank stirred up general political concern. Towns and families throughout Massachusetts split between 'Old Lights' who defended the traditional religious establishment and 'New Lights' who favoured more emotional preaching, which was to be judged by popular appeal rather than mere competence. Other differences set off the New Lights as potential threats to social order: salvation came all at once to an utterly depraved soul rather than as the culmination of 'good works' and socially acceptable 'preparation'. Itinerant ministers and preachers of different denominations were welcomed by the New Lights. These innovations clearly undermined the absolute position of each community's own established cleric. Young people, women, and the less well-to-do tended to support the Awakening. Also, three generations of high birth rates and low death rates had led to a substantial decline in economic opportunity in the province's older communities. The Awakening provided those who were worth less in worldly terms with the means to assert their superiority over those more elevated than them in the traditional socio-economic structure. For instance, the Second Church of Boston, the Mathers' congregation, split in two: the wealthier and older members followed 'Old Light' Samuel Mather when he was ousted by the younger, less affluent majority. The coincidence of overcrowding, economic distress, and a religious revival with a demonstrable social basis suggests that Massachusetts was sitting on dynamite by the early 1740s.[19]

That these social problems did not produce an explosion, it may be tentatively postulated, can be attributed to the outbreak of war between England and Spain in 1739 and England and France in 1744. The pressure of a common enemy redirected religious enthusiasm into another crusade, provided an outlet for young men with limited prospects, and brought ideological sparring within the General Court to an end for approximately two decades. Yet it can be argued that war did not so much solve these problems as mask them, since they re-emerged with even greater intensity in the 1760s. Furthermore, Anglo-American disagreement over the conduct of the war led to increasing popular discontent with Britain.

Massachusetts' limited involvement in the war with Spain from 1739 set several patterns for the greater conflicts which followed. In 1740 Governor Belcher issued a call for volunteers to serve as support troops for a British fleet destined to attack Cartagena in the West Indies. The response, thanks to promises of liberal pay, bounties, and plunder, was overwhelming despite the almost total decimation of a similar New England expeditionary force in 1703. Belcher raised one thousand men instead of the six hundred requested; this produced some embarrassment when Britain only supplied arms for the number originally planned. Surviving muster rolls indicate that young men from the long-settled towns of eastern Massachusetts supplied most of the enlistments. The campaign was a total fiasco and few of the men returned, but it set a precedent which held throughout the mid-century wars: Massachusetts raised most of its forces through bounties and the inducement of receiving military pay, room, and board.[20]

Warfare also helped to relieve the monetary crisis. As early as October 1741, Governor Shirley had managed to persuade the ministry to revoke its instructions that all issues of paper money in excess of £30,000 must be approved by the Privy Council. When war with France broke out in 1744, all restrictions were waived for the duration of the conflict. Despite 'the extreme heavy burden' of which the General Court complained in 1748, Massachusetts financed the bulk of King George's War simply by rolling the presses: in 1749, £1.9 million were extant and the currency's value had depreciated to one-tenth of sterling.[21]

Finally, the war fever caused New Lights and Old Lights to bury the hatchet between themselves. Beginning with the Louisbourg expedition of 1745, Puritan millennial confidence revived for the first time since the 1630s and 40s. Conquest of the French and Indians was viewed as a prelude to the final triumph over the Anti-Christ (Popery), the universal spread of true religion, and the second coming of Christ. The millennium would come about as a capstone on the efforts of God's chosen people, rather than as a punishment for their declension and depravity as millenarians in the intervening century, such as Cotton and Increase Mather, had feared.[22]

The imperatives of war resolved political tensions between the governor and the legislature in addition to defusing potential social conflict. Throughout the 1740s and 1750s, a powerful prerogative faction headed by Thomas Hutchinson and Andrew Oliver of Boston obtained nearly all the troops requested by Britain, successfully implemented a currency backed by specie in 1749, and prevented inflation throughout the French and Indian War by imposing heavy taxes to finance current expenditures. This faction first appeared in Bostonian politics in the late 1730s: following the death of Elisha Cooke in 1737, the town began to elect supporters as well as opponents of the governor to office for the first time in a quarter-century. Even though Hutchinson and Oliver sought to alter Boston's town meeting government to a self-selecting corporation, the town recognised their administrative competence as the only alternative to the politics of the Caucus, which had wasted its energies quarrelling with governors while the town's economy and quality of life drastically declined. Composed of relatively young men, born mostly around 1710, the prerogative faction dominated provincial politics until it was dethroned during the revolutionary crisis.[23]

The rise of the prerogative faction coincided with a drastic change in the activities of the legislature. Attention shifted from resolving local problems to matters of defence. In 1745, 224 of the 324 resolves passed by the house involved provincial interests, an almost exact reversal of the ratio of general to local business of two years before. In 1757, at the height of the French and Indian War, the proportion was 202 bills to 94. Furthermore, the number of representatives involved in the house's committee work grew dramatically.

In the absence of a paid bureaucracy, and given the fact that many of the Massachusetts local justices and militia officers sat in the house, the activity of the so-called back-benchers had to increase as the legislature changed from an ideological forum and court of appeals to an organ of policy formation and public administration. Between 1740 and 1764, 70 per cent of all represented towns (86 out of 123) supplied deputies who sat on more than fifteen committees per year, as opposed to 26 per cent in peacetime. Boston's share declined to 15 per cent, and no other town had more than three per cent. The responsibility of power diffused itself throughout the province as effectively as government imposed itself on the general population. No longer could most political figures be cousins, uncles, and brothers-in-law; even within Boston itself, apart from the Hutchinson-Oliver connection, few leading legislators of either faction were related.[24]

The prerogative's success in the provincial sphere can in part be explained by the reason that it dominated Boston. Governor Belcher's willingness to meet the old country faction more than half-way caused its members to dissipate their energy in a dispute between Belcher and Cooke which disenchanted many of the back-benchers in the assembly. Furthermore, as with solving Boston's economic problems, the task of running a war required the patience and attention to detail which the free-wheeling Cooke and his followers had never possessed. Negotiations with Indians and other colonies, preparation of endless accounts and muster-rolls, and supervision of supply shipments transformed leading politicians into full-time civil servants as well. Massachusetts willingly overlooked the prerogative's mistrust of popular government and conspicuous consumption in the face of local hardship in the light of the overwhelming necessity required by the great 'crusade'.

Prerogative rule possessed even less savoury elements. Over three-quarters of the deputies held commissions either as justices of the peace, militia officers, or both. In addition to their pay, officers had the privilege of selling supplies to their troops. Especially recalcitrant opponents of the war could be removed from their posts by the governor with the council's consent. Governor Shirley and his supporters also used dubious parliamentary manoeuvres—warning that British displeasure and punitive measures would follow if the war were not fought with all possible vigour, holding the legislature in session until their opponents went home, and even expelling the country faction's most effective remaining leader—to get their way. Prerogative strength must be explained by a combination of consensus and coercion: to stress either unduly converts men like Hutchinson and Shirley into either villains or heroes, and leads to excessively partisan interpretations of provincial politics as either stable or conflict-ridden.

The manner in which Britain's promised financial compensation for Massachusetts' Louisbourg expenditures became a prerogative tool to obtain additional troops and funds provides an excellent example of how the lower house could be persuaded to act in spite of its own best judgment. Having launched the expedition and plunged themselves £50,000 into debt, the deputies begged 'His Majesty's favor and compassion ... in relieving them from such part of the expenses and burden as to His wisdom should seem reasonable.' Once the representatives put themselves in this position, Shirley could extort further grants of troops and money by threatening that if the war effort proceeded with insufficient vigour, Britain might think twice about paying for Louisbourg. When he proposed the reduction of Canada on 31 May 1746 Shirley warned that 'a wrong step in the affair will endanger our being disappointed in our expectations'. The following July the governor impressed men who had enlisted for frontier garrison duty into the expedition contrary to the vote of the house. When the representatives refused to pay them, he obtained a reversal of this decision by promising to explain to his superiors that he was obliged to pay them from drafts on the British treasury. The house again acquiesced rather than lose all chance of receiving the Louisbourg grant.[25]

Tension between Shirley and the assembly also arose over the posting of soldiers and the duration of their service. Troops who had volunteered or been impressed for one theatre of war were sometimes transferred to a less attractive post, or else enlisted to obtain a more favourable one. These practices necessitated additional impressments to fill the vacated commands. The house protested in vain that 'we have always looked upon the impressing of men even for the defence of their own inhabitants as a method to be made use of in cases of great necessity only'. A second difficulty occurred when the governor held provincial soldiers on garrison duty long after their enlistments had expired. Some men were kept at Annapolis in Nova Scotia from mid-1744 until January 1746, and the entire 3000-men Louisbourg contingent (of whom more than 900 died from exposure and disease) remained at Cape Breton from June 1745 until a long-awaited British garrison arrived in April 1746. The assembly complained that such extended service reduced 'due confidence in the promises of government'.[26]

Discouragement with Shirley's conduct of the war brought it to a halt sooner than he would have preferred. He failed to obtain a second expedition to Canada in 1747. When Louisbourg was returned to France by the Peace of 1748, the assembly commented 'it affords us a very melancholy reflection when we consider the extreme heavy burden brought upon the people of this province, and the small prospect there is of any good effect from it . . . we have been the means of effectually bringing distress, if not ruin, upon ourselves'.[27]

In addition to side-stepping the legislature's wishes in mobilising forces, Shirley dealt harshly with opponents of his policies. Dr. William Douglass, the province's only European-trained physician, attacked the governor for permitting the impressment of sailors into the British navy, allowing sanitary conditions to deteriorate at Louisbourg, and authorising the issue of more paper money in eight years to finance his schemes than all his predecessors combined over the previous fifty. In a monumental *Summary, Historical and Political . . . of North America*, which he published serially in the *Boston Gazette* beginning in 1747, Douglass roundly attacked Shirley's military strategy and 'governors in general, who may by romantic (but in perquisites profitable) expeditions, depopulate the country'. Shirley instituted a libel suit for £10,000 on behalf of the British Admiral Charles Knowles, another target of Douglass' venom; Douglass answered with a counter-suit and ultimately won £750 in damages against the absent admiral. Shirley also sued Samuel Waldo, the Boston merchant and land speculator to whom he owed his job, for £12,000. The governor blamed Waldo, commander of the aborted Canada expedition, for failing to keep adequate accounts and thereby denying Massachusetts compensation for its efforts from the British treasury.[28] Although Waldo too was ultimately acquitted, the governor's leading opponents could count on the threat of enormous and potentially ruinous lawsuits for their pains.

After the war ended, Shirley and his supporters continued to use unsavoury tactics to persuade the assembly to adopt and maintain a specie currency. The Speaker of the House, Thomas Hutchinson, took the first step in this direction by convincing the assembly that compensation for Louisbourg would never be forthcoming unless the province pledged to use the money to sink its paper currency. However, once the money arrived, a specific plan for redeeming the outstanding bills only passed on 20 January 1749 by a vote of 40–37 after five weeks of debate. To effect this vote, Hutchinson waited until about one-quarter of the assembly had drifted away and ensured that James Allen, Shirley's principal antagonist who had accused him of trading with the enemy, would be expelled.[29]

Reaction to the new currency was overwhelmingly negative. Hutchinson lost the next Boston election to Samuel Waldo by a margin of almost three to one. His house burned down, mysteriously, and the fire companies refused to put out the blaze.[30] Allen published a list of the supporters of the currency plan: the next year, on 5 April 1750, the assembly responded by voting 46 to 33 to issue a new form of paper money. But once again, the hard money advocates had greater staying power. After the backcountry opponents of silver melted away, seven deputies were persuaded to change their minds and the new bills were rejected 31–28 on 20 April. In 1751 the house again voted an inflationary supply bill by 36–26. That year only the council's adamant refusal to concur ensured the survival of a stable currency.[31]

The ability of the prerogative faction to outlast and intimidate the majority of the representatives caused opposition spokesmen to adopt, for the first time, the Old and New Whig ideology with which the leaders of the Revolution ultimately justified their cause. Shirley's administration presented the novel phenomenon of a House of Representatives conducting an unpopular and costly war against the wishes not only of individuals but—as some of its messages and reversed votes made perfectly clear—against its own better judgment. It therefore became necessary for the country faction, for the first time, to detach itself from the assembly and go beyond the mere defence of the deputies' right to make their own laws. Once the assembly itself was conceived to be an instrument of oppression, an appeal to a higher standard was required which explained how the people's own representatives could betray their constituents.

Whig ideology suited the Massachusetts situation perfectly. The *Independent Advertiser*, America's first anti-war and protest newspaper was founded one month after the great anti-impressment riot of 17–20 November 1747 by the twenty-five-year-old Samuel Adams, among others.[32] These opposition writers cited John Locke to argue that a government which failed to protect the inhabitants' 'lives, liberties, and estates' by forcing them to fight against their wishes, impressing them into the navy, and taxing them oppressively could be opposed legitimately—even violently. Similarly, the New Whig ideas of William Trenchard and John Gordon were adapted to explain how only a morally and fiscally corrupted government would so betray its people, and that only an equally corrupted people would tolerate such oppression. The *Advertiser* blamed the war on representatives who had been corrupted by Sir Plume (Governor Shirley) and his 'prime minister' Alexander Windmill (Thomas Hutchinson) by being given military commissions, which paid officially from about £50 sterling per year for a captain to about £80 for a colonel. These, however, also entitled them to supply and pay their men and thereby opened the door for padded accounts and illegal profits.[33] Most of the complaints of corruption were directed against Shirley personally, who was alleged to have made an enormous sum of money by being granted the right to raise a royal regiment of colonials to garrison Louisbourg. New Whig ideology made sense in wartime because, unlike peacetime, real opportunities for making large sums of money in government service existed.[34]

There is little hint in The *Independent Advertiser* that the French and Indians were a real threat to Massachusetts: the 'Popish' refurbishing of King's Chapel by Shirley and the Boston Anglican community was a far greater menace. Colonists constantly denouced England as a den of iniquity and corruption instead. After the mother country gave Cape Breton back to France,[35] the most extreme critique of the war and its engineers occurred:

> Why is the security of the brave and virtuous . . . given up to purchase some short-lived and precarious advantages for lazy—f[oo]ls and idle All[ie]s? The security was purchased with the blood of the former and sacrificed to the indolence of the latter. The first won it by bravery; the latter forfeited it by Tr[e]ach[e]ry and Cow[ar]dice. As if our Min[i]stry . . . had determined to counteract the essential laws of equity, as much as possible, as they have done the rules of policy and prudence.

Reaction to British and prerogative policies not only took verbal form: wartime crowds began to focus on political issues. Between the Glorious Revolution and the 1740s, political violence in Massachusetts was committed by individuals against individuals—a bomb thrown through Cotton Mather's window, a pot shot taken at Samuel Shute, an assault against Elisha Cooke —whereas crowds restricted themselves to remedying local emergencies which could not conveniently be handled in courts of law. For example, mobs tore down bawdyhouses and market stalls under construction in the 1730s, and stopped ships trying to export food during shortages from sailing. A corrupt and brutal jailor found himself the target of a prison riot. Beginning in the 1740s, however, mobs for the first time directed themselves against imperial power and clashed with British rather than local authorities. The occasion was naval impressment: despite an Act of Parliament of 1707 forbidding impressment in American waters without the consent of local authorities, and in spite of Massachusetts' willingness to authorise the impressment of non-native seamen who happened to be in the province, British captains provoked hostility by their disregard for such points of law. Angered that their sailors deserted with local connivance, they sometimes simply impressed people indiscriminately and then sailed for the West Indies. In 1741, Captain James Scott seized over forty men and narrowly escaped with his life. A press gang killed two veterans of the Louisbourg campaign in 1745 for resisting efforts to seize them; in 1747 virtually the entire populace of Boston held many of the officers in Commodore Knowles' British fleet hostage pending the release of forty-six impressed men. Instead of negotiating Knowles threated to bombard Boston while a mob of several thousand people surrounded the governor's mansion and General Court to press their demands. The *Independent Advertiser* justified such violence as the legitimate response to lawless acts of nominally lawful authorities. Where the government could not protect its inhabitants, 'they have an undoubted right to use the powers [of self-defence] belonging to that state [of nature]'. Just before the paper closed down, it responded to critics of the Knowles Riot, 'that the sober sort, who dared to express a due sense of their injuries, were invidiously represented as a rude, low-lived mob'.[36]

The French and Indian War revived the same tendencies manifested in King George's War. The province was even more cooperative and self-sacrificing, but the prerogative faction's efforts to coordinate provincial and imperial policy again provoked resentment against British officials. Taxes, which the province had considered heavy at under £10,000 sterling in the 1740s, rose to £60,000 sterling or more from 1756 to 1760 and remained at over £30,000 for the rest of the provincial period.[37] Protesting against the fact that most of this money was raised from land taxes, the rural majority in the assembly struck back at the Boston-based prerogative faction by passing the infamous Excise Tax of 1754 and a Stamp Tax in 1755 (remarkably similar to the one Britain would later impose on the colonies) to shift the tax burden towards the urban communities. The new excise differed from the province's long-standing tax on liquor by taxing the consumption of spirits by individuals rather than the amount sold by retailers. To discover the quantity, the government appointed excise farmers who could then hire deputies to demand an account 'of all and every persons whomsoever in this government, of all the wine, rum, and brandy, and other distilled spirits expended by them (on oath if required)'; a penalty of £10 was established for false swearing. The prerogative faction and the Boston community joined forces (Boston was already paying 20 per cent of the taxes even though it had under 10 per cent of the population) to protest against this 'Total Eclipse of Liberty' and 'Monster of Monsters', as two pamphlets attacking the bill were entitled. Governor Shirley, who signed the bill under protest, himself took up the natural rights argument that had previously been used by his opponents, criticising the tax as 'altogether unprecedented in the English governments' and 'inconsistent with the natural rights of every person in the community'. The country's revenge on the court faction was short-lived: the people of the province were so angered by the excise that only 19 of the 52 deputies who approved it were re-elected, whereas 10 of the 17 who opposed it (they came from the Boston area, Salem, Marblehead, Plymouth, Maine) retained their seats.[38]

Taxes and economic difficulties during the French and Indian War rose to unprecedented heights. The legislature placed embargoes on exports of food which compelled farmers to sell provisions to British and American military commissaries at lower than usual prices; British commanders-in-chief also prohibited colonial overseas shipping intermittently when they considered trading with the enemy to be excessive. These restrictions continued until 1763: Massachusetts' new governor Francis Bernard (1760–1769) joined the legislature and protested to General Jeffrey Amherst that 'this public spirited province can ill afford to lose the small trade remaining to it' and that in any event illegal trading simply did not exist in Massachusetts. Things became so bad in 1758 that sixteen leading Bostonian merchants, all of whom paid taxes of between £95 and £540 per year, threatened to leave the province and take their business elsewhere. Bernard later argued that British taxation was unjust because Massachusetts itself had spent 'an immense sum for such a small state, the burden of which has been grievously felt by all orders of men.'[39] Economic hardship drove a large number of people into bankruptcy. To combat this problem, in 1757 the legislature passed the first major bill reforming the treatment of bankrupts in Massachusetts history. Instead of being forced to forfeit their entire estates and possibly go to debtors' prison, all persons who advertised bankruptcy in the Boston newspapers, did not try to hide any of their wealth, and permitted their affairs to be investigated by commissioners could begin life with a clean slate. Insolvents able to pay at least half their debts could retain five per cent of their wealth up to £200; those able to pay two-thirds could keep 7½ per cent up to £250; anyone who could satisfy three-fourths of the claims against him was allowed ten per cent of his estate under £300. The reform was timely: joyous news of British victories were always tempered by lists of the financially distressed in the same issues of the province's journals. For instance, twenty-eight persons filed for bankruptcy the week Louisbourg was recaptured in 1758. As late as February 1765 the default of Nathaniel Appleton on £189,000 set off a chain reaction because his creditors in turn could not pay their debts.[40]

In addition to shouldering these burdens, Massachusetts had to bear with the arrogance of British commanders-in-chief who seemed determined to infringe provincial rights and sensibilities to the maximum while winning the war. Naval impressment continued, and Massachusetts again protested against this grievance in vain.[41] Britain and Massachusetts disagreed over the number, disposition, and ability of the provincial soldiers. Each year, the prerogative faction struggled long and hard to obtain the deputies' endorsement of the full number of troops requested by Britain. Even then, the assembly confined the troops to particular posts and enlisted them for limited periods of time which coincided poorly with military necessity. As Lord Loudoun, commander-in-chief during 1757 and 1758, complained at an intercolonial conference: 'The confining of your men to any particular service appears to me a preposterous measure. Our affairs are not in such a situation as to make it reasonable for any colony to be guided by its own

particular interest'. Other problems included soldiers sent to the frontier
without arms; men enlisting and deserting several times to collect bounties;
and officers and sutlers profiteering from the right to supply men with
provisions. The province's insistence that impressment should only be used
as a last resort ensured that each year's supply of men took several months
to be mustered. Recruiting parties met with resistance in Boston and Marblehead. Loudoun also wanted colonial troops to be led by British officers and
subjected to regular army discipline. His insistence that no provincial
officer should rank higher than a British captain threatened local autonomy
and insulted the province's military capability.[42]

When in camp, British officers frequently assigned colonials only the
most onerous and demeaning work instead of committing them effectively to
battle. General James Wolfe expressed the general British attitude: 'The
Americans are in general the dirtiest, the most contemptible, cowardly
dogs that you can conceive. There is no depending upon them in action.
They fall down in their own dirt and desert by battalions, officers and all'.[43]

The most spectacular instance of Anglo-American animosity was the
quartering dispute of December 1757 and January 1758. Massachusetts
gladly offered to billet the troops for the winter, but Loudoun insisted that
any legislative action was unnecessary because the British Quartering Act
of 1694, which gave commanders such authority in England, applied to the
colonies. The assembly could not see the reason for his indignation: 'We are
really at a loss what steps to take to terminate this affair since His Lordship
does not seem dissatisfied so much from the insufficiency of what we have
done, as from the matter of its being done by a law of the province.'
Loudoun, on the other hand, argued that if quartering were discretionary
rather than automatic, 'my acquiescence under it would throw the whole
continent into a turmoil, from South Carolina to Boston. and turn three-
quarters of the troops at once into the streets to perish'. At stake was
whether the commander-in-chief could conduct the war independently of
local interference. Loudoun complained that 'even if the town of Boston
was attacked, it would not by their rule be in my power to march the troops
to its relief'. He then threatened that if things were not settled he would
'instantly order into Boston the three battalions from New York, Long
Island, and Connecticut, and, if more are wanted, I have two in the Jerseys
at hand besides those in Pennyslvania'. Loudoun also hinted that Britain
would not think it reasonable to pay the colonies for their 'very extravagant'
war expenses if they did not even provide lodging for the troops sent to
protect them.[44]

While it lasted, the French and Indian War provoked less discontent than
King George's: the country faction did not oppose any expeditions or the
war itself this time, only the proportion to be shouldered by Massachusetts
rather than by Britain. However, the peculiar manner in which the war ended
led to increased political strife, both within Massachusetts and between
Massachusetts and Britain, after hostilites were concluded. With respect to
the New England colonies, the French menace ended forever when British
forces raised the Union Jack over Quebec in 1759. But the war dragged on
four more years, both in the West Indies and on the frontier of the middle

and southern colonies. Britain expected all the mainland colonies to contribute soldiers for frontier duty so that the more valuable redcoats could be sent to Europe or the islands. Thanks largely to persuasive speeches by Massachusetts' popular new governor Francis Bernard, the Bay Colony complied and supplied 3000 soldiers per year until 1763 and also sent 700 men to the Ohio Valley in the wake of Pontiac's rebellion as late as 1764.[45] Because the war ended in 1759 in the Northeast while elsewhere it continued until 1764, Massachusetts felt little urgency or need for further sacrifices, and yet she was still required to maintain embargoes, levy taxes, and raise troops.

These difficulties were exacerbated by Britain's plans for imperial reorganisation which were implemented before the war's end. Despite the embargoes and taxes suffered by the Boston merchant community, British customs officials in Boston could not leave well enough alone and provoked the famous challenge to their general search warrants, the Writs of Assistance Case in 1761. The Sugar Act and Proclamation of 1763 were promulgated while Massachusetts still had several thousand men in service.

The manner in which Parliament's promised reimbursement finally arrived did not help matters. Massachusetts always insisted that its exertions went far beyond those of the other colonies. As a result the province was entitled to special treatment. This was not forthcoming: Jasper Mauduit, the province agent in the early 1760s, did little to force the issue. He urged acquiescence with British policy: since the other colonies were content with requesting compensation for about half their wartime expenditures, Massachusetts would appear 'in a very disadvantageous light to present a petition to Parliament setting forth that we are content with nothing less than the whole of ours'. Massachusetts ultimately received only £390,000 out of some £818,000 spent.[46]

Internal strife also broke out while the war was ending. Religious controversy between the province's Congregational establishment and a small but influential community of wealthy Anglicans began in 1761. The latter belonged mostly to wealthy Boston area families which had strongly supported and profited from the war. Charles Apthorp, a young Anglican cleric, established a 'mission' at Cambridge, causing many of the clergy to think that the long-feared Anglican bishopric was finally upon them.[47] In Maine, two land companies, the Kennibeck and the Waldo heirs, the former composed largely of future patriots, the latter of future loyalists, squabbled for control of vast tracts of land.[48] Western Massachusetts, which staunchly supported a maximum war effort, began to develop a sense of regional consciousness and in 1762 tried unsuccessfully to obtain its own college.[49] These disputes tended to coincide with divisions between the prerogative faction and its opponents: once war ended, regional, religious, and economic differences between the two factions began to take political form.

The conclusion of war also brought the problem of underemployment and overcrowding to the fore again. Massachusetts had developed something approaching a European standing army. Youths from overcrowded towns and lower class men enlisted year after year under the command of an officer class consisting of the province's leading men.[50] Battle deaths had also helped to alleviate population pressure. But beginning in 1765, the first year since 1754 Massachusetts and its fellow colonies did not muster forces for battle, the situation drastically changed. A postwar decline in overseas trade and the catastrophic drought of 1763–4 let loose an unprecedented wave of rootless persons throughout the province.[51] Boston's Warning Out records (which do not indicate who was forced to leave town, but only listed entering migrants who would then not be eligible for public relief if they became destitute) show that migration increased astronomically at precisely this time. Beginning in 1745, the first year systematic records were kept, and for the following two decades of war, migration to Boston was primarily female and mostly from Massachusetts. But in 1765, not only did the number expand greatly, but the migrants were mostly male, many men with families, and came from both Massachusetts and overseas. Eighty per cent of all male migrants to Boston from 1745–1773 arrived between 1765 and 1773. Total migration rose each decade: 458 households (1745–1755); 925 (1755–1765); 2479 (1765–1773).[52] The presence of so many additional single men in Boston undoubtedly swelled the size and added to the vigour of the Boston mob. Once again, during the revolution itself, in eastern Massachusetts long term military service was largely confined to young men who did not have sufficient wealth to pay taxes or were still dependent on their fathers.[53] But during the decade of 1765–1775, many men had nowhere to go except into the revolutionary movement.

The most notable political effect of the ending of the war was the swift demise of the prerogative faction. By 1766, its leading members were purged from the council seats some of them had held for decades. Its strength dwindled quickly from approximately half the house in 1765 to almost zero by 1768. Massachusetts would tolerate the leadership of a Thomas Hutchinson during wartime when administrative skills and capacity for hard work were of the utmost importance. Sacrifices in the interest of the common cause were tolerable, and even Hutchinson and his cohorts protested against such enormities as naval impressment and the quartering act. Once war ended, however, restrictions on Massachusetts' trade, tighter and possibly corrupt enforcement of customs regulations, and taxation by Britain rather than the province itself all appeared to undermine the prerogative's contention that Anglo-American interests were compatible.

The faction which had dominated Massachusetts for a quarter-century was swept away with remarkable ease between 1761 and 1768 largely because it had a distorted conception both of itself and of Massachusetts politics. Although most of its leaders were initially Bostonians, they disliked town-meeting politics and preferred to spend as little time in town as possible, moving to their suburban imitations of English country houses and socialising among themselves, instead of staying in contact with the common folk.[54] In consequence, they deluded themselves into thinking that they were entitled to hold office through *noblesse oblige;* they did not perceive it as a reward bestowed on them for their competent administration of the war in spite of their profiteering and aloofness. Once the war ended the sole basis of their support vanished.

The inability of the prerogative to put up a better fight can also be traced to the roots of its power. Believing that the correct role of the populace in government was passively to sanction the decisions of an administrative elite, they could not effectively use newspapers, harangue crowds, or cater to popular support through organisations such as the Boston Caucus. They had little experience in such matters, considered 'politics' as opposed to administration both a social evil and beneath their dignity, and were simply too set in their ways to adjust to a new world of politics as they approached in most cases the age of sixty.[55]

The prerogative's wartime strength was also translated into post-war weakness in another way. The opposition had been hampered throughout the war by weak or self-serving leaders; in the early 1760s, for example, Benjamin Pratt and John Tyng were respectively bought off with the Chief Justiceship of New York and an inferior court post in Middlesex County.[56] As a result of the default or death of the old popular party's leaders, a new one arose to express general indignation. Composed primarily of much younger men without previous personal or familial ties to provincial politics, the new country faction drew its strength from journalistic skills, Boston machine politics, and the 'Boston mob'. It used extreme rhetoric which equated its enemies with the anti-Christ and predicted the total suppression of American liberty if the corrupt opposition were not totally destroyed. Coming from outside the legislature, the new politics had to employ more extreme means to resist British policy in Massachusetts than in other colonies simply because in no other province did the people have to be persuaded to purge the legislature of such a strong pro-British faction.

One of the most potent arguments the revolutionaries advanced to resist British policy in Massachusetts was that it was both unfair and unnecessary because the province had indeed borne more than its share of the war. In Massachusetts requisitions had most certainly worked. For instance, when James Otis protested against the Stamp Act with his 'Rights of the British Colonies Asserted and Proved', he not only appealed to natural rights, but also to past experience:[57]

> We have spent all we could raise, and more; for notwithstanding the parliamentary reimbursements of part, we still remain much in debt. The province of the Massachusetts I believe, has expended more men and money in war since the year 1620, when a few families first landed at Plymouth, in proportion to their ability, than the three Kingdoms together. The same, I believe, may be truly affirmed of many of the other colonies, though the Massachusetts has undoubtedly had the heaviest burden.

Otis's argument was taken up by other colonials. In 1764 the New York assembly protested against British taxation because 'in many wars we have suffered an immense loss of both blood and treasure, to repel the foe, and maintain a valuable dependency on the British crown'. And when Benjamin Franklin appeared before the House of Commons in February 1766 to make his famous false distinction between the colonies' objection to internal taxes and their willingness to acquiesce in external, he was right on the mark when he argued that 'the colonies raised, clothed, and paid, during the last war, near 25,000 men, and spent many millions'.[58]

Even leading Massachusetts Tories agreed with this analysis although not with the deduction that resistance and revolution were the only correct responses. Thomas Hutchinson argued forcefully though privately that the Stamp Act was unjust because the colonies had contributed more men to the 'Great War for Empire' in proportion to their population than the mother country. Secondly, the colonies had defended themselves for the century before 1754 without much British assistance, and through their own exertions had increased the strength and prosperity of the empire. Third, whatever contribution the colonies had made as a whole, Massachusetts' efforts deserved special mention: 'No other government has been at any expense to set against this', with the result that during the war 'the public debt increased annually thirty or forty thousand pounds lawful money.' Finally, Canada was of no economic value to the colonies and would greatly depreciate existing colonial land values.[59] Loyalist Isaac Royall, a wealthy West India planter who had lived in Charlestown and Medford since 1737, similarly remonstrated with Lord Dartmouth in 1774 that 'this province Sir has always been foremost even beyond its ability and notwithstanding the present unhappy disputes would perhaps be so again if there should be the like occasion for it in promoting the Honour of their King and Nation. Witness their twice saving Nova Scotia from falling into French hands, the reduction of Louisbourg . . . and many other expensive and heroic expeditions against the common enemy'.[60]

Yet the loyalists also insisted that whatever the colonists' own exertions, British aid had still been necessary. Even if taxation were unfair or onerous, the indisputable fact remained that without Britain Canada could not have been taken. In his *History of Massachusetts*, Hutchinson argued the opposite position to that which he adopted in his letter on the Stamp Act. Without help, the colonies 'would have been extirpated by the French', and even at Louisbourg in 1745, the deciding factor was 'the superior naval power of Great Britain'. Hutchinson agreed with the patriots that the mother country had no altruistic motives for aiding the colonies—'fear of losing that advantageous trade' rather than 'paternal affections' was the true cause of intervention. But Britain had undeniably 'expended a far greater sum' rescuing the colonies during the final war 'than the whole property, real and personal, in all the colonies would amount to'. Therefore, 'in a moral view, a separation of the colonies which must still further enfeeble and distress the other parts of the empire, already enfeebled by exertions to save the colonies', was reprehensible.[61] Of course, the revolutionaries argued that Hutchinson and his fellow loyalists' real motive for defending British policy was that their own careers and pocketbooks had benefited greatly through their participation in the war, whereas many of their countrymen had lost sizeable portions of their estates or even their lives.

A persuasive case can be made that serious popular resentment against British imperial policy—which had been loosely enforced during the age of 'Salutary Neglect' between Queen Anne's and King George's Wars— occurred because in two decades Massachusetts had launched a war effort which to be effective required a major transformation of its political system. War greatly increased the role of government in Massachusetts society and transformed the nature of the General Court. Increased taxation, regulation of the economy in the form of food embargoes and requistion of needed supplies, and the drafting of perhaps a fifth of the male population into the army and navy characterised military policy in mid-eighteenth century Massachusetts. To manage King George's and the French and Indian Wars, the house's committee work involved a large majority rather than a small minority of representatives. War proved a centralising experience in that the legislature no longer spent most of its time reacting to petitions from the towns and inhabitants and then settling disputes. Beginning in the 1740s and 1750s, deputies from throughout the province, not just a few leading men from Boston and some of the larger towns, initiated and shaped government policy instead of merely voting on issues laid before them by the leadership.

Perhaps even more importantly, as Lawrence Henry Gipson has noted, the American Revolution was an aftermath of the 'Great War for Empire'. Gipson stresses that Britain's effort to regulate the colonies originated in unsolved problems of the Anglo-American connection (frontier defence, trading with the enemy, effective inter-colonial coordination of forces) which seriously hampered the war effort. Had not Canada fallen to the British, the Americans would still have depended on the mother country for defence and could not have rebelled.[62]

But the revolution was also an aftermath of Massachusetts' war for empire. Since the 1740s, the dominant faction in the province, led by men such as Hutchinson and Oliver, had staked its fortunes on whole-hearted American cooperation with British war measures. Functioning as full-time civil servants for years on end, they continued to support submission to post-war impositions even when the military necessity which had compelled such docility in the past had vanished. Convinced that the population as a whole lacked the knowledge and competence to govern itself, the future loyalists lacked any understanding that the successful careers and cordial relationships they had enjoyed with British officials during the war were not typical. They were not insensitive; they sought to alleviate impressment and imperial taxation. But if Britain proved adamant, they always counselled forbearance rather than resistance. Estranged from their suffering country-men, they emerged in the revolutionary decade as a government without a country.

NOTES

1. William Pencak is Andrew W. Mellon Fellow in the Humanities, Duke University, Durham, North Carolina. Much of the article is adapted from his dissertation, 'Massachusetts Politics in War and Peace, 1676–1776' (Columbia University, 1978). A revised version will be published by Northeastern University Press. He wishes to thank Ralph Crandall, Jack P. Greene, Alden T. Vaughan, and Chilton Williamson for their assistance.
2. *Boston Gazette,* 21 May, 1754.
3. See generally Charles Tilly, ed., *The Formation of the Nation State in Western Europe* (Princeton, 1975), esp. 5–83.

4. Good accounts of Anglo-American relations during the French and Indian War are Lawrence Henry Gipson, *The British Empire Before the American Revolution* 15 vols. (New York, 1948–1974); Stanley Pargellis, *Lord Loudoun in North America* (New Haven, 1933); and Alan Rogers, *Empire and Liberty: American Resistance to British Authority, 1755–1763* (Berkeley, 1974).
5. *Journals of the House of Representatives of Massachusetts Bay* (Boston, 1919), XXII, 17, 84, 99, 110, 116, 153; XXIII, 26, 45, 110 (hereafter cited as *House Journals*); Gipson, *British Empire*, VII, 159–163; 316–24; IX, ch. iii; Jack P. Greene, 'Social Context and the Causal Pattern of the American Revolution: A Preliminary Consideration of New York, Virginia, and Massachusetts', (unpublished paper delivered at the Colloque Internationale du Centre National de la Recherche Scientifique: La Révolution Americaine et l'Europe, February 1977), 6.
6. Accounts of the Louisbourg campaign may be found in John A. Schutz, 'Imperialism in Massachusetts During the Governorship of William Shirley, 1741–1746', *Huntington Library Quarterly*, XXII (1960), 217–36; and Douglas Leach, 'Brothers in Arms'? —Anglo-American Friction at Louisbourg, 1745–1746', *Massachusetts Historical Society Proceedings*, LXXXIX (1977), 36–54.
7. Michael Zuckerman, *Peaceable Kingdoms: The New England Towns in the Eighteenth Century* (New York, 1970), 35.
8. Abner C. Goodell and Ellis Ames, eds., *The Acts and Resolves of the Province of Massachusetts Bay* (Boston, 1869–1922), III 1107–51; IV, 1079–1116 for index of taxation and fiscal acts; for resolves for 1743, see XIII (Hereafter cited as *Acts*). Conversion of pounds Massachusetts to pounds sterling follows William Douglass, *A Summary . . . Historical and Political . . . of North America* (London, 1755), I, 493, and *Historical Statistics of the United States* (Washington, 1960), 771. After 1750 four pounds Massachusetts equalled three pounds sterling.
9. *House Journals*, II, 228–33; VII, 450 ff; various letters for 1724–1726 in the Belknap, Pepperrell, Cushing, Colman, and Saltonstall Papers, Massachusetts Historical Society; Albert C. Matthews, 'The Acceptance of the Explanatory Charter', *Colonial Society of Massachusetts Publications*, XVII (1913), 389–400.
10. *House Journals*, VII, 229; VIII, *passim*, esp. 140, 163.
11. *Ibid.*, VIII, 251–435; IX, 1–81, *passim*; various letters of William Burnet and Jonathan Belcher to Lords of Trade and the Duke of Newcastle in W. Noel Sainsbury *et. al.*, eds., *Calendar of State Papers, Colonial Series* (London, 1869), XXXVI–XLII (hereafter cited as *CSP*); Lords of Trade to Privy Council, 26 Aug. 1735, *ibid.*, XLII, no. 82.
12. *House Journals*, X, 104, 123, 256, 415; XI, 67, 73, 93, 228, 309; Belcher to Newcastle, 26 Dec. 1732 and 19 May 1733, *CSP*, XXXIX, no. 285; XL, no. 170.
13. William Dummer to Duke of Newcastle, *CSP*, 15 Sep. 1729, XXXVI, no. 904; Benjamin Prescott to John Chandler, 23 June 1729, MsC. 2041, New England Historic Genealogical Society, Boston, Mass.
14. *House Journals*, VI, 73, 93, 278, 309; Massachusetts Archives, Office of the Secretary of the Commonwealth, State House, Boston, XX, 248–9.
15. John A. Schutz, 'Succession Politics in Massachusetts, 1730–1741', *William and Mary Quarterly*, 3rd ser. XV (1958), 508–20.
16. Pencak, 'Massachusetts Politics', 445–53 for names of house leaders and statistical tables.
17. Information on kinship connections among the elite are most conveniently found in the appropriate biographies in Oliver O. Roberts, *The History of the Ancient and Honorable Artillery Company* (Boston, 1854–8), I, II; and John L. Sibley and Clifford K. Shipton, *Biographical Sketches of Those Who Attended Harvard College* (Cambridge, 1873), III–VIII.
18. Good descriptions of the crisis are found in Andrew M. Davis, *Currency and Banking in Massachusetts Bay* (New York, 1901), I, 111–51; II, 102–218; 'Boston Banks and those who were Interested in Them', *New England Historic Genealogical Register*, LVII (1903), 279–81; and 'Provincial Banks, Land and Silver', *Colonial Society of Massachusetts Publications*, III, (1905–07) 2–41; George A. Billias, *Massachusetts Land Bankers of 1740* (Orono, Me., 1954); For specific information see *House Journals*, XVIII, 42–8, 185–6; Thomas Hutchinson to Benjamin Lynde, 12 Aug. 1741, in

Fitch E. Oliver, ed., *Diaries of Benjamin Lynde and Benjamin Lynde, Jr.* (Boston, 1880), 222–3.

19. J. M. Bumsted, 'Revivalism and Separatism in New England: The First Society of Norwich, Connecticut, as a Case Study', *William and Mary Quarterly*, 3rd. ser., XXIV (1967), 588–612; Philip Greven, 'Youth, Maturity, and Religious Conversion: A Note on the Ages of Converts in Andover, Massachusetts, 1718–1744', *Essex Institute Historical Collections*, CVIII (1972), 119–34; John C. Miller, 'Religion, Finance, and Democracy in Massachusetts', *New England Quarterly*, VI (1933), 29–58. I am indebted to Frank Granato, in a seminar paper written at Tufts University, 1979, for the information on the Second Church of Boston. For overpopulation, see Philip Greven, *Four Generations: Land, Population, and Family in Colonial Andover, Massachusetts* (Ithaca, 1970); Kenneth Lockridge, 'Social Change and the Meaning of the American Revolution', *Journal of Social History*, VI (1973), 403–39.

20. *House Journals*, XVIII, 103; Jonathan Belcher to William Shirley, 12 July 1740, Belcher Papers II, *Massachusetts Historical Society Collections*, 6th. ser. VII, 360; William Shirley to Duke of Newcastle, 4 Aug. 1740, in C. H. Lincoln, ed. *Correspondence of William Shirley* (New York, 1912), I, 24–6. For a profile of the soldiers, see Myron Stachiw's excellent introduction to the forthcoming *Massachusetts Officers and Soldiers During French and Indian Wars, 1722–1743*, to be published by the New England Historic Genealogical Society.

21. Shirley to Newcastle, 17 Oct. 1741, 23 Jan. 1742, and to Lords of Trade, 10 Aug. 1744, *Shirley Correspondence*, I, 76, 80, 140; Lords of Trade to Shirley, 9 Sep. 1744, *ibid.*, 144.

22. See, among other sources, Nathan O. Hatch, 'The Origins of Civil Millennialism in America: New England Clergymen, War with France, and the Revolution', *William and Mary Quarterly*, 3rd. ser., XXXI (1974), 417–22; Alan Heimert, *Religion, and the American Mind from the Great Awakening to the American Revolution* (Cambridge, 1966), 82–4; George A. Wood, *William Shirley: Governor of Massachusetts, 1741–1756* (New York, 1920), 169–70; 275–6.

23. G. B. Warden, *Boston, 1689–1776* (Boston, 1970), ch. vii; William Pencak and Ralph Crandall, 'Metropolitan Boston Before the American Revolution: An Urban Interpretation of the Imperial Crisis', (unpublished paper delivered at the Colonial Society of Massachusetts, February 1979).

24. See n. 8, 16, 17 above. Many leading supporters of the prerogative who had withdrawn from politics—especially those who became Anglicans—were related. But they exercised no influence in the legislature.

25. *House Journals*, XXI, 198; XXII, 162, 182; XXIII, 42.

26. *Ibid.*, XXII, 207, 246, 252.

27. *Ibid.*, XXV, 37, 52, 66; XXVI, 307–8.

28. John Noble, 'The Libel Suit of Knowles v. Douglass, 1748, 1749', *Colonial Society of Massachusetts Publications*, I (1895–7), 213–40; quotation from *The Independent Advertiser*, 4 July 1748; William Shirley to Samuel Waldo, 28 June 1748 and 7 July 1748; Waldo to Shirley, 28 June 1748; The Case of Waldo vs. Shirley, 22 April 1749; and Waldo to Christopher Kilby, 24 April 1749; all in Henry Know Papers, L, Massachusetts Historical Society.

29. *House Journals*, XXV, 116, 148, 150, 157; James Allen, *Letter to the Freeholders and Other Inhabitants of Massachusetts Bay* (Boston, 1749).

30. Thomas Hutchinson, 'Hutchinson in America', 58, 59, Egremont Mss. no. 2664, British Museum, Microfilm at Massachusetts Historical Society; Hutchinson to Israel Williams, 17 May 1749, Israel Williams Papers, Masachusetts Historical Society.

31. Allen, *Letter to Freeholders; House Journals*, XXVII, 35, 47, 56, 62, 97, 198, 234; XXVIII, 42, 52, 56, 69.

32. For a general discussion of the riot and its aftermath, see John Lax and William Pencak, 'The Knowles Riot and the Crisis of the 1740s in Massachusetts', *Perspectives in American History*, X (1976), 153–214.

33. For these nicknames, see *The Independent Advertiser*, 27 March, 1 April and 21 Nov. 1748. For salaries, see, for example, *Acts*, IV, 218; for government contracts, William T. Baxter, *The House of Hancock: Business in Boston, 1724–1775* (Cambridge, 1950),

92–110; 118–23; 129–41; 150–6; 253–5. Soldiers in out-of-province military expeditions were not liable to be sued for debt, a further inducement to enlist.
34. For a similar interpretation of why an ideology stressing government corruption appeared at this time, see Jack P. Greene, 'Political Mimesis; A Consideration of the Historical and Cultural Roots of Legislative Behavior in the British Colonies in the Eighteenth Century', *American Historical Review*, LXXV (1969), 337–67.
35. *The Independent Advertiser*, 4 Jan., 10 Oct. and 14 Nov. 1748; 17 July, and 17 Aug. 1749.
36. See Lax and Pencak, 'The Knowles Riot', for discussions of these mobs and bibliographical footnotes. Quotations from *The Independent Advertiser*, 8 Feb. 1748 and 5 Dec. 1749.
37. See n. 8 above.
38. *House Journals*, XXX, 43; XXXI, 38, 63–72; 202–3, 283–8; XXXII, 10, 56–9, 340–53; XXXIII, 294, 304, 307. For a discussion of the pamphlet literature see Paul Boyer, 'Borrowed Rhetoric: The Massachusetts Excise Controversy of 1754', *William and Mary Quarterly*, 3rd, ser., XXXI (1964), 328–51. For Boston's tax problems, see Warden, *Boston*, ch. vii., and William Pencak, 'The Social Structure of Revolutionary Boston: The Evidence From the Great Fire of 1760 Manuscripts', forthcoming in *The Journal of Interdisciplinary History*.
39. For embargoes, see, for example, *House Journals*, XXXII, 87, 93, 249, 305, 404; Francis Bernard to Jeffrey Amherst, 30 May, 2 June, 29 Aug. and 5 Sep. 1762, Bernard Papers, II, 155, 157, 280, 282, Sparks Manuscripts, Houghton Library, Harvard University; Bernard to Lords of Trade, 1 Aug. 1763, Bernard Papers, III, 162; Massachusetts Archives, LV, 301.
40. *Acts*, IV, 29–38; Francis Bernard to Lords of Trade, 18 April 1765, Bernard Papers, III, 203; Carl Bridenbaugh, *Cities in Revolt* (New York, 1955), 252–3.
41. Impressment during the French and Indian War is discussed in William Pencak, 'Thomas Hutchinson's Fight Against Naval Impressment', *New England Historic and Genealogical Register*, CXXXII (1978), 25–36.
42. Lord Loudoun to [Massachusetts House of Representatives], 29 Jan. 1757, Israel Williams Papers; *House Journals*, XXXV, 351f; Thomas Hutchinson to Loudoun, 21 Feb. 1757, Loudoun Papers, Huntington Library, San Marino, California, photostat at the Massachusetts Historical Society; various letters in Massachusetts Archives, LVI, Pargellis, *Lord Loudoun*, 175–6; 185–6; 214–5; 269–78; John A. Schutz, *Thomas Pownall: Defender of American Liberty* (Glendale, California, 1951), 125, 130.
43. Quoted in Rogers, *Empire and Liberty*, 63.
44. Lord Loudoun to Governor Thomas Pownall (1757–1760), 8 and 15 Nov., 8 Dec. 1757, Massachusetts Archives, LVI, 256–66; Pownall to Loudoun, 26 Dec. 1757, *ibid.*, 278, 286; *House Journals*, XXXIV, 208, 256.
45. *House Journals*, XXXVII, 250; XXXVIII, 302; Francis Bernard to Lords of Trade, 17 April 1762, Bernard Papers, II, 180.
46. Jasper Mauduit to Massachusetts House of Representatives, 8 Feb. 1763, Mauduit Papers, *Massachusetts Historical Society Collections*, LXXIV (1918), 100; Gipson, *British Empire*, IX, ch. ii.
47. Carl Bridenbaugh, *Mitre and Sceptre: Transatlantic Faiths, Ideas, Personalities, and Politics, 1689–1775* (New York, 1962), ch. vii; Mauduit Papers, *passim*, esp. 30, 76, 104–19; Francis Bernard to Richard Jackson, 23 Jan. 1763, Bernard Papers, II, 249–50; for families which profited from the war, see Gary Nash, 'Social Change and the Growth of Pre-Revolutionary Urban Radicalism', in Alfred E. Young, ed., *The American Revolution*, (DeKalb, Ill., 1976), 21–3.
48. Warden, *Boston*, 356–57; Gordon E. Kershaw, *'Gentlemen of Large Property and Judicious Men': The Kennebeck Proprietors, 1749–1775* (Somersworth, N. H., 1975); also see various documents in Henry Knox Papers, L–LI, Massachusetts Historical Society.
49. Henri Lefavour, 'The Proposed College in Hampshire County in 1762', *Massachusetts Historical Society Proceedings*, LXVI (1936–41), 53–80; Mauduit Papers, 70–3; Oxenbridge Thacher to Benjamin Pratt [1762], Thacher Papers, Massachusetts Historical Society.
50. John Shy, *A People Numerous and Armed* (New York, 1976), 30–1, 173.

51. Joseph Ernst and Marc Egnal, 'An Economic Interpretation of the American Revolution', *William and Mary Quarterly*, 3rd. ser., XXIX (1972), 3–32; Anne Cunningham, ed., *Diary and Letters of John Rowe*, (Boston, 1903), 61, 67–70; Warden, *Boston*, ch. viii.

52. Warning Out Records in Overseers of the Poor Mss., Massachusetts Historical Society. These themes are developed further in William Pencak, 'The Revolt Against Gerontocracy: Genealogy and the Massachusetts Revolution', *National Genealogical Society Quarterly*, LXVI (1978), 291–304.

53. David Ader, Arthur Landry, and David Peete, in course papers written at Tufts University, 1979, have studied the Medford and Roxbury contingents in the continental army during the Revolution. In gerneal, young men who did not pay taxes comprised the rank-and-file of those who enlisted for more than a few days when the British were in the neighbourhood. See also B. Michael Zuckerman, 'Neighbours Divided: The Social Impact of the Continental Army—Massachusetts, 1774–1786', (Wesleyan University, A. B. honors thesis, 1971).

54. For a detailed discussion of the residences and migration pattern of the prerogative faction, see Pencak and Crandall, 'Metropolitan Boston'.

55. John A. Schutz, 'Those Who Became Tories: Town Loyalty and the Revolution in New England', *New England Historic Genealogical Register*, CXXIX (1975), 94–105. For age of loyalists, see Pencak, 'Revolt Against Gerontocracy'.

56. Waldo died in 1759, Allen in 1754; for Pratt and Tyng see Shipton, *Harvard Graduates*, VI, 540–49; VII, 595–600.

57. James Otis, *The Rights of the British Colonies Asserted and Proved* (Boston, 1764), 72.

58. Quoted in Jack P. Greene, *Colonies to Nation, 1763–1789* (New York, 1967), 34, 72.

59. Edmund S. Morgan, 'Thomas Hutchinson and the Stamp Act', *New England Quarterly* XXI (1948), 488, 489; Hutchinson to William Bollan, 14 July 1760, Massachusetts Archives XXV, 14–17, pagination to typescript copy at the Massachusetts Historical Society prepared by Catherine Barton Mayo.

60. Isaac Royall to Lord Dartmouth, 18 Jan. 1774, Ms., L., Massachusetts Historical Society.

61. Thomas Hutchinson, *History of the Colony and Province of Massachusetts Bay* (Cambridge, 1936), III, 253.

62. Lawrence Henry Gipson, 'The American Revolution as an Aftermath of the Great War for Empire, 1754–1763', *Political Science Quarterly*, LXV (1950), 86–104.

British Government Spending and the North American Colonies 1740-1775

by

Julian Gwyn

I

One of the more intractable problems facing historians of the pre-industrial economy relates to the balance of payments. There is the usual problem of the absence of suitable statistics. There is, for instance, an abundance of data about commodity trade especially with foreign states, which include imports and exports as well as re-exports. But data on the other element in a nation's current account—invisible trade—were not collected by governments in most cases until the twentieth century. As a result, historians have tended to confine themselves to comments about the balance of trade, and to ignore the more important question of the balance of payments. Moreover, as in so many aspects of economics, the theory of the balance of payments is presently subjected to much discussion and some dispute. In general it was (and perhaps still is) assumed that a positive balance of payments is good, and an endemic adverse balance is bad, for an economy. Yet a deficit in the balance of payments is not necessarily bad nor a surplus good for a state. A deficit is a form of borrowing which could be employed to enhance domestic savings to boost investment to the benefit of future growth. By contrast if the deficit is occasioned by an excess of aggregate demand, an economy could be said to be heading for trouble, if the practice became chronic. A knowledge of aggregate demand then becomes crucial, for it largely determines the levels of production and employment, and thus becomes the critical measure of the relative health of an economy at given intervals. To estimate aggregate demand for pre-industrial economies, where governments collected none of the necessary statistics, is an almost hopeless task for economic historians. Marginally less difficult are estimates of invisible trade.

The economy of British North America in the generation before the War of Independence is a case in point. Useful statistics of merchandise trade, except for a five-year interval from 1768 to 1772,[1] exist only for commerce between the colonies and the mother country. In general they show a large commodity trade deficit, for most colonies in most years, in favour of Great Britain. The traditional but erroneous explanation of how such deficits were met was found in American commodity trade to the West Indies.[2] Thus it was argued, again wrongly, that there was little need for movements of bullion in the North Atlantic commerce, as there was, for instance, in the trade to Russia, India and the East generally.

Adequate discussion of invisible trade, and hence the balance of payments in colonial America, dates only from research begun fifteen years ago. Such research found that the colonial deficit was met partly by trading favourably elsewhere, especially in Europe south of Cape Finisterre, partly by the income from services to overseas customers, and partly by capital inflows into America. For 1768–1772, by way of example, the annual average deficit on commodity trade was first estimated at £1,331,000. With £610,000 earned annually from shipping services, £400,000 from defence spending in America by Britain and £220,000 from other invisible earnings, all but £99,000[3] of this huge annual deficit was accounted for. From an accountant's viewpoint this was more or less a balanced budget.

It will surprise no one, least of all the authors of this original research, that each of these figures needs correcting. Such is the fate of all worthy pioneering works! It is one of the certain indications of the importance of their work that it should have stimulated new attempts to analyse the colonial economy of the eighteenth century. Much of the revisionary work has been undertaken by Dr Price of the University of Michigan. It was he who first made available to historians the data for Scotland's trade with America.[4] When that is added to the trade of England and Wales, the American deficit was reduced for the years 1768–1772 by 14 per cent, or £189,000 annually. For certain colonies, such as the tobacco colonies of the Chesapeake, his Scottish data turned what had been regarded as colonial deficits into trade balances favouring the colonies.[5] More recently his analysis of the sale of American-built ships in Britain has added (at the very least) £40,000 annually to Shepherd's and Walton's estimates of invisible earnings by Americans.[6]

II

The first main purpose of this contribution is to refine the earlier estimates of defence spending by Britain *in* America. British spending in the colonies by the government, though largely for defence, was not confined to the army and navy and the Board of Ordinance. Estimates contained here include as well expenditures for Indian services, and payments administered by certain colonial governors and agents for such important frontier colonies as Nova Scotia and Georgia, Quebec (from 1760), and the Floridas, West and East after 1763. It also takes note of reimbursement by Parliament of certain colonial wartime expenditures, and finally some small payments made from the King's privy purse.

The sources for this more refined data are available mostly in the Public Record Office at Kew. They include the audited accounts of the army and Board of Ordnance in Audit Office papers, and for the navy the Navy Board and Victualling Board bill books in the Admiralty Papers, as well as the in-letters of the Navy Board. In addition the papers of the Treasury Board were studied for this thirty-six year interval. Two important printed sources were also employed, the appropriate volumes of the *Journals of the House of Commons,* and a parliamentary session paper for 1868–69, Vol XXXV, which summarised year by year, public expenditure for the eighteenth century. All information relating to spending in America was recorded and arranged annually under general headings: army, navy, ordnance, colonial administration, parliamentary reimbursements, privy purse. It was not found possible to distinguish precisely where the expenditure took place. This was especially the case for army expenditures, the largest single category. Clearly though, the bulk must have occurred in New York, the headquarters of the British Army in America from 1755 onwards, and on whose frontiers so much of the fighting occurred and where the bulk of the troops were stationed. Finally the data were totalled and arranged in intervals of war and peace: 1740–8, 1749–55, 1756–63, 1764–75.

The period 1740–8 was one of war with Spain and (after 1744) France. As far as the American colonies were concerned the years until 1744 were characterised by rather low levels of British governmental expenditure. Thereafter, especially as a result of the successful siege of Louisbourg and the establishment of a North American naval squadron in 1745, spending rose rapidly to heights never before attained in North America. With the decision in 1745 to garrison Louisbourg with regular British regiments brought from Gibraltar, together with the preparations throughout 1746 for an invasion of Canada, a project not abandoned until 1747, governmental spending remained at a high level until hostilities ended.

Though the years 1749–55 were ostensibly ones of peace, British public spending in America continued well above pre-1740 levels. This arose partly from the decision to compensate the colonies for their 1745–7 wartime expenditures, and partly from the decision to garrison Nova Scotia, after Louisbourg was restored to the French. The cost of maintaining regulars in Nova Scotia together with the expenditures incurred in building the new town of Halifax ensured that costs would rise when compared with the period 1740–8.

The return of war between 1756 and 1763 necessitated outlays in America on a scale that dwarfed the war effort between 1744 and 1748. They represented the greatest imperial expenditure at any time before the War of Independence. With unprecedentedly large bodies of troops stationed in America and large squadrons of warships, demands for funds from Parliament seemed endless. The policy of reimbursing colonies for at least a significant part of their own costs also added to the overall expenditure. The peak was reached in 1759–1760. Yet even afterwards, owing to the need to maintain an army of occupation in Canada, and on the western frontier, spending levels remained higher than had been experienced before 1755.

The years 1764–75 were ones generally of retrenchment, at first somewhat delayed by the need to contain the Indian threat led by Pontiac, and later by the decision to maintain a standing army in America, not on the frontier but in the cities and against the Americans. There was an abrupt reversal of policy from rebates to the colonies out of taxes collected by Parliament in Britain to a demand that part of the cost of this standing army in America be borne by the colonists themselves. Average spending in this period was swollen by the build-up of forces in Massachusetts in 1774 and 1775. In all, this kept spending levels substantially above those of the earlier periods 1740–48 and 1749–55. The details for the entire period 1740–1775 are summarised below in Table I.

TABLE I
BRITISH GOVERNMENT SPENDING IN AMERICA, 1740-75
(000's of £s)

	1740-48	1749-55	1756-63	1764-75	Totals 1740-75	%
	£	£	£	£	£	
Army	756	660	5,489	3,369	10,274	63.5
Navy	274	220	966	672	2,132	13.2
Parliamentary Reimbursements	—	467	1,078	—	1,545	9.5
Colonial Administration	210	316	261	391	1,178	7.3
Ordnance Board	82	182	160	552	976	6.0
Privy Purse	9	31	30	18	88	0.5
Totals	1,331	1,876	7,984	5,002	16,193	100.0
Yearly Averages	148	268	998	417	450	
% of Total	8.2	11.6	49.3	30.9	100.0	

What can be learned from these figures? The importance of spending on the Seven Years' War is clear. Almost half the total spending for the thirty-six years of this study occurred during that brief period 1756-3. Annual expenditure reached an average of almost £1 million, when the overall 1740-75 average was only £450,000. Wartime spending between 1756 and 1763 was almost six times as large as spending during the earlier war of the Austrian Succession 1740-8. Furthermore, while annual spending for 1764-75 dropped to about 40 per cent of the annual wartime totals, nevertheless it continued at a level almost 65 per cent higher than for the pre-war years of 1749 to 1755.[7] Thus the change of British policy in America, if the serious spending of money by Parliament is a reasonable guide, can be said to date not from 1756-63, as is traditionally recorded, but from 1745-6 with the Louisbourg expedition and the planned invasion of Canada. From that moment onwards spending levels acquired an altogether new momentum, from which the British government did not free itself for the rest of the eighteenth century, even after 1783, owing to the need to defend Canada. Moreover, the data show that it was the expense of the army, with its ancillary arms of the artillery and engineers under the Board of Ordnance, which constituted the bulk of the cost, a shade under 70 per cent, or more than five times the expenditure on the navy in America. Of the £1.2 million spent in America for colonial administration, the bulk went on Nova Scotia, some £618,000, or about 53 per cent. By contrast Georgia received about £252,000 and Quebec £125,000, or about 21 and 11 per cent respectively of that item of expenditure. A great deal of the Nova Scotia expenditure was for goods and services supplied by New Englanders, chiefly from Massachusetts, and those of Georgia by South Carolina merchants.

Though there have been estimates of defence spending made by other historians, perhaps the most interesting by John Shy,[8] it is naval spending that most confused earlier attempts to come to some sort of reasonable conclusion. It might therefore be useful to provide a few more details concerning naval spending in America. The first thing to notice is that the total naval expenditure in America were but a relatively small fraction of the estimated total cost of maintaining the navy in American waters.[9] The cost of shipbuilding was a benefit to English shipbuilders, while Americans were given the crumbs when ships on the North American station needed repairs. The pay of seamen was largely effected in England and was thus of no benefit to Americans. Usually the first six months' victuals were taken on board warships leaving England for America. It was only after these rations needed replenishing that American suppliers were called upon. Still the principal expenditures by the navy in America were for provisions, administered by the Victualling Board under the Navy Board by contract with suppliers in various specified American ports, and for repairs to naval vessels, administered by the Navy Board, and carried out at the request of naval captains on the spot and without benefit of fixed price contracts. Of less significance were the annual expenditures for sick and wounded seamen, who recuperated ashore, or for Americans who acted as pilots on entering and leaving American ports, in the St Lawrence river and along the entire American coast. Other significant expenditures in America focused from 1759 on the building of a naval base at Halifax, and on the hiring of transport vessels from American owners to move both troops as well as their equipment and provisions. In addition the Navy Board ordered yearly payments to American suppliers of naval stores, either shipped directly to England or to the West Indies squadron, based at Jamaica or Antigua. Such stores included masts and bowsprits, pitch, tar and turpentine, and, increasingly from mid-century, American iron. The Admiralty also paid bounties to American captors either of enemy warships or privateers, based on the complement of the captured enemy vessel. In this way American privateers, especially from New York, earned occasional sums, quite independent of prize money. Details are found in Table II below.

TABLE II
BRITISH NAVAL SPENDING IN AMERICA, 1740–1775.

	1740–48	1749–55	1756–63	1764–75	Totals 1740–74	%
	£	£	£	£	£	
Navy Board	162,150	139,169	627,110	421,266	349,665	63.3
Victualling Board	112,032	80,967	339,093	250,569	782,661	36.7
Totals	274,182	220,136	996,203	671,835	2,132,356	100.0
Yearly Average	30,465	31,448	124,525	55,986	59,232	

A word of explanation is perhaps needed for seamen's pay. For the purpose of these estimates it has been assumed that the few seamen, privileged with shore leave while serving off North America, managed to steal as much as they spent from the minute sums they were allowed before their ships were paid off in England.[10] In this way the economic impact on America of naval pay was neutral. This is in marked contrast to soldiers and sappers, whose pay was given them more or less regularly in America and who disposed of it locally to the great benefit of the colonists. Naval officers, by cash or through credit, obviously spent some of their income ashore in America. It has been assumed here that, as with public servants everywhere, they charged most of their expenses to their government, which left their private spending at such a low level that it can safely be ignored. If a guess was required, an additional amount of perhaps £2,500 a year (or £90,000 for the entire thirty-six year interval) might be added, a sum which would add about 4 per cent to overall naval expenditure in America.

Another little considered but important aspect of American invisible earnings were the reimbursements to the colonies for part of their military costs, rebated to them by Parliament, as so-called 'free gifts'. In 1749–1750 Parliament voted some £467,000 to compensate the colonies for their costs relating to the defence of Nova Scotia in 1744, when Annapolis Royal was under attack, the attack and garrisoning of Louisbourg in 1745–1746, and the planned, but abortive, assault on Canada in 1746–7. Details of these and later grants are noted in Table III below.

TABLE III

GROSS PARLIAMENTARY REIMBURSEMENTS TO THE COLONIES, 1749–1763.

	£		£
1749	237,749	1759	200,000
1750	231,296	1760	200,000
1756	120,000	1761	200,000
1757	50,000	1762	133,333
1758	41,118	1763	133,134
	Total:	£1,544,830	

Sources: P.R.O. A01/67/86, 73/96, 74/97, 75/98, 458/1; T1/408, 415, 423, T64/44; Great Britain, Statutes at Large, 21 Geo II c. 23, xxi; 23 Geo II c. 21, xvii; 29 Geo II c. 29, xiii; 30 Geo II c. 26, xiv; 31 Geo II c. 29, xv; 32 Geo II c. 36, xv; 33 Geo II c. 18, xvii; 1 Geo III c. 19, xvii; 2 Geo III c. 34, xv; 3 Geo III c. 17, xv.

The first point to note is that these are gross figures, and thus somewhat overstate the amounts actually sent to colonial treasurers. It is known, for instance, that of the £183,649 granted to Massachusetts in 1749, some £179,260 or 97.6 per cent of the gross sum actually reached the province, the balance going in fees and commissions.[11] Again, of the £120,000 voted by Parliament in 1756 for the colonies, about £114,659, or 95.5 per cent actually reached the shores of America.[12] If these figures are an accurate guide then perhaps it can be assumed that not less than 2.5 per cent of the gross grants made by Parliament remained in the hands of English agents and officials, and Royal Navy officers by way of fees, commissions and freight money, for a total of £38,621, thus reducing the reimbursements to £1,506,209 net. The lion's share naturally went to those provinces most deeply involved in the war efforts. Massachusetts received over £624,000 gross, with Connecticut and New York trailing far behind both with less than £250,000 each. The least active, of course, were the southern colonies, far removed from the principal theatres of war. It might also be suggested that later complaints in the 1760s over Parliament's attempts to tax Americans directly to support the cost of maintaining a squadron off the continent and an army ashore were in direct proportion to the degree of largesse they had enjoyed from that same Parliament for precisely the same purpose. Such a drastic change in policy between 1764 and the year earlier, carried out without consultation with the colonial assemblies, could only have been pursued by ministers insensitive to American experiences.

It remains to be seen how British spending in America was conducted. There were two principal methods: by drawing bills of exchange on various government offices in England, and by shipping specie to America. As to the first method, a number of colonial governors regularly drew sterling bills to meet local government needs. Such, for instance, was the case of Georgia throughout its colonial history, where there is no evidence that any specie shipments were ever officially forwarded. The same practice was followed when Louisbourg was occupied between 1745 and 1749, though part of the demand for specie was offset by the ready availability in 1745 of Spanish dollars seized from prize vessels condemned there. Later, when the government of Nova Scotia established itself at Halifax, expenditure was carried on in large measure by drawing sterling bills, though again some specie circulated—indeed the first governor brought out a small quantity with him. All the colonies involved in the abortive Canada expedition in 1746–7 paid for their costs by drawing such sterling bills. Later, after the conquest of Canada in 1759–1760 and the session of the Floridas in 1763, the practice spread as by far the more convenient and secure method of making international payments. All the commanders-in-chief in America, from Braddock in 1754 to Gage in 1775, adopted this practice, which incidentally both ordnance and Royal Naval officers in America had traditionally followed. Whatever the office named in the bill of exchange, whether the Paymaster General, the Navy Board, the Victualling Board, the Transport Board, the Sick and Hurt Board, the Board of Ordnance, ultimately all bills drawn in America had either to be accepted or rejected (for lack of adequate vouchers) by the Treasury Board, and balances struck, all of which accounts were then eventually approved by the officers of the Audit Office.

The proportion of British spending in America met by shipping specie to the colonies is somewhat difficult to determine. In general, contractors to the Treasury for the supply of pay, subsistence or victuals in America were reluctant to send coin across the Atlantic, even when they were able to charge their costs of freight, handling and insurance to the government. Normally, through their agents in America, they drew bills which were sold to American merchants or British officers in America either for cash or for goods or services rendered. From time to time, when the specie situation became difficult in America, whether at Quebec or Montreal, Louisbourg or Halifax, Boston, New York or Albany, early notice was given and shipments were dispatched from England carrying Spanish milled silver and Portuguese (Brazilian) gold coin. Such shipments amounting to at least £1,885,426 or £52,373 for each of the thirty-six years under analysis here, can be verified. This amounted to roughly 12 per cent of overall British spending in America. The bulk of such payments occurred during the Seven Years' War, though the first significant shipment of this kind had been made in 1749, when Massachusetts received more than £179,000 in specie by way of parliamentary rebate for the cost of taking and garrisoning Louisbourg. It ended, as far as this study is concerned, with the rapid build-up of troops in the colonies late in 1775, and by the shipment of large additional amounts of specie to meet the requirements of army pay and subsistence. 1775 was in many ways, from the administrator's and contractor's view, a repetition of 1755, except this time it was unclear how eager the merchant communities of the port towns would be to feed at the trough provided by the Treasury Board, as it carried out the orders of Parliament. It quickly transpired, of course, that at all times American and Canadian merchants were eager to do business with the Crown's agents, who together represented the most considerable merchant banking business on the continent.

III

The data on overall British government spending in America could be analysed at much greater length, but their more important significance will be illustrated rather when that expenditure is related to the overall current account of the American colonies. The £16.2 million spent between 1740 and 1775 by Britain to administer and defend her colonies went a very long way to balance the continent's deficit in commodity trade with the mother country. In a word, much of the government's spending in America was employed to pay for imports from Britain. The aggregate adverse balance of trade is detailed in Table IV below. Data is arranged as in Table I, in the same intervals of war and peace. The total deficit, amounting to more than £20 million, developed principally from 1756 onwards. Of this huge sum fully 89 per cent was generated by the Thirteen Colonies, about 5 per cent by Nova Scotia and 3.5 per cent by Quebec. Historians are generally wary of these official values for trade; and it is my considered opinion that in general they seriously underestimate the value of American goods imported into Britain. Nevertheless they remain the best available data.[13] If they bear any relation to the flow of commodity trade, then the Thirteen Colonies per

TABLE IV
ADVERSE BALANCE OF AMERICAN COMMODITY TRADE WITH BRITAIN, 1740–1775.
(Official values in 000's of £s)

	1740–48	1749–55	1756–63	1764–75	Totals 1740–75
	£	£	£	£	£
The Thirteen	665	2,085	7,287	7,709	17,746
Quebec	—	—	120	580	700
Nova Scotia	9	145	462	378	994
Newfoundland	(45)	58	46	341	400
Florida	—	—	10	324	334
Hudson Bay	(64)	(33)	(71)	(51)	(219)
Total	565	2,255	7,854	9,281	19,955
Yearly Average	63	322	982	773	554
%	2.8	11.3	39.4	46.5	100.0

Sources: C. R. Mowat, *East Florida as a British Province, 1763–1784* (Berkeley and Los Angeles, 1943), 153. BT/185, fol. 106–117v.; House of Lords R.O., Main Series, 20 Nov. 1775; Jacob M. Price, 'New Time Series for Scotland's and Britain's Trade with the Thirteen Colonies and States, 1740 to 1791', *William and Mary Quarterly*, XXXII (1975), 322–5. Quebec estimates prepared from Customs 16/1 (1768–72) by Paul McCann, University of Ottawa.

capita had a far lower trade deficit than had Quebec, Nova Scotia or Newfoundland.

However, of far more importance than any prolonged discussion of the distribution of that deficit, is the relation it bears to the overall balance of payments. So let us now compare these net deficits in the colonial trade with Britain (an economic outflow) with net spending by Britain in America to administer and defend the empire (an inflow of invisibles). The comparative data, in simplified form, is presented in Table V. From the Table it is clear,

TABLE V

BRITISH SPENDING IN AMERICA AS A PORTION OF AMERICAN TRADE DEFICIT WITH BRITAIN, 1740–1775.

(in 000's of £s; trade figures in official values)

| | Inflow 1. Spending | | Outflow 2. (Deficit) | | Balance 1–2. Surplus (Deficit) | |
	Total	Yearly Average	Total	Yearly Average	Total	Yearly Average
	£	£	£	£	£	£
1740–48	1,331	148	(565)	(63)	766	85
1749–55	1,876	268	(2,255)	(322)	(379)	(54)
1756–63	7,984	998	(7,854)	(982)	(130)	(16)
1764–75	5,002	417	(9,281)	(773)	(4,279)	(357)
Totals	16,193	450	(19,955)	(554)	(3,762)	(105)

if the trade figures have any approximate relationship to the real value of the goods in transit,[13] that at least until 1763, except for the period 1748–55, inflows into the North American economy of British government funds to pay for defence and administration more than made up the deficit of American colonial trade with the mother country. Between 1740 and 1763 overall British spending in America was an estimated £11,191,000 while the estimated deficit in American trade with Britain was £10,674,000 for a surplus of £517,000, or about £22,000 annually.

The shift in the North American balance came with the restoration of peace after 1764, when a relatively sluggish export trade from America was overtaken by a high aggregate demand for imports from Britain. Thus it was in the dozen years before the outbreak of the War of Independence that British government expenditures in America, for the first time, failed to act as the crucial element in reducing America's historic trade deficit with Britain. Though North American imports continued to outstrip exports to Britain, the annual gap between 1764 and 1775 was actually lower than it had been during the Seven Years' War: £773,000 compared with £982,000. At the same time British spending after 1764, though at £417,000 yearly still far above the pre-1756 annual level of £268,000, fell by 42 per cent below the war years, 1756–63. For the period 1764–75 this meant that, though more than £5 millions were spent in America, the trade deficit still surpassed this huge amount by £4,279,000, or £375,000 annually. Such a figure, though large in comparison with earlier years, was hardly ruinous, and when calculated on a per capita basis, in view of the greatly enlarged colonial population by the 1770s, was actually rather small. Moreover, it is clear from the research of Shepherd, Walton and Price, among others, that on the whole the North

American colonies, as a result of their commodity trade to southern Europe and their invisible earnings in the West Indies, probably experienced with great regularity in the 1760s and 1770s a generally favourable balance of payments. Thus the trade deficit with Britain, however important, was no longer crucial to overall economic growth in the colonies.

In all of this the role of British government spending in America, a matter largely misunderstood and inaccurately estimated, became an important element. It was more than a temporary windfall, more than a passing economic feature, but, from 1740 until 1763 a decisive factor in maintaining a balance of payments favourable to the colonies. Thereafter during the 1760s and 1770s in the context of a rapidly maturing colonial economy, the importance of British government spending as an aspect of American invisible trade declined both absolutely and relatively. Yet its diminished role in no way weakened that economy, as merchants redirected their products to alternative markets, with assets greatly expanded by the Seven Years' War, and with a confidence given clear expression in the numerous enlarged new houses that they built themselves in the growing colonial cities.[14] This underscores perhaps the general success, despite political uncertainty, which North American merchants experienced in international commerce in the dozen years before the outbreak of the American War of Independence.

NOTES

* Research was undertaken with support from a Canada Council grant in 1975–6. An earlier version was read to the Department of Economics, University of Illinois at Urbana, in April 1977.

1. P.R.O. London, Customs 16/1, data for which was computerised by Professor Lawrence A. Harper, Department of History, University of California, Berkeley, to whom we all are indebted.
2. There was actually a deficit of some £18,000 annually on America's commodity trade with the West Indies between 1768 and 1772.
3. See especially James F. Shepherd and Gary M. Walton, *Shipping, maritime trade and the economic development of colonial North America* (Cambridge, 1972), 116.
4. Jacob M. Price, 'New Time Series for Scotland's and Britain's Trade with the Thirteen Colonies and States, 1740 to 1791', *William and Mary Quarterly*, XXXII (1975), 307–25.
5. See Price's review of Joseph A. Ernst, *Money and Politics in America, 1755–1775. A Study in the Currency Act of 1764 and the Economy of Revolution.* (Chapel Hill, N.C.: 1973) in *Reviews in American History*, II (1974), 367–8.
6. Price, 'A Note on the Value of Colonial Exports of Shipping', *The Journal of Economic History*, XXXVI (1976), 704–24. He estimates that between 1763 and 1775 'shipbuilding in the Thirteen Colonies totalled about 40,000 measured tons annually and was worth about £300,000 sterling, of which at least 18,600 tons worth £140,000 were sold abroad'. p. 722. See Shepherd's and Walton's estimates of between £45,000 and £106,000 annually in Appendix VI of their book, *op. cit.*, 241–5.
7. For the period 1768–72 Shepherd and Walton roughly estimated annual defence spending at £400,000. My data are slightly different. If the cost of the army, navy and ordnance office alone are taken into account, the total is £341,000, or a difference of 15 per cent. If all civil and military expenditure by Britain in America is calculated the annual figures rise to £365,000 a 9 per cent difference from their estimates. See Shepherd and Walton, *op. cit.*, 150–1.
8. John Shy, *Toward Lexington. The Role of the British Army in the Coming of the American Revolution* (Princeton, 1965), especially 338–40. Shepherd and Walton

based their estimates on an unpublished Ms by Maclyn P. Burg, 'An Estimation of the Cost of Defending and Administering the Colonies of British North America, 1763–1775', a copy of which Dr Burg was good enough to send me. He was concerned with overall costs to the British taxpayer rather than the proportion spent in America. He concluded that £8.4 million was the cost between 1763 and 1775. For another estimate see Walter Scott Dunn Jr., 'Western Commerce, 1760–1774', (Unpubl. Ph.D. diss., University of Wisconsin, 1971). See Charts H–I, pp. 253–4. His estimate is £7.7 million for the period 1759–1774, and he makes no attempt to estimate naval expenditure in America.

9. In answer to a request by the Treasury Board of 4 Feb. 1767, arising from a House of Commons order on 22 Jan. 1767, the Navy prepared estimates of the cost of the Navy between 1756 and 1766 inclusive for North America and the West Indies. The totals for the West Indies came to £6,227,759, and for America £4,736,295. Of this sum of £4.7 million, I have found at least £1,493,189 actually expended *in* America —31.5 per cent. The official estimate of £4.7 million included for wear and tear, £1,012,408, for flag officers' pay and table money £22,180, for officers' pay and seamen's wages £1,287,394, for victualling seamen and officers £1,053,233, for sick and hurt seamen and officers £71,090, for transports £967,712, victualling land forces carried on board £322,279. P.R.O., Adm 49/1, fol. 5.

10. Daniel A. Baugh, *British Naval Administration in the Age of Walpole* (Princeton, 1965).

11. For details see Massachusetts Archives, Vol. XX, fol. 588: 'The Province of the Massachusets Bay in America in Account Current with Sir Peter Warren Knight of the Bath and William Bollan Esqr'.

12. There is little use in employing current rather than official values for trade. The current values have been calculated by multiplying the official values by a highly suspect commodity price index, but the one only available, and which applies only to England. Scotland has no such commodity index, and much of the American exports in tobacco were sent there, while every colony conducted some trade with Scotland. For the current values of American trade to Britain and their method of calculation, see John J. McCusker, 'The Current Value of English Exports, 1697 to 1800', *William and Mary Quarterly*, XXVIII (1971), 607–28.

14. Evidence for this can be found in all American colonial cities from Boston south to Charleston. Much of it can be seen readily by comparing evidence of city maps in the 1740s with those of the 1760s. This subject deserves special attention.

The Seven Years' War and the American Revolution: The Causal Relationship Reconsidered

by

Jack P. Greene

I

That there was a causal connection between the Seven Years' War and the American Revolution has been so widely assumed as to become a scholarly orthodoxy. The close temporal relationship between the formal conclusion of the war in 1763 and the Stamp Act crisis in 1764–6, the first dramatic episode in the chain of events that would, a decade later, lead to separation, immediately raises the question of whether either the *experience* or the *outcome* of the war affected the events of the mid-1760s and beyond. For purposes of analysis, this question must be broken down into two parts. First, in what ways did the war contribute to those metropolitan actions that touched off the conflict? Second, how did the war affect the colonial response to those actions? Much scholarly energy has been devoted to both of these questions, albeit much of that energy has been animated by a desire to fix responsibility for inaugurating the dispute on one side of the Atlantic or the other. But no one has yet produced the comprehensive, systematic, and dispassionate analysis necessary to enable us to specify fully and persuasively the precise causal relationship between the Seven Years' War and the American Revolution.[1] What follows is a brief and preliminary effort towards that objective.

II

Perhaps the single most important result of the war in terms of the metro-politan-colonial relationship was the vivid enhancement of awareness on both sides of the Atlantic of the crucial significance of the colonies to Britain both economically and strategically. Such an awareness was scarcely new and had indeed been powerfully manifest in the heightened concern with the colonies exhibited by metropolitan officials after 1748.[2] But the decision to undertake a major national effort to protect British interests in America and the long and expensive war that followed inevitably contributed to intensify both metropolitan and colonial sensitivities to the importance of America for Britain. Thereafter, no one who was 'the least acquainted' with either the colonies 'or the concerns of the nation in them' could possibly doubt that they 'must absolutely be of the utmost conciquence to the defence,

wellfare & hapiness of These Kindoms'. 'To be convinced of their importance
at first sight', one had only to look at the 'sum total of the yearly produce
of our plantations'. That sum, 'upon a moderate computation', amounted
to between five and six million pounds sterling per annum, in addition to
which the colonists employed between forty and fifty thousand seamen and
nearly two thousand ships each year. To be sure, the colonial trade amounted
to no more than *'one third* Part' of Britain's foreign commerce, but the mere
fact that all other branches of foreign trade could be obstructed while the
colonial trade 'must still continue soley our Own' made it 'of greater
advantage to us than all other Foreign Trades we are in possession of'.[3]

The truth of this proposition seemed to be evident in both the growing
wealth and international status of Britain and the obvious envy of its colonial
possessions by its European rivals. 'Every body knows', said the New York
lawyer William Smith, Jr., after the war, that the population, wealth, and
power of Britain had been 'vastly inhanced since the Discovery of the New
World'. Simple comparisons 'of the number and force of our present fleets,
with our fleet in Queen Elizabeth's time before we had colonies', of 'the
antient with the present state of our towns and ports on our western coast,
Manchester, Liverpool, Kendal, Lancaster, Glasgow, and the countries round
them, that trade with and manufacture for our colonies, not to mention
Leeds, Halifax, Sheffield and Birmingham', or of the difference 'in the
numbers of people, buildings, rents and the value of land' within living
memory, wrote Benjamin Franklin, were sufficient to indicate that to a very
significant degree it had been the colonies that had made 'this nation both
prosperous at home, and considerable abroad'. To what else other than its
colonies could be attributed Britain's extraordinary rise from 'the third or
fourth Place in the Scale of *European* Powers' to 'a Level with the most
Mighty in Europe'? Why else would Britain's 'most daingerous Rivalls in
Trade, and most implacable Enemies the French' make 'every effort in their
power to wrest this inestimable Fountain of wealth & strength out of our
hands'?[4]

More and more during the war, commentators asserted that the American
colonies had obviously 'become a great source of that wealth, by which this
nation maintains itself, and is respected by others'. If they were indeed 'the
great support, not only of the trade and commerce, but even of the safety
and defence of Britain itself', then it followed that without them 'the people
in Britain would make but a poor figure, if they could even subsist as an
independent nation'. 'Every body is agreed', said one observer, that 'our
existence as a . . . commercial and independent Nation' as well as 'a free and
happy people' depended upon America: 'by trade we do, and must, if at all,
subsist; without it we can have no wealth; and without wealth we can have
no power; as without power we can have no liberty'. The chain of logic was
inexorable: trade was the very essence of both British greatness and British
liberty, and the great extent to which that trade depended upon 'our dominions
in *America'* necessarily meant that for Britain America was 'an object of
such magnitude as' could never 'be forgot[ten] or neglected'.[5]

If the war stimulated the emergence of a heightened realisation of the
'Infinite Advantage our American Collonys are of to these Kingdoms', it

also focused attention more directly than ever before upon a welter of problems that seemed to point to both the structural weakness of the empire and the fragility of metropolitan authority in the colonies. As Josiah Tucker had predicted at the very beginning of hostililities, the war turned out to be a rich 'Harvest for Complaints'.[6] Foremost among the problems revealed by the war was the difficulty of mobilising the military potential of the colonies. At best, the system of royal requisitions to individual colonies that was used throughout the war to supplement the men and supplies sent from Britain in ever larger numbers beginning in 1756 seemed to yield but spotty returns. Many colonies voted less than requested or encumbered appropriations with annoying restrictions, while a few failed to give any assistance at all and even refused quarters to metropolitan troops. To British commanders in the colonies, such behaviour was extraordinarily vexatious, and in their strident reports to London authorities they made few distinctions between those colonies that had and those that had not cooperated with them. 'The delays we meet with, in carrying on the Service, from *every* parts of this Country, are immense', the Commander-in-Chief, Lord Loudoun, complained to his superior, Cumberland, in August 1756. 'In Place of Aid to the Service every impediment, that it is possible to invent', he wrote to Halifax, head of the Board of Trade, a few months later, 'is thrown in the Way'. Colonial legislators 'assumed to themselves, what they call Rights and Priviledges, totaly unknown in the Mother Country . . . for no purpose', it seemed to Loudoun, 'but to screen them, from giving any Aid, of any sort, for carrying on, the Service, and refusing us Quarters'. Reports of such self-interested behaviour reached London with sufficient frequency as to become commonplace even outside official government circles.[7]

The great extent to which colonial legislators had already managed to undermine metropolitan authority by their assumption of such extravagant rights and privileges was a second and, from a long-range point of view, potentially even more worrying problem underscored for London authorities by the experience of the war. It was a rare governor who, like Charles Pinfold of Barbados, could at any time during the war write home that 'Every thing proposed to me in England has been carried into Execution and with an Unanimity that exceeded the Example of former times'. Indeed, the common report was precisely the opposite. 'At present I have His Majesties Commission and Instructions for my Government, and direction, in all public Concerns', lamented Benning Wentworth from New Hampshire, 'but from the incroachments Made by the Assembly, both are in a manner Rendered useless'. 'Such is the defective State of the Governments', echoed Thomas Pownall of Massachusetts, 'that there can not on the Continent be produced an instance of the Governors being able to carry his Majesty's Instructions into Execution where the People have disputed them'. Even in the new and more closely supervised colonies of Georgia and Nova Scotia, the legislatures were 'industriously attempting to usurp the same power[s]' as those already exercised with such 'great Licence' by their counterparts in the older colonies. Everywhere in the colonies, the '*leading* People' appeared to raise disputes with metropolitan representatives merely 'to have a merit with the others, by defending their Liberties, as they call them'. So long had the colonists thus been 'suffered to riot in privileges' that royal governors had become little more than *'Cyphers'*, 'Pompous Titled Nothing[s]' of very little use "to those who employ[ed]" them, while metropolitan authority had obviously been by far 'already too much weakened'.[8]

The same conclusion could be drawn from mounting evidence of colonial disregard for metropolitan economic regulations. For several decades prior to the war, complaints had filtered into London of a growing 'illicit trade which all the colonies have run more or less into.' In New York and New England and particularly in Rhode Island, it was charged, there was 'scarce a man in all that country who' was 'not concerned in the smuggling trade' in Dutch, French, and French Caribbean goods, a trade, moreover, that had long since been 'sanctified with the name of *naturalising* foreign goods'. What had seemed so patently 'destructive of the national interests' of Britain in peacetime came to appear totally pernicious—and self-serving—during the war, which brought a marked increase in reports of colonial violations of the navigation acts. Military and naval commanders, royal governors, metropolitan customs officials: all described a brisk trade throughout the war not only with the neutral Dutch but with the enemy French in the West Indies, either indirectly by way of neutral ports or directly under the guise of flags of truce to exchange prisoners of war. The result was that the French islands were 'provided with a Sufficient Stock of provisions' and everything else they needed 'in spite of all the Regulations'. Metropolitan efforts to curtail this trade were largely ineffective, and at the end of the war, one customs official estimated that smuggled molasses from the French West Indies into the northern colonies had increased 500 per cent during the war, while another observer asserted that nearly 90 per cent of the tea consumed in the colonies was being smuggled from the Netherlands. In the face of such reports few in Britain could any longer doubt by 1763 that 'a spirit of Illicit trade' prevailed 'more or less throughout the Continent[al]' colonies, in America and that there was 'almost a universal desire in the People [there] to carry on a trade with foreigners not only in America but in Europe'.[9]

But these were only the most flagrant examples by which the colonists acted 'wholly in conformity to their own selfish or rapacious views', and obstinately refused to do what was 'necessary for the good of the whole' during the war. Unscrupulous traders and land developers cheated Indians in utter disregard for either fairness or the safety of the older settlements and thus created a highly unfavourable disposition among the Indians to the 'British Interest'. Colonial assemblies used metropolitan needs for military assistance to extract still further privileges from Crown officials and, in many cases, financed their war contributions by issuing massive amounts of paper currency, at least some of which was so inadequately secured as to depreciate rapidly and thereby to exacerbate fears among metropolitan mercantile interests that the colonists would seek to pay their debts in depreciated currency. In one area after another during the war, the colonists thus behaved in ways that seemed to make it perfectly obvious that they had but slight regard for either the interests or the authority of the metropolis.[10]

At least since the beginning of the century, metropolitan officials and traders had exhibited what seemed to Americans an 'unnatural Suspicion' that the colonies would 'one Time or other' rebel and throw 'off their dependence on Britain'. Increasingly evident in the decade just prior to the war, such fears, Americans insisted, were both 'groundless and chimerical'. But colonial behaviour during the war with its many manifestations of a 'general disposition to independence' only seemed to belie their protestations and to provide growing evidence that they would seek 'a Dissolution' of the empire at the earliest opportunity.[11] Not just the experience but the result of the war operated to heighten metropolitan fears of colonial independence. For it had been frequently argued by students of colonial affairs both before and during the war that only 'their apprehensions of the French' and their dependence upon Britain for protection kept the colonists 'in awe' and prevented their 'connection ... with their mother country from being quite broken off'. To 'drive the French out of all N. America', Josiah Tucker had declared in 1755, 'would be the most fatal Step We could take'. By eliminating the one certain 'guarantee for the[ir] good behaviour' towards and 'dependence on their mother country', such a move, it was widely suggested, would both further 'their love of independence' and place 'them [entirely] above controul' by Britain, which they would subsequently ignore, rival, and perhaps even destroy.[12]

Fear of such an eventuality was obviously not deep enough to cause metropolitan officials to return Canada to the French at the conclusion of the war, though many later observers from John Lind in 1775 until Lawrence H. Gipson in the twentieth century have argued that it was precisely the 'great change ... in the strength and situation of the colonies' brought about by the removal of the French from North America in 1763 that was primarily responsible for the American decision for independence thirteen years later.[13] Whether, given the rising awareness of the strategic and economic importance of the colonies to Britain, the many predictions of colonial independence actually filled metropolitan officials 'with Terror,' as William Smith, Jr., charged, the evidence, piled up during the war, that both stimulated and sustained such predictions, certainly contributed to further the disposition, already 'pretty general in the nation' prior to the war, 'to enquire into the affairs of the plantations' and to make sure that 'at a proper oppertunity'—that is, at the conclusion of hostilities—'the settlement of America', that 'greatest and most necessary of all schemes', would become a serious 'Object ... of Attention' in London.[14]

Nor was the 'settlement of America' perceived only or even primarily in terms of solving the immediate problems arising out of the need to secure, organise, and administer the new territories; to finance the large American military establishment; and to begin to pay off the vast debt accumulated by Britain during the war, as historians have been wont to emphasise.[15] Of far 'more fundamental importance' was metropolitan dissatisfaction with the state of British authority in the colonies. For the war had removed all doubt that in America, 'a Country long neglected' by the metropolis, 'many Disorders' had 'crept in, in some Instances dangerous and detrimental to the Colonies, and their British Creditors, ... derogative of the just Rights, and many Prerogatives of the Crown', and totally subversive of that 'dependance which the Colonies ought to be kept in to the Government of the Mother Country'. In both the internal civil and external commercial spheres, the Board of Trade repeatedly asserted during and after the war in reiterating, with growing conviction, a conclusion it had already reached over the previous decade, that the authority of Britain 'and the Sovereignty of the Crown' stood 'upon a very precarious foot' and was 'in great Danger of being totally set aside'. Indeed, by the late 1750s and early 1760s, it seemed to be a valid question as to whether the colonists had not to a considerable degree already 'arrived at an Independency from the Government of the Mother Country', and the sense of urgency implicit in such remarks pervaded metropolitan counsels following the expulsion of the French from Canada in 1759. What the Treasury argued in October 1763 on behalf of proposals to tighten the trade laws was being said over and over about colonial civil administration: 'some effectual Remedy' was an 'immediate Necessity, lest the continuance and extent of . . . dangerous Evils' might 'render all Attempts to remedy them hereafter infinitely more difficult, if not utterly impracticable'. If remedial steps were not taken soon, Britain might eventually lose 'every inch of property in America!'[16]

By the concluding years of the war, the question was no longer whether imperial administration would be reformed at the conclusion of the war but how. Many advocates of reform counselled a mild approach. Arguing that measures specifically calculated to 'cement friendships on both sides' would 'be of more lasting benefit to both countries, than all the armies that Britain can send thither', they contended that the most effective way to secure the dependence of the colonies was 'by promoting . . . their welfare . . . , instead of checking their growth, or laying them under any other inconvenience', and warned against all 'violent innovations'.[17] But the tide of metropolitan sentiment was running powerfully in a contrary direction. There was no desire either to oppress or stifle the colonies. 'The increase in our Colonies', said Secretary of the Treasury Charles Jenkinson in early 1765, 'is certainly what we wish', and most people seem to have recognised with Thomas Whateley that the 'Mother Country would suffer, if she tyrannized over her Colonies'. Yet, it was widely agreed, as Bute reportedly observed immediately after the Treaty of Paris in 1763, both that it was essential 'to bring our Old Colonies into order' and that the best way to accomplish that end was through the imposition of stricter controls. Thenceforth, in Jenkinson's words, the colonies were to be administered 'in such a manner as will keep them useful to the Mother Country'.[18]

Thus, as Bernhard Knollenberg has shown, virtually every metropolitan measure undertaken in reference to the colonies not simply from 1763 but from the defeat of the French in Canada in 1759 was calculated to restrict their scope for economic and political activity.[19] In even more detail, Thomas C. Barrow has demonstrated to what a great extent the new trade regulations of 1763–4, including the use of the navy and royal vice-admiralty courts as agencies of enforcement, an increase in the size of the customs establishment, and the introduction of a residence requirement for customs officials, were designed not only to produce a revenue but to destroy 'the long-continued commercial independence of the American colonies' by eliminating all except certain specifically permitted commerce between them and Europe and making it more expensive to trade with foreign islands in the Caribbean.[20] Similarly, the decision to exercise caution in the authorisation of settlement to the west of the Appalachians was intended not simply to prevent clashes between Europeans and Indians or to establish a foundation for better relations with the Indians but also, as former Georgia governor Henry Ellis remarked, to prevent settlers from 'planting themselves in the Heart of America, out of the reach of Government, and where, from the great Difficulty of procuring European Commodities, they would be compelled to commence Manufacturs to the infinite prejudice of Britain', a possibility that had worried observers since before the war.[21]

In the civil sphere, metropolitan officials were less systematic and more tentative. They revealed no disposition to try to do away with representative institutions in the colonies. They were willing to entertain a variety of proposals for the extensive 'amendment of Government' in the colonies by act of Parliament, including the establishment of a single governor general for the colonies together with an annual congress of deputies from each colony, the resumption by the Crown of the charters of Connecticut and Rhode Island, and the creation of a permanent revenue to put royal governors 'upon a more respectable and independent Footing'. But, although the Board of Trade favoured the last two of these proposals, metropolitan officials did not immediately act upon any of them. Perhaps because of the complexity of the problem, they eschewed, for the time being at least, any effort to undertake the comprehensive alteration of the colonial constitutions recommended by many.[22] But in dealing with the separate colonies after 1759 they rarely failed to act upon the conclusions, first reached by the Board of Trade between 1748 and 1756 and further reinforced by the experience of the war, that the colonies were 'not sufficiently obedient' and, as Granville told Franklin in 1759, had 'too many and too great Privileges; and that it' was 'not only the Interest of the Crown but of the Nation to reduce them'. To that end, metropolitan officials sought to correct as many as possible of the 'many Errors and unconstitutional Regulations & practices' that had 'taken place and prevailed' in all the old colonies by 'Clipping the Wings of the Assemblies in their Claims of all the Privileges of a House of Commons' and holding them to an 'absolute Subjection to Orders sent from' London 'in the Shape of Instructions', objectives they sought to accomplish primarily by strictly requiring suspending clauses in all colonial legislation of unusual character and disallowing all laws that appeared in any way to be 'injurious to the prerogative', detrimental to metropolitan authority, or conducive to the establishment in the colonies of 'a greater measure of Liberty than is enjoyed by the People of England'.[23]

If the Seven Years' War intensified metropolitan appreciation of both the value of the colonies and the weakness of metropolitan authority over them, it also contributed to three structural changes that would have an important bearing upon metropolitan calculations concerning the colonies after the war. First, the war brought Parliament more directly and intimately into contact with the colonies than at any time since the late seventeenth century.

The huge expenditures required for American defence as well as the smaller annual appropriations for the new royal colonies of Georgia and Nova Scotia helped to fix Parliamentary attention upon the colonies more fully than ever before and contributed to an increasingly widely held assumption that Parliament should be directly involved in reconstructing the imperial system after the war. Such an assumption was scarcely novel insofar as it applied to the commercial relationship between Britain and the colonies: since the 1650s Parliament had taken responsibility for regulating trade and other aspects of the economic life of the colonies. Prior to the war, however, administration had involved Parliament in the internal affairs of the colonies only in very exceptional circumstances.[24] Yet, with their growing frustration over their inability to enforce colonial compliance with their directives during their reform attempts between 1748 and 1756 metropolitan authorities had been more and more driven to threaten Parliamentary intervention to force the colonies into line, and in 1757 the House of Commons, in an important precedent, intervened in the purely domestic affairs of a colony for the first time since 1733 when it censured the Jamaica Assembly for making extravagant constitutional claims while resisting instructions from London. By carefully informing all the colonies of the Commons' action in this case, metropolitan authorities made it clear that they were no longer reluctant to support similar actions against other colonies whenever necessary.[25]

During the war, moreover, a chorus of proposals from both inside and outside the government called for 'the legislative power of Great Britain to make a strict and speedy inquiry . . . to remedy disorders . . . and to put the government and trade of all our colonies into' a 'good and sound . . . state'. Not just the commerce but the internal civil affairs, it came to be very widely assumed, required Parliamentary attention. 'Nothing', declared Thomas Pownall, could 'restore the Authority of the Crown & settle the Rights of the People according to the true Spirit of the British Constitution but an Act of Parliament' because, William Knox added in spelling out the lessons of the war and immediately pre-war period, 'no other Authority than that of the British Parliament will be regarded by the Colonys, or be able to awe them into acquiescence.' Such sentiments revealed a well-developed conviction that in 'the perpetual struggle in every Colony between Privilege and Prerogative' the metropolitan government would thenceforth no longer hesitate to turn to Parliament to achieve what it would be unable to accomplish through executive action alone. As Isaac Norris, speaker of the Pennsylvania Assembly appreciated in trying to understand the new Grenville measures of 1764–65, the idea of resorting to the 'Power of Parliament to make general Colony Laws' and otherwise intervene in the internal affairs of the colonies was 'no new Scheme'. It had been often suggested during the decade prior to the war. But as Norris understood, it was 'the War in America' that had 'brought it to the Issue we now see and are like to feel both now and hereafter'.[26]

Though some thought that the colonists would not resist any Parliamentary effort to 'new model the Government' and trade of the colonies, metropolitan officials were not blind to the possibility that even the august authority of Parliament might be contested in America. 'From their partial Interests and Connection', the colonists could in fact be expected to 'give all the Opposition on their power to ... any ... matter ... for the General Good'. During the war, metropolitan civil and military representatives had taken note of the 'slight [regard] people of this Country affect to Treat Acts of Parliament with', and Lord Loudoun had reported that it was 'very common' for colonists to say, defiantly, that 'they would be glad to see any Man durst Offer to put an English Act of Parliament in Force in this Country'.[27] But a second structural change brought about by the war gave London authorities confidence that any opposition to Parliamentary measures could be easily overcome. The idea of using royal troops in a coercive way against the colonies had been considered during the late 1740s and early 1750s, but no significant body of troops was readily available. Only with the rapid buildup of an American army beginning in 1756 did the metropolis have, for the first time in the history of the North American empire, significant coercive resources in the colonies. During the war, several governors, including Robert Hunter Morris of Pennsylvania, had argued that it was 'next to impossible without a standing force to carry the Laws [of Parliament] into Execution' and, like Thomas Pownall and Henry Ellis of Georgia, he had urged the necessity of using the military to reinforce civil authority. 'A military force is certainly necessary to render Government respectable, & the Laws efficacious', wrote Ellis in June 1757, '& perhaps not more so in any country upon earth than this, which abounds with ungovernable and refractory people'. Pownall agreed: 'tis necessary', he wrote to Halifax less than a month later,' that the Military should carry into effect those matters which the Civil thro it's weakness cannot'.[28] Others wrote in a similar vein. Thus, in urging the quick adoption of a plan to reduce the colonies to a 'state of subordination and improvement' near the end of the war, customs comptroller Nathaniel Ware warned that 'if an effectual reformation be not introduced before those troops are withdrawn which could have been thrown in [to the colonies] upon no less occasion [than the war] without giving a general alarm, one may venture to pronounce it impossible afterwards'. With the colonies 'now surrounded by an army, a navy, and ... hostile tribes of Indians', Maurice Morgann, adviser to Shelburne, agreed, there would be no better 'time (not to oppress or injure them in any shape) but to exact a due deference to the just and equitable demands of a British Parliament'.

The decision to keep a large contingent of troops in America following the war was almost certainly not the result of the sort of calculated deception suggested by Captain Walter Rutherford, a British officer in the colonies, who proposed in 1759 that troops be retained in the colonies 'apparently for their defence, but also to keep them in proper subjection to the Mother Country'. But neither, as some later historians have contended, were security of the new conquests against their former possessors nor the desirability of distributing troops 'amongst the several Members' of the 'Empire, in proportion to their ability to support them' the only considerations behind this decision. As William Knox explained in a long memorandum in 1763, 'one great purpose of stationing a large Body of Troops in America' was 'to secure the Dependence of the Colonys on Great Britain' by, another observer remarked, 'guarding against any Disobedience or Disaffection amongst the Inhabitants . . ., who already begin to entertain some extravagent Opinions, concerning their Relations and Dependence on their Mother Country'. With such a large military force in the colonies,—7,500 troops in all—metropolitan officials at the end of the Seven Years' War could now proceed with the business of imperial reconstruction with reasonable confidence that they had the resources near at hand to suppress any potential colonial opposition.[29]

But there seemed to be little reason to fear extended colonial resistance. For, people in Britain believed, the war had shown Americans to have little stomach for a fight. Not only had they proved to be 'execrable Troops', they had also shown themselves unwilling to stand up to military power. As Loudoun concluded from his successful use of the threat of force to overcome colonial opposition to providing quarters for troops in 1756–7, the colonists 'wou'd invade every Right of the Crown, if permitted, but . . . if the Servants of the Crown wou'd do their Duty, and stood firm, they wou'd always Submit'.[30] Even if they were braver than they appeared during the war, however, the 'mutual jealousies amongst the several Colonies would always', Lord Morton observed, prevent a united resistance and thus 'keep them in a state of dependence'. With fourteen separate colonies in the continent in 1763, all with 'different forms of government, different laws, different interests, and some of them different religious persuasions and different manners', it was no wonder that they were 'all jealous of each other. Indeed, as Benjamin Franklin reported, their 'jealousy of each other was so great that' they would never be 'able to effect . . . an union among themselves' and there was therefore absolutely no possibility that they could ever become '*dangerous*' to Britain.[31]

But perhaps the most important structural change produced by the war was not the increasing involvement of Parliament in American affairs or even the introduction of an army into the colonies but the elimination of France and Spain from eastern North America. Following contemporaries, historians have emphasised the importance of this development as a precondition for colonial resistance after 1763. Of far greater importance, in all probability, was its effect upon the mentality of those in power in the metropolis. For the destruction of French power not only made the colonies less dependent upon Britain for protection; it also left Britain with a much freer hand to proceed with its programme of colonial reform by removing the necessity that had operated so strongly during the first half of the war for conciliatory behaviour towards the colonies to encourage them to cooperate against a common enemy. Colonial leaders appreciated this point quite fully in the wake of the Grenville programme. Many people, found an anonymous Frenchman visiting the colonies in 1765, were saying that if the 'french . . . were [still] in Canada the British parlem't would as soon be D[ea]d as to offer to do what they do now'. John Dickinson agreed. The colonists, he declared in 1765, 'never would have been treated as they are if Canada still continued in the hands of the French'.[32]

If the structural changes produced by the war—the intrusion of Parliament

into colonial matters, the presence of a metropolitan army, and the removal
of international pressures for conciliating the colonies—provided metropolitan officials with favourable conditions for undertaking a sweeping
reformation of the imperial system, while their heightened awareness of both
the value of the colonies and the fragility of their authority over them
served as a motive, they were pushed even more strongly in this direction
by their own interpretation of the purposes of the war and the relative
contributions of Britain and the colonies. For the belief was widespread
in London that the war had been undertaken not on behalf of any specifically
metropolitan objectives but for the protection of the colonies. As Shelburne
put it in a speech in the House of Lords in December 1766, the 'security of
the British Colonies in N. America was the *first* cause of the War'. Britain's
generosity, in fact, seemed to contrast sharply with the colonies' parsimony.
Britain, wrote Thomas Whateley, had certainly 'engaged in the Defence of
her most distant Dominions, with more alacrity than the Provinces themselves that were immediately attacked', while the colonists had repeatedly
refused 'to sacrifice their own partial Advantages to the general good' and
brazenly taken 'advantage of their Countrys distresses' to cram 'their modes
down the throat[s] of the Governor[s]' in shortsighted and selfish disputes
over privileges. In return for such generous treatment, metropolitan leaders
expected the colonists to show both a deep appreciation and a strong sense
of the great 'obligation they owe[d] her'. Instead, they received nothing but
ingratitude, the sting of which was made all the more painful by the fact
that Britain had accumulated a huge debt of between £100,000,000 and
£150,000,000 and a high annual rate of taxation as a result of the war and
had even reimbursed the colonies for their own military appropriations by
nearly £1,100,000. Nor was such recompense made any less galling by the
colonists' vaunted prosperity. While the parent society wallowed in debt and
groaned under high taxes, its 'vigorous Offspring' in America seemed to be
enjoying low taxes and a flourishing economy that enabled them to riot in
opulence and luxury.[33]

III

The colonial response to the war could scarcely have been more different.
Scholars have traditionally emphasised the extent to which the war contributed to colonial discontent with British rule. Thus, Alan Rogers has
recently argued that their experiences during the war made the colonists
rebellious and filled them with anxieties about the power of the metropolis.
'While the struggle to drive France from the North American continent
was being waged', he contends, 'Americans from every social class experienced
firsthand, or had some cause to fear the use of arbitrary [metropolitan]
power'. Some of their discontent derived from Crown attempts to centralise
Indian administration and still more from the overt condescension of British
regulars towards American provincials and a discriminatory military
structure that assigned American officers and soldiers to subordinate roles.
Most, however, arose from the insistence by British military commanders
that military necessity overrode all other considerations. 'Granted sweeping

powers by the Crown', they 'imposed embargoes on shipping, ordered press gangs into the street and countryside to seize men and property, forced citizens to quarter soldiers in their homes, and insisted that the authority of colonial political agencies was subordinate to their own military power'.[34]

Well before the war, of course, the colonists had learned to be wary of metropolitan power and intentions. 'From some hard usage, received in former times', principally from 'the governors and other officers sent among them', they had long 'entertained an opinion that *Britain* was resolved to keep them low, and [was] regardless of their welfare', and their rejection of the Albany Plan of Union in 1754 on the eve of the war can be interpreted at least in part as an expression of this wariness. That the many examples of objectionable behaviour by the metropolis and its representatives cited by Rogers exacerbated these longstanding colonial fears is clear. Thus, Thomas Pownall reported in December 1757 that Loudoun's high-handed tactics in his efforts to quarter British troops in Massachusetts had created 'Mischevious Suspicions & Suggestions' that Pownall was 'in league with the Army to turn the Constitution of this Province into a Military Government'. Against the background of the new aggressiveness towards the colonies exhibited by London authorities during the decade preceding the war, moreover, metropolitan behaviour during the war appeared even more ominous, and some colonists, like William Smith, Jr., worried that the 'long hand of the Prerogative' would 'be stretched over to us, more than ever, upon the conclusion of the next general peace'. Nor did the colonists respond entirely favourably to the rising chorus of suggestions both immediately before and throughout the war for Parliamentary intervention in the internal affairs of the colonies, and at least one colonial leader, Stephen Hopkins, the elected governor of Rhode Island, reportedly declared in 1757 'that the King & Parliament had no more Right to make Laws for us than the Mohawks' and that whatever might be said 'concerning the Arbitrary Despotic Government of the Kingdom of France, yet nothing could be more tyrannical, than our being Obliged by Acts of Parliament To which we were not parties to the making; and in which we were not Represented'.[35]

Similarly, as Knollenberg has shown, the many restrictive policies implemented by the metropolis during the later stages of the war following the conquest of Canada in 1759 elicited considerable colonial discontent. Colonial legislators resented the demonstrable increase in metropolitan limitations upon the supervision of their law-making powers. By effectively 'strip[ping] us of all the Rights and Privileges of British Subjects', complained Colonel Richard Bland, the Virginia lawyer and antiquarian, such limitations threatened to undermine the customary constitutions of the colonies and 'to put us under' a 'despotic Power' of the sort usually associated with 'a French or Turkish Government'. At least in the northern colonies, colonial merchants were equally unhappy with metropolitan efforts to enforce the trade laws more systematically and especially with their attempts to suppress colonial trade with enemy islands. Far from being 'pernicious and prejudicial' to either Britain or the war effort, such trade, they argued, was 'of the greatest benefit to the kingdom, and the mein sourse from whence we have been enabled to support the extraordinary demands for cash, that have been made upon us in order to enable his majesty to carry on the present just and necessary, but most expensive war.' Even to interfere with, much less to suppress, a trade that was ultimately responsible for bringing the British nation annual profits of over 600 per cent and cash in the amount of £1,500,000 seemed to colonial traders incomprehensible. Because there had never been a total prohibition of trade between the home islands and France at any time during the war, moreover, it also seemed to be patently discriminatory against colonial merchants, who professed to find it explicable only in terms of the 'undue influence of the [British] *West-Indians*' and metropolitan partiality for their interests over that of the continental colonists. In addition, some colonists were sceptical about metropolitan intentions to keep a standing army in the colonies after the war. They wondered with Cortlandt Skinner of New Jersey why, 'when a few independent Companies' had been 'sufficient for the continent' for over a century when the French were in possession of Canada, Britain suddenly required a permanent garrison of 'so many regiments when every [European] enemy is removed at least a thousand miles from our borders' and worried that the army was really intended 'to check us'.[36]

In the final analysis, however, the anxieties with which the colonists emerged from the war appear far less important than the high levels of expectations. For on balance the war seems to have been for the colonists a highly positive experience. For one thing, the war had brought large sums of specie into the colonies through military and naval spending and successful privateering and had been highly profitable for many people, especially in the northern colonies where most of the troops were stationed.[37] But the psychological benefits the colonists derived from the war would seem to have been far more significant than these material ones. That so much of the war had been fought on colonial soil and that the metropolitan government had made such an enormous effort and gone to such a great expense to defend them were extraordinarily reinforcive of colonial self-esteem and gave rise to an expanded sense of colonial self-importance.) Moreover, the colonists took great pride in the fact that they had themselves made an important contribution to the war. Historians have often taken at face value contemporary metropolitan opinion that, with a few notable exceptions, the colonies had not exerted themselves in voting men and money for the war, and that the requisition system through which the administration had sought to mobilise colonial contributions to the war was, in the judgment of George Louis Beer, 'largely a failure'. Yet, as John M. Murrin has recently pointed out, the subsidy policy adopted by the metropolitan government beginning in 1756 by which it reimbursed the colonies with specie voted by Parliament according to the amounts they actually expended for the war worked with 'reasonable efficiency'. 'By offering valuable rewards to specie-poor colonies, it actually stimulated competition among them in support of imperial goals', he argues: 'At an annual expense to Britain of £200,000 (later reduced to £133,000), the colonies raised about twenty thousand provincials per year through 1762, paying about half the cost themselves'.[38]

The following table not only reinforces Murrin's point but shows that the colonial contribution to the war was both more evenly distributed and far more substantial than historians have appreciated. Massachusetts and Virginia, the two colonies that subsequently took the lead in the resistance movement after 1763, were together responsible for half of total net expenditures, but Pennsylvania, New Jersey, New York, Connecticut, and, in terms of taxes per adult white male, even South Carolina all expended respectable sums. Besides the new colony of Georgia, only New Hampshire, North Carolina, Maryland and, to a lesser extent, Rhode Island did not vote substantial amounts and thereby place their inhabitants under significantly higher tax burdens than they had been used to before the war.

COLONIAL CONTRIBUTIONS TO THE SEVEN YEARS' WAR[39]

A. Expenditures

Colony	Expenditures	% Total	Reimbursed by Parliament	% Reimbursed	Net Expenditures	% Total
	£		£		£	
Massachusetts	818,000	31.8	351,994	43.0	466,006	31.1
Virginia	385,319	15.0	99,177	25.7	286,142	19.1
Pennsylvania	313,043	12.2	75,311	24.1	237,732	15.9
New Jersey	204,411	8.0	51,321	25.1	153,090	10.2
New York	291,156	11.3	139,468	47.9	151,688	10.1
South Carolina	90,656	3.5	10,226	11.3	80,430	5.4
Maryland	39,000	1.5	0	0.0	39,000	2.6
Rhode Island	80,981	3.2	51,480	63.6	29,501	1.9
Connecticut	259,875	10.1	231,752	89.2	28,123	1.9
North Carolina	30,776	1.2	11,010	35.8	19,766	1.3
New Hampshire	53,211	2.1	47,030	88.4	6,181	0.4
Georgia	1,820	0.1	0	0.0	1,820	0.1
Totals	2,568,248	100.0	1,068,769	41.6	1,499,479	100.0

B. Tax Per Adult White Male

Colony	Tax	Colony	Tax	Colony	Tax
	£		£		£
South Carolina	10.94	Virginia	7.20	North Carolina	1.28
Massachusetts	10.70	Pennsylvania	6.62	Georgia	1.51
New Jersey	8.77	Rhode Island	3.51	Connecticut	1.01
New York	7.52	Maryland	1.91	New Hampshire	0.84

For the colonists, the knowledge that they had, for the first time in their histories, made such an important contribution to such a great and glorious national cause increased the immediacy and strength of their ties with Britain and produced a surge of British patriotism. They had long had, in Thomas Pownall's words, a 'natural, almost mechanical affection to Great Britain', an affection that was deeply rooted in ties of blood and interest, satisfaction with their existing prosperous condition, and pride in being linked to a great metropolitan tradition that, they believed, guaranteed them the same 'privileges and equal protection', the same 'liberty and free constitution of government', that were the joyous boast of Britons everywhere and the jealous envy of the rest of the civilised world. The extraordinary British achievements in the Seven Years' War could only intensify this deep affection for and pride in being British, which came pouring out during the later stages of the war in a veritable orgy of celebrations, first, of the great British victories in Canada, the West Indies, and Europe; then of the accession of a vigorous, young, British-born king, George III, in 1760; and, finally, of the glorious Treaty of Paris in 1763, a treaty that made the British Empire the most extensive and powerful in the Western world since Rome. British national feeling among the colonists had probably never been stronger than it was in the early 1760s.[40]

The feeling of having been a partner in such a splendid 'national' undertaking, even if only a junior partner, not only intensified the pride of the colonists in their attachment to Britain, it also heightened their expectations for a larger—and more equivalent—role within the Empire, a role that would finally raise them out of a dependent status to one in which they were more nearly on a par with Britons at home. It also stimulated visions of future grandeur—within the British Empire. 'Now commences the Aera of our quiet Enjoyment of those Liberties, which our Fathers purchased with the Toil of their whole Lives, their Treasure, their Blood', ecstatically declared Reverend Thomas Barnard of Salem, Massachusetts, in one of many similar sermons celebrating the conclusion of the Seven Years' War: 'Safe from the Enemy of the Wilderness, safe from the griping Hand of arbitrary Sway and cruel Superstition; Here shall be the late founded Seat of Peace and Freedom. Here shall our indulgent Mother, who has most generously rescued and protected us, be served and honoured by growing Numbers, with all Duty, Love and Gratitude, till Time shall be no more'. The expulsion of the French had at once both rendered the colonies safe and opened up half a continent for their continued expansion. Now that this vast and rich area had finally been 'secured to the British Government', the colonists confidently expected that as a matter of course liberty would 'be granted to his Majestys Subjects in' the 'Colonies to Settle the Lands on Ohio' and elsewhere in the west. Once these lands had been settled, prospects for Britain, and America, colonists predicted with assurance, would be almost without limits. 'The State, Nature, Climate, and prodigious Extent of the American Continent' obviously provided 'high Prospects in favor of the Power, to which it belongs'. With all of eastern North America for its granary, Britain could become one extended town of manufacturers, and this powerful Anglo-American partnership would enable the British Empire to 'maintain and exalt her Supremacy, until Heaven blots out all the Empires of the World.' Given their crucial role in these developments, the colonists had no doubt, as an anonymous pamphleteer had phrased it early in the war, that they would 'not be thought presumptuous, if they consider[ed] themselves upon an equal footing with' Englishmen at home or be 'treated the worse, because they will be *Englishmen*'. Conscious of the strenuous and critical character of their exertions during the war, they now thought that they had every 'reason to expect that *their* interest should be considered and attended to, that *their* rights . . . should be preserved to them'. 'Glowing with every sentiment of duty and affection towards their

100 THE BRITISH ATLANTIC EMPIRE

mother country', they looked forward at war's end to 'some mark of tender-
ness in return'. As soon as the metropolitan government recognised their
great 'services and suffereings' during the war, they felt sure, it would be
compelled even 'to enlarge' their Priviledges'.[41]

IV

The experience of the Seven Years' War thus sent the postwar expectations
of men on opposite sides of the Atlantic veering off in opposite directions.
More aware than ever of the value of the colonies, increasingly anxious
about the fragility of metropolitan authority over them, and appalled by
their truculent and self-serving behaviour during the war, the metropolitan
government was determined to bring them under tighter regulations at the
end of the war and willing to use the authority of Parliament to do so. By
contrast, the colonists, basking in a warm afterglow of British patriotism,
minimised evidence accumulated before and during the war that metropolitans had other, less exalted plans for them, and looked forward
expansively to a more equal and secure future in the Empire. At the same
time, the removal of the Franco-Spanish menace from the eastern half of
North America had both made the colonists somewhat less dependent upon
Britain for protection and left subsequent British governments much freer
to go ahead with a broad programme of reform, while the presence of a large
number of royal troops in the colonies gave them confidence that they could
suppress potential colonial resistance and seemed to make the caution and
conciliation they had traditionally observed towards the colonies less
necessary. In combination, these psychological consequences and structural
changes produced by the war made the relationship between Britain and the
colonies far more volatile than it had ever been before.

Given this situation, it was highly predictable that British officials in the
1760s would take some action, probably by bringing Parliamentary authority
to bear upon the colonials in new, unaccustomed, and hence, for the
colonists, illegitimate ways and that such action, so completely at variance
with the colonists' hopes and expectations, would be interpreted by the
colonists as both a betrayal and a violation of the customary relationship
between them and Great Britain. For the colonists, it was not only the new
taxes and restrictive measures in themselves that so deeply offended them
in the mid-1760s but the injustice, ingratitude, and reproach those measures
seemed to imply. When they discovered through these measures that their
obedience during the war would be rewarded not by the extension but the
'loss of their freedom', that, as the Massachusetts lawyer Oxenbridge
Thacher exclaimed, they had been 'lavish of their blood and treasure in the
late war only to bind the shackles of slavery on themselves and their children'
and that Britain intended to treat all the colonies, regardless of whether
they had contributed heavily to the war or not, without distinction, with
'the rude hand of a ravisher', they felt a deep sense of disappointment,
even betrayal, as if, in the words of Richard Henry Lee, they had 'hitherto
been suffered to drink from the cup of Liberty' only that they might 'be
more sensibly punished by its being withdrawn, and the bitter dregs of

Servility forced on us in its place'.[42] Perhaps more than any other single factor, the sense of betrayal, the deep bitterness arising out of the profound disjunction between how, on the basis of their performance during the Seven Years' War, they thought they deserved to be dealt with by the metropolis and the treatment actually accorded them, supplied the energy behind their intense reaction to the Grenville programme in 1765–6. For metropolitans, on the other hand, the colonists' powerful resistance to the Grenville measures only operated to confirm ancient fears that the allegiance of these valuable colonies to Britain was highly tenuous, that their authority in the colonies was dangerously weak, and that the ungrateful colonists were bent upon escaping from their control and establishing their independence.

By contributing so heavily to the creation of the intellectual and psychological climate and a structural situation that produced these actions and reactions, the Seven Years' War thus had a profound, if complex, bearing upon the emerging confrontation between Britain and its North American colonies and served as an important component in the causal pattern of the American Revolution.

NOTES

1. The only recent exception is John M. Murrin's brief but penetrating 'The French and Indian War, the American Revolution, and the Counterfactual Hypothesis: Reflections on Lawrence Henry Gipson and John Shy', *Reviews in American History*, I (1973), 307–18.

2. Jack P. Greene, ' "A Posture of Hostility": A Reconsideration of Some Aspects of the Origins of the American Revolution', American Antiquarian Society *Proceedings*, LXXXVII (1977), Part I, 5–46.

3. John Mitchell, *The Contest in America between Great Britain and France with Its Consequences and Importance* (London, 1757), vii; John Thomlinson to Lord Granville, 13 Dec. 1756, in Stanley M. Pargellis, ed., *Military Affairs in North America, 1748–1765: Selected Documents from the Cumberland Papers in Windsor Castle* (New York, 1936), 257; William Smith, Jr., 'Some Thoughts upon the Dispute between Great Britain and her Colonies', 1765–67, in Robert M. Calhoon, 'William Smith, Jr's Alternative to the American Revolution', *William and Mary Quarterly*, 3d ser., XXII (1965), 111–12.

4. Smith, Jr., 'Some Thoughts upon the Dispute', 118; Benjamin Franklin, 'The Interest of Great Britain Considered', 1760, in Leonard W. Labaree, *et. al.*, eds., *The Papers of Benjamin Franklin* (New Haven, 1959–   ), IX, 79; Thomlinson to Granville, 13 Dec. 1756, in Pargellis, ed., *Military Affairs*, 257; *The Comparative Importance of Our Acquisitions from France in America* (London, 1762) 42 E, as quoted by Fred J. Ericson, 'British Motives for Expansion in 1763: Territory, Commerce, or Security'? *Papers of the Michigan Academy of Sciences, Arts, and Letters*, XXVII (1942), 583.

5. Mitchell, *Contest in America*, vii–viii, xx; [Peter Williamson], *Occasional Reflections on the Importance of the War in America* (London, 1958), 7–8.

6. To ———— on French possessions in America, 1761, Peter Force Papers, IX, Box 9, Library of Congress, Washington, D.C.; Josiah Tucker to Rev. Thomas Birch, 1 Sept. 1755, Additional Manuscripts, 4326–B, ff. 64–7, British Library, London.

7. Loudoun to Cumberland, 29 Aug. 1756, in Pargellis, ed., *Military Affairs*, 230, and to Halifax, 3 Oct. 1756, Loudoun Papers (hereafter, LO) 1956A, Henry E. Huntington Library, San Marino, Calif.; Halifax to Loudoun, 11 Mar. 1757, LO 3018–A; Malachy Postlethwayt, *The Universal Dictionary of Trade and Commerce* (2 vols., London, 1757), 473–4. Italics added.

8. Pinfold to Halifax, 31 May, 1757, Force Papers, IX, Box 7; Wentworth to Board of Trade, 15 Jan. 1758, Colonial Office Papers (hereafter, CO) C/927, Public Record

Office, London; Henry Ellis to Board of Trade, 1 Jan. 1758, CO 5/646; Board of Trade to Charles Lawrence, 14 Dec. 1759, CO 218/5, 374–6; Pownall to Loudoun, 7 Dec. 1756, 28 Nov. 1757, LO 2321, 4908; Loudoun to Cumberland, 26 Dec. 1756, in Pargellis, ed., *Military Affairs*, 272–3; Board of Trade to Privy Council, 28 July, 1758, in William L. Saunders, ed., *The Colonial Records of North Carolina* (10 vols., Raleigh, 1886–1900), V, 959–61; Thomas C. Barrow, ed., 'A Project for Imperial Reform: "Hints Respecting the Settlement for our American Provinces", 1763', *William and Mary Quarterly*, 3d. ser., XXIV (1967), 118.

9. *State of the British and French Colonies in North America* (London, 1755), 148–9; *A Short View of the Smuggling Trade, carried on by the British Northern Colonies* . . . (n.p., n.d.); Loudoun to Cumberland, 22 June, 1757, in Pargellis, ed., *Military Affairs*, 376; Charles Hardy to Board of Trade, 15 July, 1757, and Halifax to Newcastle, 4 May, 1759, Add. Mss., 32890, ff. 492, 507–10; Board of Trade to Rhode Island Governor, 9 Oct. 1756, in John R. Bartlett, ed., *Records of the Colony of Rhode Island and Providence Plantation, in New England* (10 vols., Providence, 1856–65), V, 546; Board of Trade to Privy Council, 31 Aug. 1759, CO 138/20, 447–57; Francis Bernard to John Pownall, 5 May, 1761, Bernard Letter Book 1758–61, 309–12, Houghton Library, Harvard University, Cambridge, Mass.; Commissioners of Customs to Treasury, 21 July, 1763, Treasury, Papers 1/426, ff. 269–73, Public Record Office; Nathaniel Ware to ————————, 22 Aug. 1763, Stowe Mss. (hereafter STG), 12/14, Huntington Library; 'An Estimate of Tea, Sugar, and Molasses, Illegally imported into the Continent of North America . . .', 17 Nov. 1763, Add. Mss., 38335, f. 243; 'General Thoughts with Respect to such Regulations . . .', 1763–64, STG 12/28; Robert Hunter Morris to Pitt, c. 1758/59, Misc. Mss., William L. Clements Library, Ann Arbor, Michigan. See also Thomas C. Barrow, 'Background to the Grenville Program, 1757–1763', *Wm. & Mary Qtly.*, 3d ser., XXII (1965), 93–104, and *Trade and Empire: The British Customs Service in Colonial America 1760–1775* (Cambridge, Mass., 1967), 160–85; Oliver M. Dickerson, *The Navigation Acts and the American Revolution* (Philadelphia, 1951), 63–102; George Louis Beer, *British Colonial Policy 1754–1765* (New York, 1907), 86–131.

10. *State of the British and French Colonies*, 53–4; Halifax to Loudoun, 11 Mar. 1757, LO 3018–A; Loudoun to Halifax, 26 Dec. 1756, LO 2416C; Jack M. Sosin, *Whitehall and the Wilderness: The Middle West in British Colonial Policy, 1760–1775* (Lincoln, Neb., 1961), 3–51; Joseph A. Ernst, 'Genesis of the Currency Act of 1764: Virginia Paper Money and the Protection of British Investments', *Wm. & Mary Qtly.*, 3d ser., XXII (1965), 33–74.

11. See John M. Bumsted, ' "Things in the Womb of Time": Ideas of American Independence, 1633 to 1763', *Wm. & Mary Qtly.*, 3d ser., XXXI (1974), 533–64; Greene, 'A Posture of Hostility', 10–11; Mitchell, *Contest in America*, xxi; Franklin, 'Interest of Great Britain Considered', *Franklin Papers*, IX, 78; *A Letter to a Member of Parliament, on the Importance of the American Colonies* (London, 1757), 22–3; Calhoon, 'William Smith, Jr's. Alternative', 114; Barrow, 'Project for Imperial Reform', 111.

12. See Adolph B. Benson, ed., *Peter Kalm's Travels in North America* (New York, 1964), 138–40; Tucker to Thomas Birch, 1 Sept. 1755, Add. Mss., 4326–B. ff. 64–7; Mitchell, *Contest in America*, xxii; [William Burke], *Remarks on the Letter Addressed to the Two Great Men* (London, 1760), 50–1; Thomas Falconer to Charles Gray, 30 Nov. 1765, D/DRg 4/9 Gray-Round Archives, Essex Record Office, Chelmsford; Bernhard Knollenberg, *Origin of the American Revolution 1759–1766* (New York, 1961), 18–19.

13. See Frederic J. Ericson, *The British Colonial System and the Question of Change of Policy on the Eve of the American Revolution* (Chicago, 1943), 6, 8; Vincent T. Harlow, *The Founding of the Second British Empire 1763–1793* (London, 1952), 166; Lawrence Henry Gipson, *The Coming of the Revolution 1763–1775* (New York, 1954), xi; Richard W. Van Alstyne, *Empire and Independence: The International History of the American Revolution* (New York, 1965), 25.

14. Calhoon, 'William Smith, Jr's. Alternative', 114; *State of the British and French Colonies*, 150; [Thomas Whateley], *The Regulations Lately Made* . . . (London, 1765), 40; Board of Trade to Benning Wentworth, 15 Jan. 1758, CO 5/941, 403–7; Edmond Fitzmaurice, *Life of William, Earl of Shelburne* (3 vols., London, 1875–76), I, 148.

15. See for the classic statement of this view, which has been very widely held, Lawrence

Henry Gipson, *The British Empire before the American Revolution* (15 vols., Caldwell, Idaho, and New York, 1936–72), IX, 42–3.

16. Barrow, 'Background to the Grenville Program', 93; Calhoon, 'William Smith Jr's. Alternative', 116, 118; Board of Trade to Wentworth, 9 Nov. 1758, CO 5/941, 403–7, to Thomas Pownall, 22 Nov. 1758, CO 5/919, 5–10, and to Privy Council, 31 Aug. 1759, CO 138/20, 447–57; Thomas Pownall, 'The State of the Government of Massachusetts Bay as it Stood in the Year 1757', CO 325/2; Treasury to Privy Council, 4 Oct. 1763, W. L. Grant and James Munro, eds., *Acts of the Privy Council of England, Colonial Series* (6 vols., London, 1908–12), IV, 569–72; Malachy Postlethwayt, *Britain's Commercial Interest Explained and Improved* (2 vols., London, 1757), I, 424–5.

17. Mitchell, *Contest in America*, xxiii, 'Some Thoughts on the Settlement and Government of Our Colonies in North America', 10 Mar. 1763, Add. Mss. 38335, ff. 74–7; Thomas Pownall, *The Administration of the Colonies* (London, 1764), 22–39; John Fothergill, *Considerations Relative to the North American Colonies* (London, 1765), 48; 'General Thoughts with respect to such Regulations . . .', 1763–64, STG 12/28.

18. Whately, *Regulations Lately Made*, 40; Jenkinson to Wolters, 18 Jan. 1765, in Nineta S. Jucker, ed., *The Jenkinson Papers, 1760–66* (London, 1949), 347–8; Barrow, 'Project for Imperial Reform', 109.

19. Knollenberg, *Origin of the American Revolution*.

20. Barrow, 'Background to Grenville Program', 93–5, 102–5; Carl Ubbelohde, *The Vice-Admiralty Courts and the American Revolution* (Chapel Hill, 1960).

21. Verner W. Crane, ed., 'Hints Relative to the Division and Government of the Conquered and Newly Acquired Countries in America', [5 May, 1763], *Mississippi Valley Historical Review*, VIII (1922), 371; Tucker to Birch, 1 Sept. 1755, Add. Mss., 4326–B, ff. 64–7; Barrow, 'Project for Imperial Reform', 114–15; Sosin, *Whitehall and the Wilderness*, 3–78.

22. 'Some Thoughts on the Settlement and Government of Our Colonies', 10 Mar. 1763, Add. Mss. 38335, ff. 74–7; 'Govr. Dilwiddy [Dinwiddie's] Concern of the Settlements in North America', 17 Jan. 1763, *ibid.*, 38334, f. 300 Halifax to Loudoun, 11 Mar. 1757, LO 3018–A; Francis Bernard to Halifax, 23 May, 1759, Bernard Letter Book, 1758–61, 173–5; Barrow, 'Project for Imperial Reform', 117–25; Board of Trade to Privy Council, 31 Aug. 1759, CO 138/20, 447–57; R. H. Morris to Pitt, 1758–59, Misc. Mss., Clements Library; [John Pownall], 'General Propositions: Form and Constitution to be established in the new Colonies', 1763, Shelburne Papers, XLVIII, 559–60; Cecelius Calvert to Horatio Sharpe, 19 Jan. 1760, in William Hand Browne, *et. al.*, eds., *Archives of Maryland* (65 vols., Baltimore, 1883–   ), XXXI, 527–8; Crane, ed., 'Hints Relative to the Division', 372; Greene, ' "Posture of Hostility".'

23. See Franklin to Proprietor, 20 Aug. 1757, and to Isaac Norris, 10 Mar. 1759, *Franklin Papers*, VII, 250, VIII, 293–6; Barrow, 'Project for Imperial Reform', 117; Knollenberg, *Origins of the American Revolution*.

24. See Jack P. Greene, ed., *Great Britain and the Colonies, 1606–1763* (New York, 1970), xi–xlvii, 'Some Instances of Matters relating to the Colonies in which the House of Commons have interfered', 1757, Add. Mss., 35909, ff. 275–80.

25. Greene, ' "Posture of Hostility",' 40–1.

26. James Abercromby to Pitt, 25 Nov. 1756, Chatham Papers, PRO 30/8/95, ff. 197–208; [Henry McCulloh], *Proposals for Uniting the English Colonies on the Continent of America* (London, 1757), esp. 15–16; Postlethwayt, *Britain's Commercial Interest Expalined*, 424–5, and *Universal Dictionary* (2 vols., London, 1757), I, 373; R. H. Morris to Pitt, 1758–59, Misc. Mss., Clements Library; Pownall to Halifax, 29 Oct. 1757, Force Papers, IX, Box 7; Barrow, 'Project for Imperial Reform', 117–18; Norris to Franklin, 18 May, 1765, *Franklin Papers*, XII, 130–1.

27. 'Report on South Carolina . . . Boundaries', 1763, Add. Mss., 42257, ff. 434–56; Loudoun to Cumberland, 26 Dec. 1756, in Pargellis, ed., *Military Affairs*, 273, to Halifax, 26 Dec. 1756, LO 2416C, and to Horatio Sharpe, 3 Nov. 1757, LO 4747B; 'General Thoughts with respect to such Regulations . . .', 1763, STG 12/28; Greene, ' "Posture of Hostility",' 45–6.

28. Greene, ' "Posture of Hostility" ', 26, 43; Morris to Pitt, 1758–59, Misc. Mss., Clements Library; Ellis to William Henry Lyttelton, 23 June, 1757, Lyttelton Papers, Clements Library; Pownall to Halifax, Force Papers, IX, Box 7; Knollenberg,

Origins of the American Revolution, 87; John Shy, *Towards Lexington: the Role of the British Army in the Coming of the American Revolution* (Princeton, 1965), 3–83.

29. The Rutherford and Ware quotes are from Shy, *Towards Lexington*, 63–4; Barrow, 'Project for Imperial Reform', 122, 124–5; John M. Bumsted, 'The Paranoia of the Colonists Vindicated: the Grenville Programme for America', unpublished paper, 21; Knollenberg, *Origin of the American Revolution*, 87–96.

30. See Cumberland to Loudoun, 22 Oct. 1756, in Pargellis, ed., *Military Affairs*, 251; Loudoun to Halifax, 26 Dec. 1756, and to Thomas Pownall, 17 Nov. 1757, LO 2416C, 4853.

31. Henry Frankland to Thomas Pelham, 1 Sept. 1757, Add. Mss. 33087, f. 353; Franklin, 'Interest of Great Britain', *Franklin Papers*, IX, 90; Calhoon, 'William Smith, Jr's. Alternative', 113; Sir Lewis Namier, *England in the Age of the American Revolution* (London, 1963), 276.

32. 'Journal of a French Traveller in the Colonies, 1765', *American Historical Review*, XXVI (1920–21), 747; John Dickinson, *The Late Regulations Respecting the British Colonies* (Philadelphia, 1765), in Bernard Bailyn, ed., *Pamphlets of the American Revolution* (Cambridge, Mass., 1965), I, 690.

33. Shelburne, Speech, 9 Dec. 1762, Shelburne Papers, CLXV, 309–21, Clements Lib.; Whateley, *Regulations Lately Made*, 43–4; William Allen to Benjamin Chew, 7 Oct. 1763, in David A. Kimball and Miriam Quinn, eds., 'William Allen-Benjamin Chew Correspondence, 1763–1764', *Pennsylvania Magazine of History and Biography*, XC (1966), 215; *State of the British and French Colonies*, 129; Fred J. Ericson, 'The Contemporary British Opposition to the Stamp Act, 1764–65', *Papers of Mich. Acad.*, XXIX (1944), 503; Van Alstyne, *Empire and Independence*, 14; *The Power and Grandeur of Great Britain Founded on the Liberty of the Colonies* (Philadelphia, 1768), 7; Richard Koebner, *Empire* (Cambridge, Eng., 1961), 105–65; Gipson, *British Empire before the American Revolution*, X, 3–110, *The Coming of the Revolution 1763–1775* (New York, 1954), 10–27, 56, and 'The American Revolution as an Aftermath of the Great War for Empire, 1754–1763', *Political Science Quarterly*, LXV (1950), 86–104.

34. Alan Rogers, *Empire and Liberty: American Resistance to British Authority, 1755–1763* (Berkeley and Los Angeles, 1954). The quotations are from p. ix.

35. *State of the British and French Colonies*, 59; Pownall to Loudoun, 15 Dec. 1757, LO 5014; Smith to Thomas Clap, [1757–59], as quoted in William Smith, Jr., *The History of the Province of New-York*, ed. Michael Kammen (Cambridge, Mass., 1972), I, xxxiv; Deposition of Samuel Freebody, 15 Sept. 1758, R. I. Mss. 12/21, Rhode Island Historical Society, Providence.

36. Knollenberg, *Origin of the American Revolution*, 66, 91, 176–7; Shy, *Towards Lexington*, 141–2; Rogers, *Empire and Liberty*, 90–104; *State of the Trade Carried on with the French on the Island of Hispaniola* . . . (New York, 1760), 4–6, 10–14.

37. See Loudoun to Cumberland, 22 June, 1757, in Pargellis, ed., *Military Affairs*, 376; Robert Hunter Morris to Andrew Johnstone, 20 Mar. 1758, Robert Hunter Morris Papers, Box 3, Rutgers University Library, New Brunswick, N. J.; Marc Egnal and Joseph A. Ernst, 'An Economic Interpretation of the American Revolution', *Wm. & Mary Qtly.*, 3d. ser., XXIX (1972), 3–32.

38. Beer, *British Colonial Policy*, 52–85; I. R. Christie, *Crisis of Empire: Great Britain and the American Colonies 1754–1783* (London, 1966), 32; Murrin, 'French and Indian War', 314–15.

39. Section A of this table is based upon many sources. Except for the New Hampshire data, which is derived from William Henry Fry, *New Hampshire as a Royal Province* (New York, 1908), 412–15, the column marked expenditures is taken from 'A State of the Debts incurred by the British Colonies of North America for the Extraordinary Expenses of the last wars . . .', [1766], Add. Mss., 35909, f. 169. The column designated reimbursements by Parliament has been pieced together from the Treasury Papers (T) in the Public Record Office: the 1756 grant of £115,000 (T 54/38, pp. 254–9); the 1757 grant of £50,000 (T 1/376, f. 81); the 1758 grants of £27,380 (Massachusetts) and £13,736 (Connecticut) (T 1/388, f. 20); the 1759 grant of £200,000 (T 61/38, p. 181); the 1760 grant of £200,000 (T 52/52, p. 244); the 1760 grant of £2,979 to New York (*Journals of the House of Commons*, 28 Apr. 1760, XXVIII, 894); the 1761 grant of £200,000 (T 52/54, pp. 109–11; Audit Office Papers 1/74/97; and T 1/423);

the 1762 grant of £133,333 (T 1/423, 110); the 1763 grant of £133,333 (T 52/55, p. 430). Net expenditures have been computed by subtracting reimbursements from expenditures. Part B. has been computed by dividing net expenditures by adult white male population figures for 1760.

40. Pownall, *Administration of the Colonies,* 28; Edmund Burke, *Selected Writings and Speeches on America,* ed. Thomas H. D. Mahoney (Indianapolis, 1964), 79, 181; Richard Henry Lee to Arthur Lee, 4 July, 1765, in James C. Ballagh, ed., *Letters of Richard Henry Lee* (2 vols., New York, 1912–14), I, 11; Postlethwayt, *Universal Dictionary,* I, 535; Franklin, 'Interests of Great Britain Considered', *Franklin Papers,* IX, 85, 89–90, 94. See also Max Savelle, *Seeds of Liberty: The Genesis of the American Mind* (New York, 1948), 553–87, and 'Nationalism and Other Loyalties in the American Revolution', *Am. Hist. Rev.,* LXVII (1961), 901–23; Paul A. Varg, 'The Advent of Nationalism, 1758–1776', *American Quarterly,* XVI (1964), 160–81.

41. Thomas Barnard, *A Sermon Preached before His Excellency Francis Bernard, Esq., ... May 25th, 1763* (Boston, 1763), 44; George Mason to Robert Dinwiddie, 9 Sept. 1761, in Robert A. Rutland, ed., *The Papers of George Mason, 1725–1792* (3 vols., Chapel Hill, 1970), I, 28; Calhoon, 'William Smith, Jr's. Alternative', 118; *State of the British and French Colonies,* 64; Oxenbridge Thacher, *The Sentiments of a British American* (Boston, 1764), and Dickinson, *Late Regulations,* in Bailyn, ed., *Pamphlets,* I, 490, 690; James Otis, *Brief Remarks on the Defence of the Halifax Libel* (Boston, 1765), 9; John Watts to Sir William Baker, 22 Apr. 1763, to Robert Monckton, 16 May, 1764, and to Moses Frank, 9 June, 1764, in *Letter Book of John Watts,* New York Historical Society, *Collections,* LXI (New York, 1928), 138, 255, 263; Instructions to Jasper Mauduit, 15 June, 1762, in *Jasper Mauduit,* Massachusetts Historical Society, *Collections,* LXXIV (Boston, 1918), 53.

42. Thacher, *Sentiments,* Stephen Hopkins, *The Rights of the Colonies Examined* (Providence, 1765), and Dickinson, *Late Regulations,* in Bailyn, ed., *Pamphlets,* I, 490, 496, 520, 690; Lee to Landon Carter, Feb. 2, 1766, in Ballagh, ed., *Letters of Richard Henry Lee,* I, 13.

Old Whigs, Old Tories, and the American Revolution

by

Paul Langford

The view that the debate about British policy towards the thirteen colonies in the years preceding the American Revolution can be seen simply as an expression of the ancient rivalry of Whig and Tory has long since ceased to hold attractions for historians. No doubt a thorough reappraisal of the activities of George III and Bute and consequent reassessment of the posture of the Newcastle and Rockingham Whigs has done much to assist this development.[1] In recent years it has even been denied that the measures of the 1760s and 1770s, the policies which raised up so formidable an opposition outside Parliament, represented a significant departure from the practices of earlier Whig governments, so that the idea of a 'new Toryism' has come to seem as implausible as a revived old one.[2] Most significantly perhaps, the sophistication of modern political analysis has transformed our understanding of party politics in the period, banishing the idea of a simple and enduring two party structure, and replacing it with a complex and constantly changing pattern, dominated now by old fashioned court and country groupings, now by the jockeying of aristocratic factions, now by the machinations of the various interest groups.[3] Out of this confusion, it is recognised that there gradually appeared, first in the form of the Rockingham Whigs and their articulated philosophy of party,[4] then, in the 1790s, in the emergence of a new conservative consensus, the essential basis for the nineteenth-century two party system. But how these developments related to the events of the early years of George III's reign, and more particularly to the American Revolution, is a matter for debate. What follows is an attempt to show how two important preconditions for the establishment of the party system, the weakening of the old Whig tradition, and the forming of a new authoritarian viewpoint, were affected by the conflict with America.

Contemporaries would not have needed enlightening as to the fluidity of party politics in the 1760s and 1770s. The effective dissolution of the two historic parties in the middle years of the century was a matter of frequent comment, not least, for example, by those eminent authorities on whom later historians were to rely, but whose remarks on this point have sometimes been neglected.[5] For many political purposes, some would argue for most, it became practicable to act more or less without regard to Whig and Tory distinctions. Admittedly, at a local level, particularly in the larger constituencies, and where great landed interests could trace back a continuous tradition of loyalty to one of the great parties, the old slogans continued to be used at election time, though without much reference to the actual conduct at Westminster of those elected. Moreover, in America the party labels quickly acquired in this period a revived significance, readily applied in a rapidly polarising situation. But to many in the mother country the distinction was merely baffling, and one visiting Englishwoman, for example, was genuinely puzzled to find in New England, that 'those who are well disposed towards Government ... are termd Tories'.[6]

Despite the growing irrelevance of the old party terminology to the new political realities, the terms themselves continued to play a part in public life. The first two decades of George III's reign were not short of major issues of principle, and it was natural enough that the political protagonists should endeavour to relate them to old and well-remembered ideologies. Party slogans retained a pronounced emotional appeal, particularly out of doors. In an age deeply conservative in such matters, they also opened promising avenues, depending on the standpoint, to political respectability on the one hand or political disrepute on the other. Naturally it was among opponents of government, faced with the constant need to justify their conduct to themselves and to the public, that the effort to revive old rallying cries was most marked. The most powerful political figure of the period, the elder Pitt, himself made effective use of such tactics, in a cynical or at any rate suspiciously convenient manner, whenever he found himself in opposition. Typical was his allegation in 1763, that 'this Government ... was not founded on true Revolution principles; that it was a Tory Administration'.[7] When in office himself, as in 1766, he talked more of the need to do away with party differences than to establish the new Whig Jerusalem, but in opposition again he quickly returned to the old language, discerning, he claimed, a 'distinction between right and wrong,—between Whig and Tory'.[8] Such opportunism was perhaps as transparent at the time as in historical retrospect. However, a more consistent, more considered Whig critique of supposed court Toryism came from the Rockingham Whigs, who indeed sometimes made themselves unpopular by appearing to claim a monopoly of Whig principles, and by portraying themselves as the only true 'friends to the Revolution System of Government'.[9] Their most effective spokesman, Burke, was too subtle to stoop to the crudities of Pitt, and he always refrained from associating the policies of George III's ministers with the tainted Tory party of his predecessor's reign. But he took pride in the Whig antecedents of Rockingham and the Cavendishes, and appealed consciously to their standing as the 'great Whig families', the 'great Whig connexions'.[10] Finally, beyond the parliamentary parties, among the many radical groups, and in the popular press, there was a marked concern with the promulgation of a revived Whiggism in the fact of alleged Toryism, even Jacobitism.

The polemical importance of the search for clear Whig and Tory identities was strongly felt by contemporaries. It stimulated varying responses from the critically minded. One natural reaction was the clear analysis of the political realist, incidentally according with the verdict of historians. Thus one newspaper correspondent protested at the over simplifications of the party situation current at the onset of the American War. 'Our correspondent N. seems to mistake the matter quite. The distinction of Whig and Tory no longer exists in England. He must look for it only in America. It it now the Butean party, the Bedford party, the Chatham party, the Rockingham party, the Shelburne party, etc. etc. among whom the present contest is for power'.[11] Equally strong was the demand for precise formulations of a party creed rather than vague appeals to outdated party principles. Since most of the polemic was designed to renew the vitality of Whig ideals against a supposed recrudescence of royalist Toryism, much of this criticism centred on the relevance of the Whiggism of Shaftesbury, the Junto, or even Newcastle, to the political problems of George III's reign. The *Crisis,* the most intemperate of all the radical journals being published at the outbreak of the war with America, made strenuous attempts to specify the beliefs of real Whigs, and lambasted those who merely referred in appropriately pious but vague terms to the Bill of Rights and the Glorious Revolution. 'So many Years are now elapsed since the Revolution, that its Principles are almost forgot. They are showy in *Theory,* but obsolete in *Practice'.*[12] Such remarks were addressed primarily to the moderate Whigs of the Rockingham party, whose much vaunted loyalty to the Revolution of 1688 begged major questions. Lord Mahon, one of those eccentrically radical aristocrats who sought to revive the popular appeal of the old Whiggism, laid special emphasis on the necessity for precision in this respect. 'Saying he would act on Revolutionary Principles was saying nothing, unless he would declare what he meant thereby.'[13]

In the process of defining Revolution principles, and for that matter other elements in the old party philosophies, special attention was naturally devoted to the conflict with America, a conflict which occupied the best part of two decades in British political life, and eventually came to dominate it almost to the exclusion of all other questions. The debate on the American Revolution was of its very nature a debate about fundamentals. At its narrowest the constitutional argument turned on differing interpretations of the venerable maxim that taxation could only be laid with the consent of those taxed. At its widest it was a dispute about the nature of sovereignty and political authority, and involved the clash of two diametrically opposed philosophies. Between lay a great range of legal, constitutional, political, even religious issues which led readily to the posing of basic ideological questions. In America itself, and indeed through much of continental Europe the results were profoundly important for the development of political thought. Within England the significance of this intellectual ferment is the subject of continuing controversy. But if nothing else it made Englishmen look harder than ever at the evolution of their own political ideas. Both for government and for opposition, in and out of Parliament, it provided a profound challenge, a test of the underlying principles to which they adhered.

English allies of the American cause tended to assume that, in the context of 1776, Revolution principles were synonomous with American principles. Admittedly, the appeal made by the most intellectually adventurous Americans to natural rights theory involved an extension, perhaps a redirection of established Whig ideas. But the narrower, and equally influential reliance on traditional English notions of liberty, particularly in relation to representation and chartered rights, together with the constant stress on America's debt both to the real Whig tradition and to Lockeian political theory created a natural connection between English and American Whiggism. Certainly it was the deliberate intention of the Anglo-American radical lobby in London to establish and exploit this connection. Conscious manipulators of opinion like Arthur Lee not only appealed directly to the old Whiggism of Revolution days, but unashamedly glorified the oligarchical era of Walpole and the Pelhams, picturing George II, for instance, as 'a Whig king' with a 'Whig Minister, speaking to a Whig people'.[14] As for the men in power under George III, it followed 'that they are Tories, that they have been bred Tories, and consequently that they must have imbibed such principles as are diametrically opposite to those on which the Revolution was established.'[15]

The clamour of the radicals makes it easy to forget that America's claims were rejected as well as supported on solid Whig grounds. Governments were naturally less given than were their opponents to detailed expositions of their underlying ideology, but in Parliament there was much emphasis on the Whiggish propriety of the successive measures of taxation and coercion which led up to the American Revolution. At election time ministerial candidates were not afraid to stand on the platform of 'the Constitution upon Revolution Principles' to the slight surprise of at least one visiting American.[16] In one case, that of George Grenville, we even have a coherent and plausible defence of taxation without representation on the basis of Locke's *Second Treatise*. Grenville, who was treated by radicals like Sylas Neville as an 'arch-Tory'[17] was in fact a thoroughly conventional Whig, who consciously saw his policies and principles in a Revolution framework. His interpretation of Locke's famous statement of the invalidity of taxation raised without consent was arguably attentive both to the real intention of Locke's remarks and to their historical context. As he pointed out, Locke had been concerned to destroy the basis of Filmerian theory, not to establish the case for a representative democracy. Grenville leaned heavily on the central if at times obscure Lockeian concept of trust in explaining the relationship between both the executive and legislature on the one hand and the people on the other:

> Upon this Principle it is true that no man can be tax'd without his own Consent or the Consent of those whom the Society has empower'd to act for the whole and not by the will of anyone claiming a Right from Heaven deriv'd through the Patriarchs to govern the People and tax them as he thinks proper. From the general Doctrine which is evidently true the Idea seems to have been taken that no man could be tax'd without having a distinct Representative which is evidently untrue both in Reason and in fact.[18]

Grenvillian theory tends to be seen in terms of virtual representation and in some of his speeches Grenville seems to have employed this obvious line of attack. It would be fairer, however, to see his basic argument as one that representation was simply irrelevant to the legislative powers of Parliament. But even when he went beyond matters adequately discussed in traditional political theory, and explained the existing relationship between the colonies and the metropolitan authorities, Grenville resorted to the language of Whiggism. Relations with America he apparently saw in terms of the original contract, that familiar theme in Whig literature. 'My ideas for America have always been to give them good Laws and good Government on the one hand and to exact from them on the other Hand that just Obedience and Subordination which by the original Compact of all Society is the Return due for it'.[19] This was arguably a simplistic use of contract theory, frequently in this period used against parliamentary taxation rather than for it. Radicals even argued that the King had actually violated his coronation oath in his treatment of the colonists, and thereby broken the original contract somewhat in the sense that James II had.[20] For Grenville it was the colonists who were the contract breakers, a view which he shared with many who accepted the 'fundamental Principle of Civil Societys that Protection and Allegiance are reciprocal.'[21] Staunch Whigs found it hard to see the justice of 'new fangled and desperate Doctrines' denying the authority of a legislature which in English eyes had long carried out and continued to carry out its fiduciary duties towards the colonies.[22]

Few politicians of Grenville's standing made the conscious effort to link their conduct to first principles. But most of them believed that in taxing Americans, or coercing them in the name of taxation, they had behind them the main body of Whig beliefs. In this they were largely sustained by their belief that the central issue in contention with the colonies was the sovereign authority of Parliament. Blackstone's complete and uncompromising assertion of the omnicompetence of the legislature was relatively recent, but the supremacy of Parliament, and logically of the King in Parliament, was after all an ancient axiom of Whig theory, and at any rate for less sophisticated subscribers, its essential feature. The value to ministerial Whigs of this reflection was also much enhanced by the growing realisation that a natural consequence of the position adopted by the colonies would be appreciably to enhance the power and influence of the monarchy, that is of the King distinct from the King in Parliament.

This appreciation was neither sudden nor new. A major element in the debate about taxation during the Stamp Act crisis had been the conviction in Britain that if taxation was not within the imperial competence of Parliament, it would be difficult to establish clearly what form of legislative activity was. And some had seen that if America were effectively independent of Westminster, she must be all the more dependent on the crown. As Grenville himself put it, the thirteen colonies would come to be seen as 'Independent Communities in alliance with us, and only govern'd by the same Prince as Hanover is'.[23] The Americans had been understandably slow to reach the same conclusions themselves. The early years of the controversy over taxation saw a remorseless treading and re-treading of the worn ground of representative theory and produced ever more elaborate arguments about the lines which might be drawn between legislation in a general sense, and taxation of particular kinds. By the early 1770s, however, Americans were well on the way to dispensing altogether with the idea of parliamentary supervision and coming to rely exclusively on their link with the crown and its subordinate organs of government, principally the Privy Council. Franklin, for example, found himself increasingly persuaded by the attractions of a constitution which made the crown alone sovereign, and conferred the legislative role exclusively on a combination of the colonial assemblies and King-in-Council, thereby, providing a logically tenable line of defence against the unlimited claims made for Parliament. The argument was fully developed in James Wilson's *Considerations on the Nature and Extent of the Legislative Authority of the British Parliament* and finally emerged as a more or less accepted statement of the American position in the course of 1774 and 1775. The Declaration of Colonial Rights and Grievances, issued by the first Continental Congress in October 1774, by implication came very close to such a statement, and 'cheerfully consented' to parliamentary legislation on commercial questions, only 'from the necessity of the case' and out of 'a regard to the mutual interest of both countries'. Even this vestigial role for Westminster was finally whittled away in the reply made by the second Continental Congress in December 1775, to the King's Proclamation of Rebellion. In this manifesto, 'allegiance to Parliament' was specifically disavowed, 'allegiance to the Crown' specifically admitted. The Declaration of Independence in effect restated this final assertion of colonial allegiance to the crown, listing as it did in bizarre and colourful detail the alleged misdeeds of the King and referring to Parliament only as 'a jurisdiction foreign to our constitutions' involving 'Acts of pretended Legislation'.[24]

This important and fundamental change of stance in America caused some astonishment in the mother country. An early hint of it drew a sarcastic reaction in print from Josiah Tucker: 'Good Heavens! What a sudden Alteration is this! An American pleading for the Extension of the Prerogative of the Crown?'[25] To most Englishmen indeed the notion seemed inherently absurd, and smacked of the antiquated royalism voiced most recently by the pamphleteer Timothy Brecknock in 1764.[26] Brecknock's offending work was ritually condemned by the House of Lords and publicly burned.[27] To most contemporaries his doctrines seemed laughable rather than dangerous. But the readiness of the colonists to occupy similar ground proved a godsend to anti-Americans in Britain, for it instantly made it possible to picture their opponents as friends of the royal prerogative. At precisely the moment in 1775 when Americans were demanding from England the definitive assertion of the Whig case, the form in which they put their demands made government appear impeccably Whiggish.

The opportunity was seized upon. In the Commons, at the beginning of the decisive session of 1775–6, Fox, bitterly denouncing the cabinet as 'enemies to freedom' and 'Tories', was devastatingly answered by North:

His lordship . . . said, that if he understood the meaning of the words Whig and Tory, which the last speaker had mentioned, he conceived that it was the characteristic of Whiggism to gain as much for the people as possible, while the aim of Toryism was to increase the prerogative. That in the present case, administration contended for the right of parliament. while the Americans talked of their belonging to the crown. Their language therefore was that of Toryism, although, through the artful designs of the real enemies of freedom, the good sense of the people of England was endeavoured to be misled, and false opinions were industriously inculcated throughout the kingdom.[28]

This line was naturally taken up elsewhere, and produced an amused response in the press. 'The Tories, by the acknowledging the supreme power of the British parliament over the whole British empire, appeared to be turned Whigs — And the Whigs, in attempting to extend the power of the King's prerogative beyond the control of his parliament, shew themselves to be Tories'.[29] The ultimate irony perhaps occurred with the loyal addresses to the crown, which in the summer and autumn of 1775 reflected widespread endorsement of the government's policies, and profoundly dismayed those who looked for a demonstration of public opinion in opposition to North's policies. Some of these addresses made considerable play with the apparent inconsistency of the Whig position. That from Oxford, for example, expressed 'heart-felt Pleasure, that your Majesty has not been tempted to endanger the Constitution of Great Britain, by accepting the alluring offers of an unconstitutional Increase of your Prerogative'.[30] Maidenhead declared loftily 'we cannot but protest against the Principles of those Men, who by asserting the Dependence of America on the Crown, exclusively of the Parliament of Great Britain, endeavour to point out a Distinction, that in future Times may be productive of the most fatal Consequences to both.'[31]

For those in opposition, whose principal aim in politics generally was to criticise the supposed aggrandisement of the crown, nothing could have been more embarrassing than the direction taken by the Anglo-American debate at this critical moment. It was doubly so, because one of their great hopes had long been the possibility that their general concern with the influence of the crown might plausibly be connected with the grievances of the colonies. This possibility had emerged most strongly between the break-up of the Chatham Ministry and the partial repeal of the Townshend duties, when Hillsborough as Secretary for the Colonies seemed genuinely to be considering the employment of prerogative rather than parliamentary powers in America. It was reported: 'the language of the ministry is that they will restrain the Americans by the Powers and the authority of the crown without the Intervention of Parliament, or in other words they will make them subject to the King though not to the Legislative of Great Britain. This special Tory doctrine will certainly fail in its Effect as it ought to do'.[32] The parliamentary opposition made the best of this half-opening. When, in 1769, Hillsborough formally held out to the colonial governors the possibility that the hated Townshend duties would be repealed the following session. Burke and his colleagues were able, somewhat to the bewilderment of their American friends, to attack him on the grounds that he had violated parliamentary privilege, undertaking on behalf of the executive what actually pertained to the legislature.[33] The revival of the statute of treasons of Henry VIII, though carried through Parliament, could also be seen as an attempt to employ odious executive and judicial powers not in accord with the spirit of English law. Unfortunately for parliamentary opponents of the ministry, this approach to the Anglo-American question turned out to be a blind alley. What blocked it was not merely the instinctive preference of successive governments for working entirely through Parliament, notwithstanding Hillsborough's short-lived campaign to the contrary, but the unwavering, almost pedantic constitutionalism of the King himself. His later statement that he was fighting the battle of the legislature is well known, and accurately reflected his conduct over the years. George III personally disliked Hillsborough's schemes for unorthodox new policies in the colonies,[34] and like most of his ministers insisted on treating Parliament's unlimited supremacy over the colonies as the first and only line of defence. When the next crisis came, in 1774–6, the government's policy was taken step by step through Parliament, and at every point dealt with in parliamentary terms. Even the highly controversial Massachusetts Government Act, which was primarily designed to strengthen royal authority in New England, was seen essentially as part of the campaign to have the principle and application of Parliament's supremacy accepted. Thereafter occasional opportunities for reopening the question of the prerogative occurred. For example, in 1775, the King's action in sending Hanoverian troops to safeguard the strongholds of Gibraltar and Minorca, was portrayed by opposition as a deliberate violation of the Bill of Rights, and stimulated lively pictures of the importation of foreign mercenaries on a scale sufficient to threaten English liberty.[35] Fanned by the opposition this innocent, not to say prudent, measure flickered into life when some of the country gentlemen now supporting the crown remembered their anti-Hanoverian prejudices. It was, however, quickly extinguished by the good humoured response of North himself. In the end, the old Whigs went into the American War all too aware that it was a war not for the prerogative of the crown but for that parliamentary sovereignty which they were themselves supposed to venerate.

For some, indeed for most of those who carried the banner of moderate, mainstream Whiggism, particularly the Rockinghams, it was not only the direction taken by the debate about the royal prerogative which hamstrung them in their efforts to develop a politically viable and ideologically pure line of argument. Equally restricting was the common ground which they shared with most of the leading ministers in the period, in their attachment to the unlimited power of Parliament over the colonies. In this respect they were clearly the victims of their own actions, for it was the Rockingham Ministry, which in 1766, had promoted the Declaratory Act, flatly asserting on the lines of the Irish Dependency Act of 1720, the legislative supremacy of Parliament in all cases. To many admirers of Rockingham this seemed a dreadful hindrance to the cause of Whiggism, and one which begged to be exploited by his enemies. Ministerial hacks in Parliament and in the press never tired of pointing out that the coercion of America was carried on in order to preserve the principle of Rockingham's Declaratory Act. American observers also saw the difficulty. Typical was the verdict of one colonial visitor, Jonathan Williams, whose expectations of Rockingham were sadly disappointed when he heard him speak in the Lords in 1775:

> Lord Rockingham got up, and seemed but partly in our favour.—That Declaratory Act of his, is a great stumbling block to his patriotism, for it is impossible to take the matter up to this day without entering into the question of rights, and the whole must now turn on that single point, whether Great Britain has or has not, *a right to tax America* if she has, *in all cases whatsoever* there can be no doubt but all her Laws, are on a good Foundation, and we as the most abject Slaves, in

acquiescence of that right, must obey; on the other hand, if she has
not that right, the Americans must enjoy all the Liberties they claim.[36]
In theory it was possible to get over the stumbling block of the Declaratory
Act. Even at the time of its enactment Americans had tended to play down
its significance, encouraged no doubt by the widely reported speeches of the
elder Pitt, who vociferously opposed it while supporting the ministry's
repeal of the Stamp Act. Henry Laurens described the Declaratory Act as
'the last feeble struggle of the Grenvillian party',[37] and many other Americans
saw it simply as a meaningless piece of paper, ' a kind of salvo for the
authority of Parliament'.[38] Even in the Rockingham party itself, the more
radical elements confessed to their leaders that they regarded it 'rather as
necessary at the time, than strictly right'.[39] In due course Fox was able to
pass this interpretation on to later Whigs as the more or less official version
of the passing of the Declaratory Act. Unfortunately it simply does not
correspond with the facts. The Declaratory Act was not only passed out of
conviction by Rockingham and his leading friends, but maintained out of
conviction; throughout the difficult years before the outbreak of war, the
consistent position adopted by the party was that as a matter of right, in a
debate which largely concerned right, Parliament's powers were unlimited.
In asserting this they firmly believed that they were asserting the true
principles of their party, consciously adhering to its ancient traditions.[40]

Whether they were right in this belief is a matter for debate. It is tempting
to suggest that like most other politicians in the 1760s they were subtly
reacting to the great growth in the power and prestige of Parliament which
had marked the evolution of the eighteenth-century constitution. On this
reading there lay, in the not very distant past, a less logically demanding
position, one which acknowledged the basic primacy of Parliament established in 1688 and yet retained some semblance of self-government for the
colonies. Support for the idea that there was such a middle position may
be detected in the gulf between generations which seems to mark the views
of the Whigs on this question. The evidence is necessarily thin, but it suggests
that the immediate forbears of the Rockingham Whigs might have had
some doubts about the sweeping character of the Declaratory Act. This
seems to be true of the first Earl of Hardwicke, lifelong friend of Newcastle,
and servant successively of the Walpole and Pelham regimes. His experience
as Lord Chancellor and his political and legal standing made him as good
a representative as any of the official Whig mind in the mid-eighteenth
century. There seems no doubt that he disliked the idea of colonial taxation,
which was beginning to be discussed in Parliament in 1764, the year of his
death. According to an American agent's report, 'Mr. Grenvile was shewn
Lord Hardwicke's Opinion relative to Taxing America (Inexpedient) before
he bro't in the Act.'[41] This story gains credibility from the testimony of
Hardwicke's son, the second Earl, who told Governor Hutchinson a similar
story about his father's last months. 'When asked what he thought of Mr.
Grenville's scheme of taxing America, said—They had not been used to
taxes: told Archbishop Secker, when he proposed sending a Bishop, that
the Americans left England to avoid Bishops'.[42] Still more interesting, since
it suggests objections on grounds of impropriety as well as inexpediency,

is a letter written by the second Earl. This letter has additional value since it was plainly penned at the time that the Stamp Bill was being considered, early in 1765, before the great controversy of 1765–6 could influence his recollections. His father, he remarked, 'had doubts about the *Right*. I have no doubts but that the Colonys will be very restive'.[43]

There are other hints of old Whig attitudes, some of them of doubtful value. Stories about the superior wisdom of Walpole in the 1730s and Pitt in 1750s in refusing to have anything to do with American taxation are legion, but they all seem to reflect the benefit of hindsight. More interesting, perhaps, is the attitude of the survivors of the Hardwicke era. Newcastle did not think deeply about such matters, and was persuaded pragmatically to dwell on the repeal of the Stamp Act as the central achievement of the Rockingham Ministry. Nonetheless. he clearly had instinctive doubts about the Declaratory Act.[44] Pitt, though a good deal younger than either Hardwicke or Newcastle, was consciously atavistic in his political views, and his ringing denunciation of parliamentary taxation perhaps recalled an earlier tradition. Unfortunately Pitt's position, as so often in his political career, presents problems, not least about his basic consistency. The attack which he launched in 1766 on the internal taxation of the colonies savoured as much of characteristic opportunism and rhetoric as of deep political conviction. It also got him, whenever he attempted to define his position more precisely, into logical difficulties from which he never satisfactorily extricated himself. When challenged he tended to lapse into vague and meaningless pronouncements. Nor does his record in office in 1766 provide an easy answer.[45]

In any event Pitt's view is more significant as an exception than as a rule. Not the least interesting feature of the 1760s is the arrival in politics of a whole generation of young Whigs who quickly supplanted or succeeded their elders. Apart from Pitt, the old leaders of Whiggism disappeared from the scene in rapid succession; Granville in 1763, Hardwicke, Legge and Devonshire in 1764, Newcastle was of little importance in the years before his death in 1768, and Holland of less before his in 1774. On the American question the new leaders of mainstream Whiggism entertained none of Hardwicke's doubts or Pitt's objections. In the Rockingham party Rockingham's own clear view commanded wide acceptance. Ironically it was strongly supported by a powerful group of his connections, the Onslows, the Townshends, Grey Cooper and their like, who left him to join the court in 1766 and continued to share from an opposite political standpoint the same ideological stance. The same could even be said of the Chatham party, at least before Pitt's dramatic declaration against the internal taxation of the Colonies in January 1766. Shelburne, one of the more clear thinking of the party, was much embarrassed, for in December 1765 he had publicly adopted more or less independently, what was to become the Rockingham position, that the right existed but that, for the sake of Britain's commercial strength, it should not be exercised. Like the slightly more cautious Camden, he had some difficulty adjusting to his leader's view subsequently.[46] Among lawyers the unanimity was particularly striking. Hardwicke's second son, Charles Yorke, as Attorney-General in Rockingham's ministry, drafted the Declaratory Act and never questioned its validity. Even the Chatham party's lawyer in the Commons, John Dunning, declined to accept Pitt's theory of taxation. In fact in this matter Dunning and Yorke both subscribed to the opinion of Mansfield, the legal luminary of the age and, in the eyes of American and English radicals, the *éminence grise* of North's imperial policy.

Whether the survival into the later 1760s of the most influential of the old corps leaders would have opened the way for a more credible Whig critique of ministerial policy is a nice question. In one respect it might have actually created additional problems. For the views of ministerial Whigs of the Pelham era were associated with a way of thinking about the colonies which potentially carried the same danger of strengthening the royal prerogative as that so distressingly offered by the evolution of American thought. One pointer to this possibility is the conversation which Franklin recorded as having taken place in 1757 with Lord Granville. Granville was a Whig of great experience and seniority; moreover as Lord President of the Council he was likely to have considered in detail the constitutional relationship between mother country and colonies. The subject of his talk with Franklin was not, naturally, the extent of Parliament's authority, but rather the perennial problem of conflict between the colonial assemblies and royal governors, and in particular the standing of the latter as representatives of the Crown.

You Americans have wrong ideas of the nature of your constitution; you contend that the King's instructions to his governors are not laws and think yourselves at liberty to regard or disregard them at your own discretion. But these instructions are not like the pocket instructions given to a minister going abroad for regulating his conduct in some trifling point of ceremony. They are first drawn up by judges learned in the laws; they are then considered, debated, and perhaps amended in Council, after which they are signed by the King. They are then so far as relates to you, the *law of the land;* for THE KING IS THE LEGISLATOR OF THE COLONIES.

Franklin replied:

I told His Lordship this was a new doctrine to me. I had always understood from our charters that our laws were to be made by our Assemblies, to be presented, indeed, to the King for his royal assent, but that being once given, the King could not repeal or alter them. And as the Assemblies could not make permanent laws without his assent, so neither could he make a law for these without theirs. He assured me I was totally mistaken. I did not think so, however. And His Lordship's conversation having a little alarmed me as to what might be the sentiments of the court concerning us. I wrote it down as soon as I returned to my lodgings. I recollected that about twenty years before a clause in a bill brought into Parliament by the ministry had proposed to make the King's instructions laws in the Colonies; but the clause was thrown out by the Commons, for which we adored them as our friends and friends of liberty, till by their conduct towards us in 1765, it seemed that they had refused that point of sovereignty to the King only that they might reserve it for themselves.[47]

This exchange must obviously be treated with caution. Franklin wrote his autobiography in 1771, at a time when he was particularly interested in the constitutional relationship between crown and colonies. Granville, if he said precisely what he is represented as having said, was presumably anxious to stress to a not uninfluential American the concern of British ministers at the continuing war of attrition against the prerogatives and powers of the King's deputies in America. He can hardly have intended to cast doubt on the authority of Parliament. Even so his observations are expressive of the mentality of mid-eighteenth century Whigs. Typical of this mentality was the conviction that the colonies were peculiarly the concern of the executive, and except in matters of commercial regulation, outside the natural purview, if not the competence, of Parliament. Thus in 1754 Henry Fox objected to the introduction of parliamentary legislation to regulate American troops on lines similar to the Mutiny Act in Britain: 'as our colonies are more particularly under the eye of the crown than any other part of the British dominions, it would in my opinion, be too great an encroachment upon the prerogatives of the crown, or at least it would be an intermeddling in the affair with which we have no call to have any concern'.[48] This certainly reflected the view of successive ministers, not least in the case of Walpole twenty years earlier. Egmont, for example, had found, in connection with the affairs of Georgia, that Sir Robert 'was not willing the Colonies should depend on Parliament for their settlements, but merely on the Crown. He objected that the king's prerogative would be subjected thereby to Parliament'.[49]

This jealous protection of the prerogative was maintained by the Pelhams. As Henry McCulloch observed 'it hath not been agreable to the wisdom of the Crown to have the Parliament interfere in any matter relating to the exercise of the regal power'.[50] However, McCulloch was one of many who had doubts about this wisdom, and the latter part of George II's reign witnessed growing pressure from all levels of the imperial bureaucracy to resort to parliamentary weapons. The pressure was as old, strictly speaking, as the Board of Trade itself, but in the course of 1740s and 1750s it became almost insurmountable. Successive body blows to royal authority in individual colonies made the arguments for parliamentary intervention stronger than ever. Moreover the new interest in things American during the War of Austrian Succession and the Seven Years War seemed to make both a strengthening of the machinery of government and more systematic exploitation of colonial sources of financial and military power necessary. Right through the 1750s a succession of colonial officials and military leaders warned ministers at home of the growing insubordination of colonial institutions and the men who ran them, and appealed for the adoption of a grand strategy based on parliamentary action. These demands did much to create among the rising generation which was to provide leadership in the 1760s a climate of opinion requiring firm action, and especially firm parliamentary action, in the colonies. But on the men at the top at the time it made little impression, according to Franklin because they 'are afraid the Parliament would establish more Liberty in the Colonies than is proper or necessary, and therefore do not care that Parliament should meddle at all with the Government of the Colonies; they rather chose to carry every Thing there by the *Weight* of Prerogative'.[51]

Whether this fear was justified is perhaps doubtful. On the rare occasions when Parliament did consider the internal state of the colonies, it did not seem very interested in the maintenance of colonial liberties. The Massachusetts Bay Assembly was rapped sharply over the knuckles for its activities against government in 1733; in the same year Rhode Island's opposition on the Molasses Bill produced an indignant reaction from MPs, one of whom expostulated 'as if this House had not a power to tax them, or to make any laws for the regulating of the affairs of their colony'.[52] A decade or so later with reports of opposition to royal government growing more frequent, one onlooker warned from London that 'Every endeavour to wrest the King's Authority out of the hands of his Governour may draw on the Resentment not only of the King but likewise of a British Parliament who allready seem to have become Jealous of the Dependancies of their Colonies'.[53] Such straws in the wind suggest that even before 1760 the Commons would have been disposed rather to chastise the colonial assemblies for aping the authority of the imperial legislature, than to support their struggle against weakening royal prerogative. In any event, by the time in the 1760s that Parliament was finally brought directly into Anglo-American relations, it is easy enough to see that the approach of the Pelhamite Whigs would have seemed to their successors anachronistic and even dangerous.

If the principal representatives of the Whig tradition found themselves embarrassed by the dual need to combat the court and maintain their inherent conviction of the ultimate authority of Parliament, there remained only one means of escape from their dilemma, that offered by the radicals. There was, of course, no unified campaign on the radical front, although radicals on both sides of the Atlantic strenuously sought to make common cause. Between a sophisticated re-examination of fundamental libertarian beliefs, like Richard Price's *Civil Liberty,* and the wild ranting of the popular journals there lay a great range of viewpoints.[54] Nonetheless it is easy enough to identify elements of consistency in the wide variety of radical approaches adopted in this period. First among these was the basic assertion which made it possible for them all to oppose government, support America, and also appeal to traditional Whig values. This was the claim that whatever the rights and wrongs of the American issue, Parliament itself and the system of which it was a part no longer provided a valid expression of the will of the people or even, indeed, of the will of the propertied. Arguments for constitutional reform based on the absurdities of the existing structure of the parliamentary franchise and constituencies, and on the alleged corruption which sustained them, provided a basis for root and branch opposition to successive governments. This stance was intellectually more effective than the 'country' position of the Rockinghams who founded their case against government exclusively on the growing influence of the Crown. Radicals cheerfully absorbed the Burkeian case against influence and 'double cabinet', but also went much further, with a frontal attack on the representative credentials of a Parliament which deprived the Middlesex electors of their liberty and simultaneously abused the rights of Americans. Such a posture could readily be made to correspond with the ancient canons of the Whig constitution, and, for instance, Locke's solemn warning about the inevitable decline of any representative system was frequently quoted.[55]

Unfortunately, this formula was not for practical purposes available to the Rockingham Whigs. A few of their allies on the radical fringe, like David Hartley, [56] were prepared to follow the reforming line to some extent. But the great body of Rockingham Whigs, at any rate before their leadership passed into the hands of Fox in 1782, feebly criticised the conduct of Parliament without ever demanding fundamental change. Powerful appeals from the radicals to the effect that the American war had created 'an actual dissolution of government'[57] merely frightened them further away from real reform, and the charge of critics such as Catherine Macaulay, that Rockingham was happy to reduce the improper influence of the Crown, but bent on maintaining his own improper influence, made an obvious impact.

None of this means that the Rockinghams failed to evolve a coherent position on America. On the contrary, over the years and thanks in large measure to Burke they put together a tenable position. Their claim for a right of taxation which it was impolitic to exercise proved much easier to defend than the Chathamite distinction between legislation and internal taxation. Burke's speeches provided a steady stream of statesmanlike common sense which might well, in power, have produced a more sensitive and realistic policy, or so it could be argued. The demand for a return to 'the ancient Standing Policy of this Empire'[58] and repeal of all offending legislation subsequent to 1763 could be made to coincide, on a superficial examination at least, with the wish of Congress to return to the status quo at the end of the Seven Years War. Rockingham, in speaking of this, resorted in yet another version of the contractual relationship with the colonies, to traditional Whig vocabulary;

I don't love to claim a right on the foundation of the supreme power of the legislature over all the dominions of the Crown of Great Britain; I wish to find a consent, and acquiesence in the *governed,* and I choose, therefore, to have recourse to what I think an original tacit compact, and which useage had confirmed until the late unhappy financing project interrupted the union and harmony which had so long prevailed, to the mutual advantage and happiness of this country and its colonies.[59]

Burke seems to have been more cautious about using contract language to describe the era of salutary neglect, but he relied on it in his crucial distinction between the formal framework of the constitution and the informal network of customs and traditions which governed its operation. No doubt in these concepts latent ideas of trust and tacit contract were implicit. Particularly in his *Speech on Conciliation* he was able, characteristically, to elevate this pragmatism into something resembling a general principle of federalism such as would attract the applause of later theorists of empire.

The Rockingham position helped to keep a party of opposition in being, capable, unlike its brethren among the Chatham Whigs, of responding to the challenge of conceding American independence. But to many it seemed inconsistent, over-ingenious, and above all lacking in that vigorous assertion of basic principles which was required of the Whig case. Burke's circumvention of the ideological problems involved was sophisticated but perhaps too sophisticated. Bluff country gentlemen found his distinctions between theory and practice either baffling or objectionable, and in a rare humiliation for Burke on the floor of the Commons, in December 1774, one of them said so in a sensational scene.

> Burke was more flowery than ever; he addressed himself with a great deal of rhetorick to the young Members, cautioning them against the wiles of Administration; but was so facetious that he pleased the whole House. A short answer was given by a blunt Mr. Van. 'The Honourable Gentleman', says Van, 'has been strewing flowers to captivate children. I have no flowers Mr. Speaker to strew, all I have to say is, that I think the Americans are a rebellious and most ungrateful people, and I am for assuring the king that we will support him in such measures as will be effectual to reduce them'. The honesty of the man and his singular manner set the whole House into a halloo! and answered Burke better than Cicero could have done with all his eloquence.[60]

Even worse, the Rockinghams' posture could readily be portrayed as justifying almost any opinion. The allegations made against Burke by Henry Cruger, his fellow Bristol M.P., came from a malicious opponent, but they stirred matching feelings in others. 'Today, he will be the first great *Promoter* of a *Declaratory Bill*. Tomorrow he shall *insinuate* the Parliament have not a right to bind the Americans in all cases—and yet, put *him in power,* and the third day you shall find him asserting the supremacy of this country with a vengeance'.[61] The plausibility of this charge was the price the Rockinghams had to pay for the manifold pressures on the evolution of political theory presented by the American Revolution. Their response to these pressures was defensible, in some measure convincing and at least preserved their self respect through a difficult period. But as the considered attempt of the main representatives of old Whiggism to apply Whig principles to the great ideological issue of the day, it was a complete failure. The young Fox, joining the party in the mid 1770s, sensed this weakness and urged his friends to make it 'a point of honour among us all to support the American pretensions in adversity as much as we did their prosperity, and that we shall never desert those who have acted *unsuccessfully* upon Whig principles, while we continue to profess our admiration of those who succeeded in the same principles in the year 1688'.[62]

The intellectual bankruptcy of the mainstream Whig tradition in the face of the American question would perhaps have been less demoralising for its friends if it had been matched by similar intellectual confusion and division among its enemies. Instead, the unity and coherence of the consensus which emerged in opposition to the claims of the colonies, was a constant source of problems. Only very occasionally were there serious differences in the anti-American camp. In 1766 when the Rockingham Ministry was enjoying its brief year of office, those who opposed its policy of repeal were divided about the relative merits of enforcing the Stamp Act and modifying it, though it was also the case that the possibility of modification was a problem for the Rockingham ministers themselves. Again, nine years later there were serious divisions within the government between those who favoured North's conciliatory proposals and those who simply adhered to the policy of coercion. But with these relatively insignificant exceptions the opponents of America presented a remarkably united front. And on the central question of sovereignty, there was a striking measure of general agreement, which was to sustain the North Ministry in particular through years of expensive and demoralising war. Many of the leaders of the North regime were of sound Whiggish family for at least two generations, as in the case of North and Gower, or for a much longer period, as in the case of most of their colleagues. Doubtless it was a considerable source of comfort to these men, that it was possible to portray the struggle with America in terms which made the British government's position at least as solidly Whiggish as that of its enemies. No less significant, however, was the fact that they could simultaneously appeal to what was left of the old Tory tradition, thus having, as it were, the best of both worlds.

That the Tory contribution to the policies which provoked the American Revolution is easily forgotten is largely the result of the superficially negligible strength of the old Tory party by this time. It is difficult, for example, to point to a single minister or a single measure capable of being described simply as Tory, without resorting to the deliberate falsification which radicals engaged in when they roundly condemned all the works of George III and Lord North as Tory and crypto-Jacobite. By the 1760s the old Tory Party was effectively reduced to a rump of country gentlemen, whose distinctive identity was rapidly dissolving. The parliamentary managers of George III's reign sometimes continued to describe them as Tories. Rockingham's list of November 1766 did so, as did Newcastle's of March 1767. It was to be expected that two self-conscious exponents of old style Whiggism would describe their ancient enemies in this way. Charles Townshend, who also attempted to classify M.P.s in January 1767, referred more broadly to the 'country gentlemen', a category which matched very closely those described by Rockingham and Newcastle as Tories. Later on the term 'country gentlemen' grew universal and in time comprehended those who earlier might have described themselves as country Whigs and whose particular brand of independence was now indistinguishable for most purposes from that of their Tory compatriots. Some Tories escaped the category altogether by moving into one or other of the identifiable party groups. All the latter included one or two Tories, with the Rockinghams, for instance, attracting the support of William Dowdeswell and two of his West Country friends, Charles Barrow and Sir William Codrington. No less significant, very few of the men who carried their Toryism beyond the death of George II and into the reign of George III were of the first or even second rank in point of abilities. Rare exceptions were perhaps Dowdeswell himself, Sir Francis Dashwood, and at a lower level Norborne Berkeley. But none of them emerged as an important supporter of government in debate or in office before or during the American war. In debate indeed the old Tories were generally silent, though they had a few representatives like Sir William Bagot, M.P. for Staffordshire, Sir Roger Newdigate, M.P. for Oxford

University, and Arthur Van among the younger generation who made rather a point of claiming to speak for the country gentlemen.

Paradoxically, the role of the old Tories turned country gentlemen was almost more important in the politics of the 1770s than in those of George II's reign, when they had found themselves in unremitting opposition to the court. The largely unrecognised but none the less distinct reduction of the influence of the crown in Parliament,[63] together with the basic readiness of the Tories to vote for George III's ministers, made the court increasingly dependent on this large but unreliable body of opinion. Charles Jenkinson, an influential junior minister in successive governments, was acutely aware of this important change in the pattern of parliamentary politics. As a convinced courtier, he described to Governor Hutchinson what he saw as a source of weakness for government. He:

> laments the state of affairs in England: speaks of the Minister as not having the influence of Sir Robert Walpole. And that he has no assurance of the success of any measure until it is tried: that a failure upon any question would have been fatal to Sir Robert Walpole because he governed by party, (which is little other than bribery and corruption), but Lord North may lose three or four questions in a Session, and not affect him. He says there are 150 Members, a sort of Flying Squadron, that you don't know where they will be in a new question. This may enfeeble the executive powers of Government from the uncertainty of support from the legislative power; but it may be questioned whether this state is not to be preferred to the former.[64]

The final qualification was perhaps a wise one. For if the antics of the country gentlemen could be irritating, their underlying support for Lord North was a source of great strength, more especially since the opinions of these men reflected with considerable fidelity the thinking of the landed classes at large. As one of Rockingham's friends remarked, 'Many members support the minister who are not supported by him. In his party, you will find most of the country members. This is the true barometer of the higher orders in England'.[65]

Admittedly, in the 1760s this element was sometimes responsible for the relative instability of politics. The issues of this period which caused most concern were often 'court and country' questions, and in response to them the old Tories would sometimes draw back from their new allegiance to George III and vote with opposition. Thus general warrants, the cider excise, the Middlesex Election, all brought independent members not indeed to a desire to bring government down, but at least to a readiness to vote against its measures. One of the most celebrated ministerial reverses of the period, supposedly the first such defeat for government since the Revolution, occurred on the land tax division of 1767, in which the country gentlemen voted as one. The unpredictable character of their vote was in this manner a constant source of anxiety to those like Jenkinson responsible for managing the court's supporters in the Commons. It also held out to the parliamentary opposition the constant prospect of seriously embarrassing government, if the appropriate issues presented themselves.

Against this background, it was precisely the importance of the American

question that it dramatically demonstrated the readiness of the country
gentlemen to give their support to government on a more enduring basis.
North's appeal to them was manifold. His own temperament and family
connections, not to say his financial ability and his oratory all had their
effect. But more than anything North was sustained through twelve years
of power and almost as many of crisis by the support of these men for his
policy. That support was given freely in the great majority of cases because
he was getting one issue, that of America, in their terms largely right. Not
only could North not have fought the war without the natural heirs of the
old Tories, but his readiness to fight it actually strengthened his following
among them. And when after 1782 and the battle of Yorktown they had had
enough, their change of front was equally decisive in bringing about his fall.
Contemporaries were thoroughly aware of the importance of this element in
North's parliamentary position. Hutchinson, an engrossed observer of the
parliamentary scene in England was struck by the impact of the issues. On
court versus country questions, he noted, opposition mustered sizeable
votes: on American topics it was quite different, 'the independent country
gentlemen being generally against the Americans'.[66] Burke, as one of the
actors in this scene drew the correct but depressing lesson. 'He said it was
almost in vain to contend, for the country gentlemen had abandoned their
duty, and placed an implicit confidence in the minister'.[67]

How much this development owed to the Tory mentality of the old country
families it is impossible to gauge precisely. Even the personnel are not
easily identified. The very success of government in the 1770s rendered
nugatory the publication of division lists on American questions, and where
lists do exist they tend to be exclusively concerned with those in the minority.
Nonetheless such evidence makes it clear that those who can plausibly be
associated with the old Tory interest were as uncompromisingly hostile to
America as contemporary comment suggests. In the crucial divisions of
1775-6, marking the long descent into war, hardly any of the old Tories voted
against government. For instance in the division of 26 October 1775, with
the Commons preparing to go beyond the coercive legislation of 1774-5 and
effectively to commit itself to war, only one of those regarded by contemporaries as Tories voted with opposition. This was Tom Foley, representative
of an old Tory family from the West Midlands, but now a close friend and
political ally of Charles James Fox. In fact the Tories as a group were nothing
if not consistent in their views on America, for their opposition to the colonists
went back at least to the Stamp Act crisis. The turnout of the Tory party
against the repeal of the stamp tax was a marked feature of the divisions of
February 1766. The names as they appear in the lists read like a roll call of
the Tory families: Bagot, Bertie, Blackett, Burdett, Cotton, Curzon, Dashwood, Drake, Foley, Glynne, Grosvenor, Harley, Hpublon, Isham, Keck,
Kemys Tynte, Knightley, Newdigate, Mordaunt, Pryse, Shuttleworth,
Sibthorp, Bampfylde, Vansittart, Wodehouse—taking only the better known
of them—these were the very backbone of the Tory squirearchy of George
II's reign.[68] A decade later the same men or their successors were solidly
behind North, supporting him steadily in the Commons, and, no less important, whipping up a country campaign in favour of his policy. The loyal

addresses which in late 1775 finally made it clear that the verdict at least of the countryside and small towns was irreversibly behind coercion rather than conciliation in America owed much to such families, as the names of those M.P.s entrusted with the presentation of the addresses to the King reveal.[69]

The support of the old Tories for the principle of parliamentary supremacy and their readiness to go to war in its defence provoked much interest at the time. Many contemporaries cynically attributed it to the enticing prospect of relief for Tory purses, severely over-burdened by the land tax. Possibly this had some plausibility in the early stages of the Anglo-American dispute at the time of the Stamp Act and the Townshend Duties. But later, at the onset of the war, in the light of the heavy expenditure plainly involved even in a short armed struggle with America, and with opposition spokesmen bitterly reminding the country gentlemen that an increased land tax was the first fruit of their attitude, it carried less force. More interesting to many were the ideological implications. If it was curious for Whigs in America to be found supporting the royal prerogative it seemed no less odd for Tories to be seen supporting the sovereignty of the legislature. Their opponents characteristically attributed this to a major change at court rather than among the country gentlemen. 'Lucky has it been for many consistent Jacobites, who might otherwise have been reduced to the necessity of turning with the times, that the crown itself has taken a turn in their favour; by which means the morosest anti-courtiers of the last reign are become, without changing their political preferences, the civilist courtiers in this'.[71]

These calculations about the direction of Tory thinking were contrived and overstrained. For the deployment of traditional Tory emotions and beliefs in the service of parliamentary omnicompetence was carried out much more smoothly than the channelling of old Whig energies in a radical or reforming direction. Seventeenth-century concepts and ideas played a greater part in late eighteenth-century politics than is sometimes allowed for, but the changes in their use were as important as the fact that they were used at all. By the 1770s the surviving element in Tory thinking was not the divine right of the monarch, but rather the divine right of properly constituted authority, and the non-resistance which certainly lingered on in their political vocabulary was owed not to the King but to the King in Parliament. The speed and success with which Tories had adapted their traditional ideas in order to absorb the once traumatic impact of the Revolution of 1688 is now much better understood,[72] and certainly by the reign of George III the principle of parliamentary sovereignty was as commonplace among Tories as among their enemies. Moreover the distinctions which caused such agonies among conscientious Whigs were not at all embarrassing to the less pedantic Tory country gentlemen. For them it was sufficient to state that the power of taxation was implicit in the supreme authority necessarily found in every state. This secularised version of the ultimate omnipotence of paternal government figured strongly in Johnson's *Taxation No Tyranny*. 'There must in every society be some power or other for which there is no appeal, which admits no restrictions, which pervades the whole mass of the community, regulates and adjusts all subordination, enacts laws or repeals them, erects or annuls judicatures; extends or contracts privileges, exempt itself from question or control, and bounded only by physical necessity'.[73] Johnson was not one of the country gentlemen but he shared their political standpoint and was, unlike most of them, capable of articulating it. One of the advantages of such a simple concept was that it made speculation about the precise content of sovereignty pointless—it was in its nature all or nothing. It also permitted somewhat vague statements which jumbled together in a confused but satisfying mixture the supremacy of the nation, the crown, and the legislature. Franklin found this habitual lack of precision deeply irritating: 'Nothing is more common here than to talk of the *Sovereignty of Parliament,* and the *Sovereignty of this Nation* over the Colonies; a kind of Sovereignty the Idea of which is not so clear, nor does it clearly appear upon what Foundations it is established'.[74] Such looseness of definition incidentally permitted that sentimental expression of respect for the person of the King, which if it no longer implied doctrines of divine right, gave ample rein to Tory emotions. Most of the addresses of 1775 specifically referred to the need to maintain the lawful authority of the legislature, but most also referred to the rights of the Crown, in one form or another. Expressions such as the 'legal Authority of the Crown', the Dignity of your Crown and Person', 'our Hearts glowing with Zeal for your Majesty's Person' occurred in profusion.[75] Some critics were consequently driven to enquire 'whether passive obedience and non-resistance in all cases whatsoever be the duty of British subject'.[76]

The accusation that the language of the landed interest in this period was the language of non-resistance was not absurdly wide of the mark, at any rate outside Parliament itself, where the debate was generally conducted between different brands of Whigs and among relatively sophisticated politicians. But in settings as diverse as the Common Council of London and the Berkshire county meeting held at Abingdon, there were lively debates about the legitimacy of resistance and the duty of passive obedience to constituted authority.[77] The language of the addresses themselves was in many cases savage in its denuciation of the colonists and smacked distinctly of the old abuse by the High Churchmen of commonwealthmen and dissenters. Americans were, for some addressers, 'Sons of Anarchy', and 'Mob and Rabble led by mad Enthusiasts and desperate Republicans'; others referred to the 'base Innovations and black Ingratitude of rebellious Americans', and predicted the 'miseries of a democratical Tyranny'.[78] Loyalist journalists encouraged the tendency to make a connection between American radicals and old bogeys of Tory mythology. 'It is impossible' one declared, 'to give you a better description of the bulk of the people on this Continent (and particularly in the province of Massachusetts Bay), than every English history gives of the principles of the Independents in Oliver's time. There their pictures are justly drawn'.[79] The implied hostility to religious dissenters was deeply significant. One pamphleteer referred to 'these rebellious Republicans, these hairbrained fanatics, as mad and distracted as the Anabaptists of Munster'.[80] The American crisis came, by coincidence, at a sensitive moment for relations between the church and the non-comformists in England. The Feathers Tavern petition, in favour of modifying the requirement of clerical subscription to the Thirty-Nine articles, and a renewed demand from dissenters for an extension of the Toleration Act, had both been firmly repressed in 1772–3. Against this backdrop, the religious convictions of New Englanders and the political sympathies of leading English dissenters, were closely noted, and in the minds of Anglicans connected. It would hardly have been possible to raise the cry of 'the church in danger' on this basis, but there was no doubt where the inclinations of the Anglican clergy lay, and they made no secret of their desire to stoke the fires of anti-Americanism. In many parts of the country the pulpit reinforced a national political campaign for the first time in many years, and visiting Americans like Samuel Curwen were startled by the recrudescence of the old high Toryism, reflected in virulent sermons.[81] The holding of a general fast unleashed a flood of appeals for Anglican unity in the face of a revived dissenting threat,[82] while inflammatory addresses from the pulpit were matched by a powerful campaign in the newspapers: 'All true Churchman are desired to unite in an address to the throne on the present alarming times. It being evident that the Dissenters in general want to subvert the constitution'.[83] The taint of radicalism was also readily linked with these prejudices. The loudly expressed interest of Wilkites in the American cause was particularly damaging. Americans tended to believe that such interest enhanced their own prospects in Britain. In fact, with the propertied classes, it had the opposite effect. According to one experienced and friendly observer, Richard Champion, America would have found much more support among moderate Englishmen if the domestic challenges of radicalism in these years had never occurred.[84]

The defence of the British supremacy in the colonies could easily be portrayed as a defence of all those things which the old Tories most admired. In this respect the changes of George III's early years had utterly transformed their situation. They were now, as never under George I and George II, part of the natural and settled order of things. No longer engaged in the hopeless defence of an outdated creed against the Whig oligarchs, they once again felt fully a part of a unified ruling class. Tories rarely bothered to compete for government places at the higher levels, but their access to the patronage of the localities was once again as open as under Queen Anne. In particular their acknowledged place in the Commissions of the Peace and in the new-style militia gave them a stake in existing government which they had long lacked. In one of those deeply perceptive analyses of which he was capable, Shelburne saw distinctly the connections between a squirearchy fully restored to its leading role in local society, and the coercion of America. He commented on 'the alienation of all the landed Interest from the ancient Plan of Freedom: Every landed Man setting up a little Tyranny, and, armed with Magistracy, and oppressive Laws, spreading a Waste of Spirit and creating an intellectual Darkness around him. Thus employed the country gentlemen were willing, instead of controlling the abuse of Power, to take their Choice with that Government under which their own peculiar Tyrannies were maintained'.[85]

This was a pejorative way of describing the growing confidence, complacency, and cohesiveness, which marked the attitude of the old landed families and which was reflected not least in their view of the American conflict. It also underrated their readiness temporarily to resume their independence when circumstances dictated. Within four years of the addresses of 1775, they mutinied over the failure of the war and the bleak economic climate at home, came near to overturning the government, and briefly aroused radical hopes of major constitutional change. Nonetheless, Shelburne's assessment was a shrewd one, for it caught perfectly the mindless authoritarianism which the country gentlemen displayed in the face of the American challenge. Put at its simplest they declined to feel for colonial propertyholders, those libertarian sentiments which quickly sprang to their minds when the traditional rights and customs of propertied Englishmen were at stake. Americans indeed were in this sense the victims of a revived Tory paternalism, and seen somewhat as monied men or religious dissenters had been seen at the beginning of the century. In their case, moreover, clearly subordinate status and an outlandish identity which placed them on a level little above foreigners reinforced the hierarchical and patriotic instincts of the John Bull Englishman.[86] The essential fact was that the English landed gentry altogether rejected, without even giving it serious consideration, the proposition which for Americans was of equally obvious validity—the proposition that the residents of the colonies were indistinguishable from Englishmen in respect of their rights and liberties. Contemporary usage commonly described the plantations in terms which suggested that they were no more than the property of the British, and their inhabitants literally a subject people. This dismayed well-disposed Englishmen and shocked visiting Americans; ironically it offended not least those loyalist Americans who gave up everything for their principles, settled in England and found themselves despised and even cursed with their rebellious compatriots. Richard Price objected strongly to such attitudes: 'The people of *America* are no more the subjects of the people of *Britain,* than the people of *Yorkshire* are the subjects of the people of *Middlesex*. They are your fellow-subjects'. His plea fell on deaf ears.

The 1760s and 1770s saw the emergence of a clear consensus in favour of the principle of British imperial supremacy. Whether this consensus is justly to be termed the 'new Toryism' is perhaps a matter of semantics. The country gentlemen and the broader body of provincial opinion which they undobtedly represented, did not embrace all shades of opinion in favour of stern measures in the colonies. They did not themselves dictate or shape policy, and their leaders who did, appealed to their prejudices, but did not necessarily share them. On the other hand they provided the essential element of parliamentary and extra-parliamentary support without which an unprecedented war against colonists could not have been fought. Their alliance with the court of George III and its expression in the coercion of America also signified a growing identification of the governing class with the conservative values of the landed interest, and thereby prepared the way for the Church and King reaction of the 1790s. Perhaps significantly, the addresses demanding action against the colonies already provided glimpses of that obsession with the unchanging and unchangeable virtues of the constitution in church and state which was to be the hallmark of Toryism under Pitt and Liverpool. Americans were thus cast in the role which was finally to be allotted to reformers in the 1790s, that of the sacrilegious enemy of the purity of the English constitution. Ironically Burke, who was later to expound and articulate this standpoint with brilliant clarity and devastating force was, in the 1770s, searching conscientiously for a formula which would sidestep, if not supplant it. It is perhaps a measure of the importance of the American Revolution in British party politics that talents which were insufficient to revive the fortunes of the old Whiggism, were not even needed to reinvigorate the old Toryism.

NOTES

1. A convenient summary of the state of the debate is to be found in J. Brewer, *Party Ideology and Popular Politics at the Accession of George III* (Cambridge, 1976), parts i and ii.
2. I. R. Christie, 'Was there a "New Toryism" in the Earlier Part of George III's Reign' in *Myth and Reality in Late Eighteenth-Century British Politics and Other Papers* (London, 1970), Professor Christie accepts that colonial policy followed a different pattern from domestic policy during these years. He argues, however, that 'it is closer to the facts to analyse British colonial policy in terms of an imperialism which failed to find a way through the problem of freedom versus authority than to connect it with any general concept of toryism' (p. 213).
3. The most useful account of the structure of parliamentary politics is provided by the introduction to Sir Lewis Namier and J. Brooke, *The History of Parliament. The House of Commons, 1754–90* (3 vols., London, 1964).
4. For a recent assessment, see F. O'Gorman, *The Rise of Party in England: The Rockingham Whigs 1760–82* (London, 1975).
5. H. Walpole, *Memoirs of the Reign of King George III*, ed. G. F. R. Barker (4 vols., London, 1894), i. 4; E. Burke, *Works* (Bohn edn., 8 vols., London, 1854), i. 308.
6. *Letters of a Loyalist Lady* (Cambridge, Mass., 1927), 74.
7. *The Grenville Papers*, ed. W. J. Smith (4 vols., London, 1852), ii. 199.
8. *Cobbett's Parliamentary History of England*, xvi. 1107.
9. Henry E. Huntington Library, HM22513: Manchester to unknown, 9 January 1776.
10. Burke, *Works*, i. 318.
11. *Gentleman's Magazine*, 1776, 221.
12. *Crisis*, xxxix.
13. Quoted, B. Donoughue, *British Politics and the American Revolution: The Path to War, 1773–5* (London, 1964), 197.
14. [A. Lee], *An Appeal to the Justice and Interests of the People of Great Britain in the present Dispute with America* (4th edn., New York, 1775), 24.
15. *London Chronicle*, 20 June 1776.
16. *The Diary and Letters of His Excellency Thomas Hutchinson*, ed. P. O. Hutchinson (2 vols., London, 1886), i. 257.
17. *The Diary of Sylas Neville, 1767–1788*, ed. B. Cozens-Hardy (London, 1950), 28.
18. Huntington Library, Grenville Letter-Book, Grenville to Knox, 16 August 1768.
19. Grenville Letter-Book, Grenville to Dr. Spry, 19 August 1766.
20. *Crisis*, xlviii.
21. Address of Middlesex J.P.'s, *London Gazette*, 17 October 1775.
22. Grenville Letter-Book, Grenville to Lyttelton, 20 August 1765.
23. Grenville Letter-Book, Grenville to Hood, 30 October 1768.
24. *Journals of the Continental Congress 1774–1789* (Washington, 1904–37), i. 68; iii. 410; v. 512.
25. *A Letter from a Merchant in London to his Nephew in North America;* for this, with an equally sarcastic, but unpublished response from Franklin, see *Pennsylvania Magazine*, xxv (1901), 314.
26. *Droit le Roi: or the Rights and Prerogatives of the Imperial Crown of Great Britain* (London, 1764).

27. Walpole, *Memoirs*, i. 306.
28. *Parliamentary History*, xviii. 769, 771.
29. *London Chronicle*, 7 December 1775.
30. *London Gazette*, 14 November 1775.
31. *London Gazette*, 25 November 1775.
32. Grenville Letter-Book, Grenville to Whately, 15 November 1769.
33. *Sir Henry Cavendish's Debates of the House of Commons*, ed. J. Wright (2 vols., London, 1840), i. 441.
34. *Correspondence of King George the Third from 1760 to December 1783*, ed. Sir J. Fortescue (6 vols., London, 1927–8), ii. 82–4.
35. *Parliamentary History*, xviii. 773–837.
36. *Franklin Jonathan Williams and William Pitt. A Letter of January 21, 1775*, ed. B. Knollenberg (Bloomington, 1949).
37. 'Letters of Henry Laurens to his son John, 1773–1776', *South Carolina Historical and Genealogical Magazine*, iv (1903), 33.
38. [H. Williamson], *The Plea of the Colonies, On the Charges brought against them by Lord Mansfield, and Others, in a letter to His Lordship. By a Native of Pennsylvania* (Philadelphia, 1772), 6.
39. *Correspondence of Edmund Burke*, vol. iii. ed. G. H. Guttridge, 103.
40. See P. Langford, 'The Rockingham Whigs and America, 1767–1773' in *Statesmen, Scholars and Merchants: Essays in Eighteenth-Century History presented to Dame Lucy Sutherland*, eds. A. Whiteman, J. S. Bromley, and P. G. M. Dickson (Oxford 1973); P. D. G. Thomas, *British Politics and the Stamp Act Crisis: The First Phase of the American Revolution* (Oxford, 1975), 367–71.
41. Connecticut Historical Society, Diary of W. S. Johnson, 13 June 1770.
42. *Hutchinson Diary*, ii. 131.
43. British Library, Add. MS. 35361, f. 139: Hardwicke to Charles Yorke, n.d.
44. British Library, Add. MS. 32973, f. 344.
45. For an important clarification of what Pitt said in 1766, suggesting that his widely quoted condemnation of all taxation of the colonies was far from his real intention, see I. R. Christie, 'William Pitt and American Taxation, 1766: A Problem of Parliamentary Reporting', *Studies in Burke and His Time*, xvii (1976), 167–79.
46. *Correspondence of William Pitt, Earl of Chatham*, ed. W. S. Taylor and J. H. Pringle (4 vols., London, 1838), ii. 355. See also P. G. Walsh Atkins, 'Shelburne and America, 1763–83', upub. Oxford Univ. D.Phil. thesis, 1971.
47. *The Autobiography of Benjamin Franklin*, ed. M. Farrand (San Marino, 1964), 206–7.
48. *Parliamentary History*, xv. 387. Significantly the measure which Fox opposed was eventually adopted, at Grenville's instance, in 1765, the year of the Stamp Act, and proved deeply controversial in the colonies.
49. Historical Manuscripts Commission, *Egmont Diary*, i. 157. Political considerations, however, were apt to induce Walpole to modify his stance. See T. R. Reese, *Colonial Georgia: A Study in British Imperial Policy in the Eighteenth Century* (Athens, Georgia, 1963), chap. 3.
50. British Library, Add. MS. 11514.
51. *The Papers of Benjamin Franklin*, ed. L. W. Labaree (New Haven, 1959–), viii. 296.
52. *Proceedings and Debates of the British Parliament respecting North America*, ed. F. Stock (Washington, 1924–41), iv. 190, 214.
53. *Collection of New York Historical Society, Colden Papers*, iii (1920), 324.
54. For a valuable guide to the main themes, see C. Bonwick, *English Radicals and the American Revolution* (Chapel Hill, 1977).
55. *Parliamentary History*, xviii. 1291–2. Enthusiasts were, however, less ready to quote Locke's embarrassing reliance on the prince to decide when and how the elective basis of the legislature should be reformed.
56. *Parliamentary History*, xviii. 1171
57. *Crisis*, xlviii.
58. *Lords Journals*, xxxiv. 183.
59. *Memoirs of the Marquis of Rockingham and His Contemporaries*, ed. George Thomas, Earl of Albermarle (2 vols., London, 1852), ii. 254.
60. *Hutchinson Diary*, i. 316–17.

61. H. C. Van Schaak, *Henry Cruger: The Colleague of Edmund Burke in the British Parliament* (New York, 1859), 19.
62. *Rockingham Memoirs*, ii. 297. This letter to Rockingham was written on 13 October 1776, after the American defeat at Long Island.
63. See I. R. Christie, 'Economical Reform and "The influence of the Crown" ' in *Myth and Reality*.
64. *Hutchinson Diary*, i. 454.
65. *Correspondence of Mr. Ralph Izard of South Carolina* (New York, 1844), 87–8.
66. *Hutchinson Diary*, ii. 708.
67. *Parliamentary History*, xviii, 1026.
68. The most useful lists of the minority in the divisions of February 1766 are those at British Library, Add. MS. 32974, ff. 167, 169 and Sheffield City Library, WWM. R54–1, 11. Namier's suggestion that 34 Tories voted in favour of repeal is speculation 'on a *pro rata* basis'; it is also quite out of line with the comments of contemporaries. (See Sir L. Namier, 'Country Gentlemen in Parliament 1750–84', in *Crossroads of Power*, London, 1962, 43.)
69. The names are listed with the addresses in the *London Gazette* from 16 September 1775 to 4 May 1776. They include many M.P.s who never opened their mouths in the Commons.
70. *Parliamentary History*, xviii. 938.
71. *London Chronical*, 2 September 1775.
72. See, for example, J. P. Kenyon, *Revolution Principles: The Politics of Party, 1689–1720* (Cambridge, 1977), chap. 3.
73. *Samuel Johnson, Political Writings*, ed. D. J. Greene (New Haven, 1977), 423.
74. *Franklin Papers*, xiv. 69.
75. *London Gazette*, 4, 11, 14 November 1775.
76. *London Chronicle*, 4 November 1775.
77. *London Chronicle*, 8 July 1775; *Jackson's Oxford Journal*, 18 November 1775.
78. *London Gazette*, 17 October, 4 November 1775, 6 January, 30 Arpil 1776.
79. *London Chronicle*, 25 April 1775.
80. [M. Cooper], *A Friendly Address to All Reasonable Americans, On the Subject of Political Confusion* (New York, 1774), 31.
81. *Journal and Letters of the late Samuel Curwen*, ed. G. A. Ward (New York, 1845), 213–14.
82. *London Chronicle*, 19 December 1776.
83. *London Chronicle*, 30 September 1775.
84. *The American Correspondence of a Bristol Merchant 1766–1776: Letters of Richard Champion*, ed. G. H. Guttridge, Univ. of California, Pubs. in History, xx (1934), 49–50.
85. W. L. Clements Library, Shelburne MSS., vol. 165, 221.
86. *Chain of Friendship: Selected Letters of Dr. John Fothergill of London 1735–1780*, ed. B. C. Corner and C. C. Booth (Cambridge, Mass., 1971), 285.